CHELSEA HOUSE PUBLISHERS

Modern Critical Views

HENRY ADAMS
EDWARD ALBEE
A. R. AMMONS
MATTHEW ARNOLD
JOHN ASHBERY
W. H. AUDEN
JANE AUSTEN
JAMES BALDWIN
CHARLES BAUDELAIRE
SAMUEL BECKETT
SAUL BELLOW
THE BIBLE
ELIZABETH BISHOP
WILLIAM BLAKE
JORGE LUIS BORGES
ELIZABETH BOWEN
BERTOLT BRECHT
THE BRONTËS
ROBERT BROWNING
ANTHONY BURGESS
GEORGE GORDON, LORD BYRON
THOMAS CARLYLE
LEWIS CARROLL
WILLA CATHER
CERVANTES
GEOFFREY CHAUCER
KATE CHOPIN
SAMUEL TAYLOR COLERIDGE
JOSEPH CONRAD
CONTEMPORARY POETS
HART CRANE
STEPHEN CRANE
DANTE
CHARLES DICKENS
EMILY DICKINSON
JOHN DONNE & THE
    17th-CENTURY POETS
ELIZABETHAN DRAMATISTS
THEODORE DREISER
JOHN DRYDEN
GEORGE ELIOT
T. S. ELIOT
RALPH ELLISON
RALPH WALDO EMERSON
WILLIAM FAULKNER
HENRY FIELDING
F. SCOTT FITZGERALD
GUSTAVE FLAUBERT
E. M. FORSTER
SIGMUND FREUD
ROBERT FROST

ROBERT GRAVES
GRAHAM GREENE
THOMAS HARDY
NATHANIEL HAWTHORNE
WILLIAM HAZLITT
SEAMUS HEANEY
ERNEST HEMINGWAY
GEOFFREY HILL
FRIEDRICH HÖLDERLIN
HOMER
GERARD MANLEY HOPKINS
WILLIAM DEAN HOWELLS
ZORA NEALE HURSTON
HENRY JAMES
SAMUEL JOHNSON
BEN JONSON
JAMES JOYCE
FRANZ KAFKA
JOHN KEATS
RUDYARD KIPLING
D. H. LAWRENCE
JOHN LE CARRÉ
URSULA K. LE GUIN
DORIS LESSING
SINCLAIR LEWIS
ROBERT LOWELL
NORMAN MAILER
BERNARD MALAMUD
THOMAS MANN
CHRISTOPHER MARLOWE
CARSON MCCULLERS
HERMAN MELVILLE
JAMES MERRILL
ARTHUR MILLER
JOHN MILTON
EUGENIO MONTALE
MARIANNE MOORE
IRIS MURDOCH
VLADIMIR NABOKOV
JOYCE CAROL OATES
SEAN O'CASEY
FLANNERY O'CONNOR
EUGENE O'NEILL
GEORGE ORWELL
CYNTHIA OZICK
WALTER PATER
WALKER PERCY
HAROLD PINTER
PLATO
EDGAR ALLAN POE

POETS OF SENSIBILITY &
    THE SUBLIME
ALEXANDER POPE
KATHERINE ANNE PORTER
EZRA POUND
PRE-RAPHAELITE POETS
MARCEL PROUST
THOMAS PYNCHON
ARTHUR RIMBAUD
THEODORE ROETHKE
PHILIP ROTH
JOHN RUSKIN
J. D. SALINGER
GERSHOM SCHOLEM
WILLIAM SHAKESPEARE (3 vols.)
    HISTORIES & POEMS
    COMEDIES
    TRAGEDIES
GEORGE BERNARD SHAW
MARY WOLLSTONECRAFT SHELLEY
PERCY BYSSHE SHELLEY
EDMUND SPENSER
GERTRUDE STEIN
JOHN STEINBECK
LAURENCE STERNE
WALLACE STEVENS
TOM STOPPARD
JONATHAN SWIFT
ALFRED LORD TENNYSON
WILLIAM MAKEPEACE THACKERAY
HENRY DAVID THOREAU
LEO TOLSTOI
ANTHONY TROLLOPE
MARK TWAIN
JOHN UPDIKE
GORE VIDAL
VIRGIL
ROBERT PENN WARREN
EVELYN WAUGH
EUDORA WELTY
NATHANAEL WEST
EDITH WHARTON
WALT WHITMAN
OSCAR WILDE
TENNESSEE WILLIAMS
WILLIAM CARLOS WILLIAMS
THOMAS WOLFE
VIRGINIA WOOLF
WILLIAM WORDSWORTH
RICHARD WRIGHT
WILLIAM BUTLER YEATS

Further titles in preparation.

Modern Critical Views

JAMES MERRILL

Modern Critical Views

JAMES MERRILL

Edited with an introduction by

Harold Bloom

Sterling Professor of the Humanities
Yale University

1985
CHELSEA HOUSE PUBLISHERS
New York

THE COVER:

The cover illustrates Merrill's occult epic, *The Changing Light At Sandover,* where the fundamental setting is two young men consulting the ouija board, as they gain knowledge of the Sword of the Angels.—H.B.

PROJECT EDITORS: Emily Bestler, James Uebbing
ASSOCIATE EDITOR: Maria Behan
EDITORIAL COORDINATOR: Karyn Gullen Browne
EDITORIAL STAFF: Sally Stepanek, Linda Grossman
DESIGN: Susan Lusk

Cover illustration by James Forman

Library of Congress Cataloging in Publication Data

James Merrill.
    (Modern critical views)
    Bibliography: p.
    Includes index.
    1. Merrill, James Ingram—Criticism and interpreta-
tion—Addresses, essays, lectures.   I. Bloom, Harold.
II. Series.
PS3525.E6645Z7   1985   811'.54   85–6606
ISBN 0–87754–618–5

Chelsea House Publishers
Harold Steinberg, Chairman and Publisher
Susan Lusk, Vice President
A Division of Chelsea House Educational Communications, Inc.
133 Christopher Street, New York, NY 10014

Contents

Editor's Note

This volume gathers together what is, in my judgment, the best and most helpful criticism yet published on the poetry of James Merrill, presented here in the order of its publication. My "Introduction" attempts to isolate some of the qualities that establish Merrill as a remarkably original poet.

The chronological sequence begins with Richard Howard's pioneering essay on the early Merrill, emphasizing his technical accomplishment as a lyricist, and prophesying many later critical efforts to describe the poet's characteristic rhetorical stance. Subsequent essays by Richard Sáez, David Kalstone, and Helen Vendler center upon Merrill's complex imagery, his personal myth, and the developing cosmos of his fantasy.

Stephen Yenser's detailed commentary upon *The Book of Ephraim* illuminates Merrill's narrative prelude to his visionary epic. The emphasis moves back to lyric achievement with John Hollander's reading of "Mirror," J. D. McClatchy's account of *The Country of a Thousand Years of Peace* and David Lehman's survey of the unifying relationship between the earlier volumes and the epic. In the penultimate essays, the epic's general context is explored by Judith Moffett, while Charles Berger analyzes *Mirabell*'s very original mode of conserving the tropes of traditional epic by wittily "literalizing" them, thus returning this volume full circle to some of the concerns of the "Introduction." These concerns receive a final consideration in Leslie Brisman's essay on Merrill's Yeats, an original creation rather than the historical Yeats.

Introduction

In James Merrill's first book, *The Black Swan* (privately printed, 1946), there are intimations of his visionary epic, *The Changing Light at Sandover*, published in its complete form in 1983. Across thirty-seven years, the voice of the outsetting bard echoes in the extraordinary cadences of the matured seer. Here is the third stanza of "The Broken Bowl" from *The Black Swan*, written by a poet in his teens:

> No lucid, self-containing artifice
>   At last, but fire, ice,
> A world in jeopardy. What lets the bowl
> Nonetheless triumph by inconsequence
> And wrestle harmony from dissonance
> And with the fragments build another, whole,
>   Inside us, which we feel
> Can never break, or grow less bountiful?

Love, not unexpectedly, turns out to be the answer, early and late. Merrill, like Yeats, is both an occultist and an erotic poet, and again like Yeats he is a curious kind of religious poet, "curious" because the religion is a variety of Gnosticism, derived by Yeats from sources as troublesome and inauthentic as Madame Helena Petrovna Blavatsky, and by Merrill from sources just as troublesome and inauthentic, such as Dr. Carl Gustav Jung. I assume that Merrill would be delighted by Yeats' early defense of Madame Blavatsky: "Of course she gets up spurious miracles, but what *is* a woman of genius to do in the Nineteenth Century?" As a man of genius, rather late on in the twentieth century, Merrill insouciantly also gets up spurious miracles, which he calls *The Book of Ephraim*, *Mirabell: Books of Number*, and *Scripts for the Pageant*. They *are* miracles of poetic achievement, and if I call them "spurious" I only confess my own bewilderment or startled skepticism at being confronted by a contemporary Dante or Blake who follows Victor Hugo and Yeats by spending thousands of evenings at the Ouija Board in touch with alarmingly familiar spirits.

The stanza I quoted above, from "The Broken Bowl," displays already what several critics have noted as a fundamental trope of creation-by-catastrophe in Merrill, the ancient Gnostic and Kabbalistic image of the Breaking of the Vessels. But the image appears with a grand difference in Merrill, if only because he is a poet *for whom there are no catastrophes.*

Like Proust, his truest precursor, Merrill studies the nostalgias, but the study in each is just that; wonder, and not elegy. Grief is not a Merrillean or a Proustian emotion, and neither is guilt. Even Yeats, despite his passionate occultries, could mourn his peers, but Merrill is so wholehearted a preternaturalist that dead friends instantly manifest themselves in the Higher Keys of his Spirit World. What is most original and unnerving in Merrill is his emotional stance or metaphoric affect, which too readily can be mistaken for a psychic remoteness or a stylistic coldness. I note this in some contrition, since I myself am a late convert to Merrill, struck down upon my own road to Damascus by the blinding white light of trope in *Divine Comedies* (1976), after a quarter-century of weakly misreading Merrill with a merely technical admiration. *The Book of Ephraim* and its companion poems, such as "Lost in Translation" and "The Will," converted me, and sent me back to read again the major lyrics and meditations I had resisted too stubbornly and for too long a time, very much to my own loss.

II

The canonical judgment should be ventured that Merrill is one of the three permanent poets of his own American generation, together with John Ashbery and A. R. Ammons. His immediate precursors are the late Elizabeth Bishop, in the generation just before and, in a more engendering sense, Wallace Stevens, whose language and vision is prevalent in *The Black Swan* and in *First Poems* (1951), to become more subtly internalized in *The Country of a Thousand Years of Peace* (1959) and afterwards. Though W. H. Auden is invoked throughout Merrill's epic, both as sage and as archetype of the poet, his example and career seem to play the same part in Merrill as in Ashbery. He is a benign presence for both, precisely because he is not the true father, but more like an amiable uncle on the mother's side, as it were. Stevens, the veritable precursor, is a very dangerous poetic father, whether one takes after his formal self, as Merrill does, or comes up out of his repressed Whitmanian depths, which is Ashbery's authentic origin. Wallace Stevens, one of the dandies, an American, is not the same as Stevens the Real Me or Me Myself, Whitmanian celebrant of Night, Death, the Mother and the Sea. Merrill's Stevens is closer to Alexander Pope than to Whitman, but then Merrill himself now is, in some aspects, the reincarnation of Pope. *The Book of Ephraim* is less like Dante than it is like *The Rape of the Lock*, or rather *Ephraim* and its successors have the same relation to the *Commedia* that Pope's exquisite fantasy has to *Paradise Lost*.

Merrill is Popean as an artist, but hardly as a visionary, where the Proustian influence dominates, as early as the poignant poem "For Proust" in *Water Street* (1962). Merrill too is always in search of lost time, a quest that aims "to work / The body's resurrection, sense by sense," according to the "Venice" section of *The Book of Ephraim*. The epigraph to *Ephraim* is that extraordinary tercet in *Paradiso* XV where Dante's ancestor, Cacciaguida, addresses the poet as root to his branch:

> You believe the truth, for the lesser and the great of this life gaze into that mirror in which, before you think, you display your thought.

Whether Dante's vision can be reconciled with Proust's is a considerable difficulty, but it is characteristic of Merrill to make the attempt. That mirror, for Proust and for Merrill, is what Freud called the bodily ego, a precarious "frontier concept" on the edge between mind and body. Introjection, for Merrill, is a defense of identification almost invariably accomplished through the eye, so that sight is for Merrill the sense closest both to thinking and to sexual longing. Such an identification is more American than European, more like Emerson and Whitman than' like Dante and Proust. The mirror of the self, in Merrill, is an overdetermining mechanism, just as it is in Freud, despite Merrill's curious debt to Jung's *Answer to Job*. "There are no accidents" is the law of Freud's psychic cosmos, and this law is taught also by Ephraim and his fellow Spirits. We gaze into the mirror and behold the bodily ego, as it were, and so behold our thought before ever we think it:

> One speaks. *How superficial*
> *Appearances are!* Since then, as if a fish
> Had broken the perfect silver of my reflectiveness,
> I have lapses. I suspect
> Looks from behind, where nothing is, cool gazes
> Through the blind flaws of my mind. As days,
> As decades lengthen, this vision
> Spreads and blackens. I do not know whose it is,
> But I think it watches for my last silver
> To blister, flake, float leaf by life, each milling—
> Downward dumb conceit, to a standstill
> From which not even you strike any brilliant
> Chord in me, and to a faceless will,
> Echo of mine, I am amenable.

That is Merrill's "Mirror" ending its monologue in *The Country of a Thousand Years of Peace*, 1959. But, by then, poor Mirror is paranoid, though with the madness of mirrors, not humans. Mirror's breakdown ensues from the betrayal of convenant by the children who, at the start of the monologue, had trusted Mirror to teach them how to live. To have become amenable to a faceless will is surely catastrophe if one has been, before that, the glass in which the children beheld their thought ere cognition began. Yet Mirror, like Merrill, acknowledges no catastrophes.

III

In *Nights and Days* (1966), there is a celebrated sonnet-sequence, "The Broken Home," which takes as subject the history of marriage and divorce of Merrill's parents. Each of the seven irregular sonnets is the most astonishing at controlling what cannot be controlled, knowing what cannot be known. Led by his Irish setter, "head/Passionately lowered," the child enters his mother's bedroom, where:

> Blinds beat sun from the bed.
> The green-gold room throbbed like a bruise.
> Under a sheet, clad in taboos
> Lay whom we sought, her hair undone, outspread.
>
> And of a blackness found, if ever now, in old
> Engravings where the acid bit.
> 'I must have needed to touch it
> Or the whiteness—was she dead?
> Her eyes flew open, startled strange and cold.
> The dog slumped to the floor. She reached for me. I fled.

Is there trauma here? My question intends only the poem itself as referent, and not the poem as act of the mind. In Stevens, these are not separable, but in Merrill I think they are. I do not read hurt or pain *in the poem*, though it clearly renders what ought to be the trauma of the barely evaded Oedipal taboo. Contrast Hart Crane's beautifully oblique "Repose of Rivers" where the traumatic pain, *in the poem*, is dominant:

> How much I would have bartered! the black gorge
> And all the singular nestings in the hills
> Where beavers learn stitch and tooth.
> The pond I entered once and quickly fled—
> I remember now its singing willow rim.

Crane's pond is Merrill's shut bedroom, yet Crane's lyric is compounded of hurt, with its superb images of mammoth turtles mounting one another in a terrible love-death, and of his own homosexual initiation: "With scalding unguents spread and smoking darts." Where Crane obliquely renders the evaded Oedipal trespass, with a traumatic affect, Merrill directly presents it, without any intense affect at all. I do not contrast the two poems or poets in terms of aesthetic achievement; few poets, I believe, can survive a close comparison with Hart Crane, and Merrill has no poetic affinities to Crane whatsoever. It is Merrill's strangeness that is my concern. Oedipal catastrophe is for Crane catastrophe, psychic trauma does not become poetic gain. But for Merrill, trauma and grief do become precisely poetic gains, "Ill-gotten gains," as he calls them with his customary wit and self-knowledge:

> A sense comes late in life of too much death,
> Of standing wordless, with head bowed beneath
>
> The buffeting of losses which we see
> At once, no matter how reluctantly,
>
> As gains. Gains to the work. Ill-gotten gains. . .
> Under the skull-and-crossbones, rigging strains
>
> Our craft to harbor, and salt lashings plow
> The carved smile of a mermaid on the prow.

Merrill is *not* an elegiac poet, as he keeps making clear, yet nothing about his work is more difficult than its stance. Erotic poetry always has been elegiac, but Merrill is the grand and unnerving exception. In a very sensitive essay upon what he calls "elegiac aspects" of *The Changing Light at Sandover*, Peter Sacks reads the decasyllabics I have quoted above as a "balance of loss and gain," but such a reading reflects the consequences of bringing a profound experience of poetic elegy to the consideration of Merrill's very different mode. At the close of his huge poem, Merrill movingly contrasts his gain to a close friend's loss, as if to admit again that traditional elegiac consolation is not revelant to his occult sublimities:

> . . . our poor friend's
> Somber regard—captive like Gulliver
> Or like the mortal in an elfin court
> Pining for wife and cottage on this shore
> Beyond whose depthless dazzle he can't see.

Some part of Merrill's *otherness*, of his authentic uncanniness as a poet, is more attuned to an elfin court than to a wife and cottage on this shore. What is most original and valuable in Merrill's poetry comes out of this otherness, out of a quality that transcends even a sensibility from the highest Camp, as it were, let alone the witty homosexual onto-theology of the *Sandover* epic. A temperament for which there are no accidents and no catastrophes, a consciousness somehow beyond trauma and beyond mourning, is also astonishingly capable of an erotic wisdom that can balance experiential contraries that cannot be balanced:

> Where I hid my face, your touch, quick, merciful,
> Blindfolded me. A god breathed from my lips.
> If that was illusion, I wanted it to last long;
> To dwell, for its daily pittance, with us there,
> Cleaning and watering, sighing with love or pain.
> I hoped it would climb when it needed to the heights
> Even of degradation, as I for one
> Seemed, those days, to be always climbing
> Into a world of wild
> Flowers, feasting, tears—or was I falling, legs
> Buckling, heights, depths,
> Into a pool of each night's rain?
> But you were everywhere beside me, masked,
> As who was not, in laughter, pain, and love.

The heights of degradation presumably are the only possible habitation of that illusion where a god breathes through one's lips. Not even paraphrase, this is the ancient formula of a Gnosticism that forsakes asceticism and chooses instead the upward release of the sparks.

IV

It would comfort me to say that the central trope of *The Changing Light at Sandover* is the Ouija board, and that Merrill's spooks, like Yeats', have come to bring him metaphors for poetry. Unhappily, this is not so. Merrill quests for the truth at the Ouija board, and receives a heap of gorgeous nonsense, dreadful science fiction and a considerable swatch of the best poetry written during the past thirty years, or since the death of Wallace Stevens in 1955. My own experience as a reader is that *The Book of Ephraim* is almost continuously superb, and can sustain endless rereadings. But *Mirabell's Books of Number* can numb one, in between bouts of sublimity, while *Scripts for the Pageant* all too frequently compels me to believe I may be an invited guest at a post-Wildean tea-party, where I wander lost among the cucumber sandwiches and hashish fudge, plaintively mewing for something closer to my usual unhealthy diet. And yet Milton and Blake also have their expositional excesses, and Merrill never ceases to surprise and even astonish, more even in *Scripts* than in *Mirabell*, more in *Mirabell* than in *Ephraim*. Uncommon readers like Richard Saez and Stephen Yenser evidently do not experience my difficulties, but then, like my own hero, Dr. Samuel Johnson, I seem to age into a common reader, and fretfully I wince at yet another upper case angelical revelation coming at me, and long instead for more lyric interludes and intercessions by the voice of Merrill himself.

The fullness of time doubtless will settle these matters, and reveal whether *Mirabell* and *Scripts* are wholly successful in their own terms, or magnificent and picturesque poetic ruins, where one can wander almost endlessly, beholding giant splendors simply not available anywhere else. That many of these splendors are comic enhances their value, though the comedy is often rather specialized. I do not share the anticipation of Richard Saez that in this "masterpiece of sustained camp . . . the camp element may distract some readers from the seriousness of the work." That seems unlikely in an apocalyptic epic whose true starting-point is Hiroshima. Charles Berger suggestively has compared *The Changing Light at Sandover* to *Gravity's Rainbow*. The comparison is just, encompassing as it does the shared thematicism, the equal aesthetic dignity and the comic apocalypticism of the two works. Though the emergent theology of these two essentially religio-erotic seers is a mutual Gnosticism, Merrill's sexual vision is considerably healthier than Pynchon's sado-anarchism, while Pynchon's Tarot coal-tar Kabbalism impresses me spiritually more than Merrill's Ouijan revelations.

Like Pynchon (and John Ashbery) Merrill is clearly the poet of our moment, a great artist perfectly consonant with what insist upon seeming perpetually the very last days of mankind. If there is a civilized future, then the poet of "Lost in Translation" and "McKane's Falls" (both in *Divine Comedies*, 1976), of *The Book of Ephraim*, of the canzone "Samos" in *Scripts*, and of "The Ballroom at Sandover," which transcendentally fulfills as well as ends the epic, cannot fail to constitute part of what will be civilized in that future. Though he himself has scoffed at what he calls his earlier "word-painting," he is indisputably a verse artist comparable to Milton, Tennyson and Pope. Surely he will be remembered as the Mozart of American poetry, classical rather than mannerist or baroque, master of the changing light or perfection that consoles, even though, like every true manifestation of the strong light of the canonical, it is also necessarily the perfection that destroys.

RICHARD HOWARD

James Merrill

"Y ou bitch," squealed Ezra Pound, not surprisingly to the author of the just-completed *Wasteland* which had been submitted to his assessment, "I am wracked by the seven jealousies and cogitating an excuse for always exuding my deformative secretions in my own stuff . . . I go into nacre and objets d'art. Complimenti." That—especially the casting about for an excuse, but also the metaphor of secretion, whether nacre or amber, to represent a part of the self which has become precious by hardening—that is the artisan's honest resentment of the artist; that is the poet who can see no more than the design in *things* envying the poet who can also see things in a design. Pound's version of his own limitation, with its characteristically shrewd diagnosis of his mode, helps us to understand better the whole sense of Keats' beautiful remark that we hate poetry which has a palpable design upon us—poetry, that is, which would enforce the *design*, the restrictive pattern and the decorative detail, at the expense of the ongoing enterprise, the poem's project which is "evermore about to be." But the jealous voice of a man capable of no more than objets d'art addressing a man capable of an art transcending objects might easily be the voice of the early James Merrill apostrophizing the writer he was to become: one who managed to make what was merely his poetry into what was necessarily his life. For such is the case of an American writer whose several books of poetry stand upon one another like "huge pale stones shining from within," the latest affording the widest view of the country which had hitherto been seen only by wisps and pebbles, never as—in the entire sense of the word—a *prospect*.

From *Alone With America*. Copyright © 1980 by Richard Howard. Atheneum Publishers.

In 1951, Merrill published a numbered edition of his *First Poems*, a nacreous volume indeed, which prompted Howard Nemerov in a review to the wicked but supported comment that the work was certainly very good for first poems, "probably some of them would do even for second poems." And, as we shall see, Merrill has made some of them do. But for all their exquisiteness, these early poems have a strength of their own, the strength of standing against an undecided element, initiating "valors of altitude." The things that make them precious make these poems precise as well, and the bright conjugation of his triviality, or at least his frivolity, with his truth makes Merrill's gently nurtured voice, from the first, one we listen to with more than just a concession to grace:

> . . . Luminous in these schools
> Language is a glittering of flint rituals
> And a race of sober children learns long smiles.

In so many poems about the perishable, though, there is a polite and almost impenetrable patina on these pretty things "that in / such curious vividness begin," a glassy lacquer evident in Merrill's vocabulary—"gracile," "chryselephantine" and "idlesse" suggest the baubles plucked from "the shallowest stratum of the past"—as in his diction. The articulation of an abstractive sensibility round an armature of minimal *given* excitations— "roulades of relinquishment," or better and worse still, "the night was a warm nubility"—is this poet's characteristic verbal gesture. The real but unrelenting wit is a matter of local color, often so incidental as to arrest or surely distract the attention that is trying to get on with it:

> . . . Consider other birds: the murderous swan
> And dodo now undone . . .

or again:

> . . . fine red sand brought
> From where sun makes a stab at majesty . . .

We do not feel that the poet's enjoyment of his devices (often invented by trusting to the language, letting the experience accumulated in words shine through, as when Merrill speaks of "hillsides *original* with joy") has ever been sacrificed to a development of his understanding. He indulges the finite, or anyway the finished. Hence a good number of emblem poems ("The Peacock," "The Parrot," "The Pelican," "The Black Swan"), in which everything is given from the start, nothing allowed to happen or become. Indeed, the problem this poet rather languidly wrestles with and does not always resolve in these *First Poems* is how to get the reader through his poem to its end (always, in such instances, something elegiac and anguished, something decorative and heartbreaking:

Love's monuments like tombstones on our lives),

how, simply, to drag "the enchanted eye, the enchanting syllable" down the page and still enact upon the reader the literally arresting design which is Merrill's original talent in both senses. One hope, though often rather a wan one, is the exploitation of baroque syntax, the long sentence looped like an anaconda upon its punctuation and pronouns in such a way that we can find no release from it, once we are within its toils, but at the stanza's close:

> Glass fragments dropped from wholeness to hodgepodge
> Yet fasten to each edge
> The opal signature of imperfection
> Whose rays, though disarrayed, will postulate
> More than a network of cross-angled light
> When through the dusk they point unbruised directions
> And chart upon the room
> Capacities of fire it must assume.

Here the quibble on "rays . . . disarrayed" and the elaborate conceit of prismatic refraction in its paradoxical relation to broken edges ("pointing unbruised directions") can be assumed—an idiosyncratic Merrill verb, offering every possibility for agnomination—by the elaborately wrought sentence, which without letting the mind settle down accommodates a (disputed) statement, an antithesis, a relative clause of detail (also antithetically modified) and a temporal clause doubled to match "unbruised directions" and "capacities of fire" with the notions of "wholeness" and "hodgepodge" introduced in the first line. Yet Merrill's serpentine sentences are too often a motionless coil to get us past the nodes in the line: the action is already over when the poem begins and, as in the stanza quoted here, when the crystal bowl has been broken and we are asked to ruminate upon the pieces, there is nothing left to do but moralize an aesthetics of the *fait accompli*. Of the accomplishment itself, there can be no question; most of these poems are successful in affording us "astounding images of order"; and if their shellac and jewelry make them seem, like the rococo armor of the Sun King, little more than machinery brought out only for festive occasions and worse than vulnerable for being invulnerable, even so "there's keen delight in what we have"—indeed the rest of Yeats' description of modern poetry is perfectly apposite to Merrill's early work, though to it only—"the rattle of pebbles on the shore, under the receding wave":

> . . . To drown was the perfection of technique,
> The word containing its own sense, like Time;
> And turning to the sea he entered it
> As one might speak of poems in a poem
> Or at the crisis in the sonata quote
> Five finger exercises: a compliment
> To all accomplishment.

For there is always a tidal undulation beneath these poems, always a fascination with the sea—the movement of water, the periodic destruction and recurrence of waves, the "makeshift waterfalls" of fountains—as the one entity and element refractory to the poet's designs, and therefore beyond any willed arrest mirroring (*reflect* is another Merrill favorite: Narcissus as Neoplatonist) the treasures of a drowned identity. In water, "change is meaningless, since all is change," and the poet can bear, for all his glossy, stilled performances, to confront "disordered gleams from under the tide (analogous to his "root's long revel under the clipped lawn"). In a capital poem, "The Drowning Poet," Merrill details this enthrallment with great care: water is an element

> Familiar as, to the musician, scales,
> Where to swim is a progression of long vowels,
> A communication never to be sought
> Being itself all searching: certain as pearls,
> Simple as rocks in sun, a happiness
> Bound up with happenings . . .

Here the sea becomes the locus of a final, farthest selfhood, that place and state where history can at last be assented to, where process is indulged if not invited, and where tautologies like "a communication never to be sought / being itself all searching" find a natural, a necessary home. Such reflexive constructions—"the gaze that of all weariness / remains unwearied" —like the encapsulated notions of Time as "the word containing its own sense," of love as "a thing in itself," and most grandly, of "time and love and doom" as

> Those great blue grottos of feeling where the rank intruder
> Is moved to think in rhyme—

suggest the problem which obsesses this poet, at least at this point in his career: how to get past the local excitement ("where every paradox means wonder") and into the stream of occurrence; past the "brim of what may be" and into the element of what is. Merrill wearily thrusts from himself these "sea's accumulations shored and salted" in favor of the sea itself, complaining that, for all his cunning in the cutting of a cameo, "alone,

one can but toy with imagery." He wants to get beyond or below what he merely enjoys and therefore repudiates, down to "the base of stone":

> . . . as one descending
> The spiral staircase of association
> Around the well of substance . . .

One way down to this lithic level is pointed to in—among other poems, but here at its most sustained articulation—the sixth variation of a series of changes rung on the phrase "The Air is Sweetest that a Thistle Guards"; it is the way of prose, of prose talk, the self soliloquizing in that reflexive, persistent babble we recognize as the bedrock of utterance, and a far cry—or rather no cry at all, but really a near and nestling murmur— from the lacquered plangencies, the bejewelled incantations of most of this volume:

> Friday. Clear. Cool. This is your day. Stendhal
> At breakfast-time. The metaphors of love.
> Lucky perhaps, big Beyle, for whom love was
> So frankly the highest good, to be garlanded
> Accordingly, without oblivion, without cure.
> His heedful botany: not love, great pearl
> That swells around a small unlovely need;
> Nor love whose fingers tie the bows of birth
> Upon the sorry present. Love merely as the best
> There is, and one would make the best of that
> By saying how it grows and in what climates,
> By trying to tell the crystals from the branch,
> Stretching that wand then toward the sparkling wave.
> To say at the end, however we find it, good,
> Bad, or indifferent, it helps us, and the air
> Is sweetest there. The air is very sweet.

What a departure—really an exodus—from the stanza of "The Broken Bowl" already quoted! How different the running, conversational blank verse, with its halts, its telegraphic notations, then its burrowing monosyllables ("love as the best there is and one would make the best of that . . .") which constitute the *Gerede* of an identity unsure of its own grounds for understanding. How startling here the dismissal of jewels and emblems in favor of happening. In "The Peacock," Merrill speaks of that figure of pride as "trailing too much of itself, like Proust"; here a different novelist is invoked, and one whose tubby "egotism" apparently represents less of a threat to continuity than the vanity of a perfect beauty. Stendhal's famous "metaphor of love," the branch dipped into the saline solution, is preferred to the "great-pearl" version—it is not the precious product which interests the poet, but the process, "saying how it grows and in what climates . . ." Of course Merrill still delights in what he knows he has, his quibbles:

> . . . love, great pearl
> That swells around a small unlovely need . . .

and the outright, even outrageous puns:

> . . . the bows of birth
> Upon the sorry present . . .

and certainly there is a fastidiousness in the diction, a knowing, *triste* music of selfishness in a phrase like "to be garlanded / accordingly, without oblivion, without cure," which reminds us that not everything has been sacrified to the Code Napoléon. Still, the effort here—and it is an issue, an exit—is "to tell the crystals from the branch" rather than to appreciate "curvings of glass artifice"; the sound of sentences, as Frost put it, utterance accountable to a limited and thereby illuminated self, transcends, or begins to transcend

> . . . that slight crystal lens
> Whose scope allows perfection to be conceived.

In 1954, three years after *First Poems*, Merrill published semi-privately (sixty copies for sale and one hundred and fifty for "friends of the poet and the printer") an even handsomer volume, or rather a pamphlet of some ten poems, with the very important title *Short Stories*. Almost all the longish poems here are blank verse recitals, someone telling something which happens, partly in the telling, partly beforehand, so that the event is enlarged or countered by the narrator's tone, as in "The Cruise":

> Poor little Agnes cried when she saw the iceberg.
> We smiled and went on with our talk, careless
> Of its brilliant fraction and, wakeful beneath,
> That law of which nine-tenths is a possession
> By powers we do not ourselves possess.
> Some cold tide nudged us into sunny gales
> With our money and our medications. No,
> Later in shops I thought again of the iceberg . . .

Of course we recognize some of the old turns—"a possession by powers we do not ourselves possess" is just that reflexive mordant Merrill prefers, especially when it involves a pun on "powers"—but the unaerated columns of print and the distrust of rhyme suggest the prose impulse in these pieces, the effort to melt down the jewel-like stanzas into a continuous discourse. As stories, the poems are not very successful, far too elliptical and emblematic as they are to articulate, even yet, "a happiness bound up with happenings." But as dramatic monologues, portraits of voices limned at a crucial corner of an incident, these poems indicate a great extension of Merrill's means, a playfulness in terms of genre and tone which will serve him more and more seriously. By varying the number of syllables—sometimes eleven, sometimes nine, rarely ten—the poet gives a nice corrugation of surface to his pentameter, and he is very good at speeding up the poem by suspensions of syntactical structure and by enjambment. "Gothic Novel," for example, begins with a swift pastiche of prose manners, disposed like a surrealist colonnade in an infinite regress of archness:

> How rich in opportunity! Part of a wall
> Gave back a hollow sound. Forthwith, intrigued,
> The Contessina knew her mind, consulted
> No one. A door! Annunziata darkly
> Swept up after the workmen and withdrew.
> Lost in thought, her mistress was already
> Rehearsing what to say in thirty years:
> 'Only after our marriage did I begin
> To fear your father'—but she broke off
> And went with a candle down the dank stair
> Leading she knew not where . . .

This is in part the poet making a mockery of his own postures in those of Wilkie Collins, but it is also his way of learning how to *recount*, a test of style which will help him on. Even when he employs rhyme in these pieces, Merrill disguises it in a device introduced, I think, by Auden in *Nones* (1950)—rhyming only the accented syllable of a feminine word with the final syllable of the next line—thereby enhancing the prose effect for the eye but keeping the ear alert to a sequestered music:

> There are many monsters that a glassen surface
> Restrains. And none more sinister
> Than vision asleep in the eye's tight translucence.
> Rarely it seeks now to unloose
> Its diamonds. Having divined how drab a prison
> The purest mortal tissue is,
> Rarely it wakes. Unless, coaxed out by lusters
> Extraordinary, like the octopus
> From the gloom of his tank half-swimming half-drifting
> Toward anything fair, a handkerchief
> Or child's face drifting toward the glass, the writher
> Advances in a godlike wreath . . .

There are still jewels here too—"glassen surface" (glassen!), vision's "dia-monds," "lusters extraordinary"—and the characteristic vocabulary of a self-deprecating urbanity, as if to tell the truth one had to be very, very tired. But there is also a truth to the *telling* (it is a real octopus Merrill shows us, though one invoked only as a figure of vision) which coaxes us through the poem, beyond the "lusters" and to the end, just as vision must for this poet be coaxed out of the "prison" of even the purest mortal tissue . . .

Alongside Current Events, poems about The Phoenix, The Vampire and Midas (all crucial figures for this poet, versions as they are of the disproportionate relations between life and artifice, but the last a paradig-matic emblem, rehearsing precisely Merrill's quandry: how to grasp the world yet somehow leave it intact) approach the myths obliquely, through a gossipy genre of runs and gushes. The narrator's occasional surrogate, an elegant and perverse Young Man named Charles introduced in *First Poems* ("Charles was like that"), is the last *persona* we might expect to meet up with in the refurbishing of such august categories, but he is evidently Merrill's first choice in escaping from the kind of emblematic stasis which fetters him:

> There followed for each a real danger of falling
> Into the oubliette of that bland face,
> Perfectly warned of how beneath it lay
> The bat's penchant for sleeping all day long
> Then flying off upon the wildest tangents
> With little self-preserving shrieks, also
> For ghastly scenes over letters and at meals,
> Not to speak of positive evil, those nightly
> Drainings of one's life, the blood, the laugh,
> The cries for pardon, the indifferences—
> It was then Charles thought to wonder . . .

What Charles wonders is what "on earth" the Vampire means by confess-ing herself a symbol of the "inner adventure." And with a teasing laugh, Merrill ends his poem: "Her retort is now a classic in our particular circle." It is not the story, not even the retort, but the notation of a world in which the retort is possible that matters to him; these poems are concerned to create a climate of opinion, a variable weather of discourse, and the provoking resonance of privacy about them—"a classic in our particular circle"—is little enough to pay for the freedom they afford the poet, though it is a freedom he cannot always himself afford. The resolu-tion of one difficulty invariably prompts another, and the decorative impulse is ever ready to capture Merrill's new beachheads:

> . . . the dread
> That, civilizing into cunning shapes,
> Briefly appeased what it could not oppose.

In 1957, Merrill published his first novel, *The Seraglio*, a good deal of which seems to have been written by Charles; though the first half is a narrowly observed account of life among the very rich and the very bored at what one Smith girl calls "the tippy-tippy end of Long Island," the remainder of the book turns into the glittering topography of a fantastic mythological opera, whose performance has overwhelming symbolic consequences for the novel's personnel as well as its prose. Two years earlier, Merrill's full-length play *The Immortal Husband*, a graceful Giralducian treatment of the story of Aurora and Tithonus, had been performed off-Broadway in New York and was later published. Both works indicate that the poet was concerned to explore the directions by which he might best work himself out of the lysis into which his *First Poems* had brought him: the direction of prose narrative and the direction of characterized speech. And in 1959 Merrill's new book of poems, *The Country of a Thousand Years of Peace*, was published, encompassing too all the *Short Stories* but "Gothic Novel." It is a brilliant, opalescent book and provides samples not only of all the accomplishments in form and decorum which *First Poems* had rather stiflingly insisted on, but realizations of the experiments in tone and identity initiated by *Short Stories*, now absorbed and even outstripped in some of the new pieces. In the eight years since his first book of poems, Merrill had made himself a "good European"—that is the first thing we notice about these poems, their wide but personal range of allusion to the experience of a transcontinental sightseer, shopper and sleeper (O the dreams in the "Hôtel de l'Univers et Portugal!"

> We had begun perhaps to lack a starlit Square.
> But now our very poverties are dissolving,
> Are swallowed up, strong powders to ensure
> Sleep, by a strange bed in the dark of dreaming),

and their ready understanding of Europe's history in the terms of Europe's myths: not only the Vampire and Salome, but an updated Marsyas, and Orpheus, even Europa herself in a couplet sonnet (one of the book's half a dozen jokes on the form) typical of Merrill's heightened method, whereby geography and puns, gossip and elegy are melted into the one vision:

> The white bull chased her. Others said
> All interest vanished. Anyhow, she fled,
> Her mantle's flowing border torn
> To islands by the Golden Horn,

Knee bared, head high, but soon to set
One salty cheek on water, let
Flesh become grass and high heart stone,
And all her radiant passage known
Lamely as Time by some she dreamt not of.
Who come to pray remain to scoff
At tattered bulls on shut church doors
In black towns numberless as pores,
The god at last indifferent
And she no longer chaste but continent.

It is a metamorphosis Ovid never dreamed of! Here the failure of classical
religion ("the god at last indifferent") and the degeneration of a Christian
successor (with its glancing reversal of Goldsmith's pious line and the
camp on papal bulls in "Who come to pray remain to scoff / at tattered
bulls on shut church doors") are wittily subsumed not only in the figure of
Europa herself turning into Europe ("her mantle's flowing border torn / to
islands by the Golden Horn"), but in puns inherent in her languages: "no
longer chaste but continent" is almost inhumanly clever in its ultimate
apprehension of the tourist's happy hunting ground. The notion of the
Continent as a vast declining bazaar:

Mild faces turned aside to let us fondle
Monsters in crystal, tame and small, fawning
On lengths of ocean-green brocade.
"These were once nightmares," the Professor said,
"That set aswirl the mind of China. Now
They are belittled . . . into souvenirs."
"Well I'm still famished," said a woman in red
Whose name escapes me now . . .

follows Merrill through all his poems henceforth, even affording him a subject
in his *refusing* to buy: the negative version of experience, the turning from
love, the renunciation of the voyage, the impatience with possessions
("tame . . . fawning . . . belittled into souvenirs"), all such rejecting moments become increasingly momentous for this "future sleuth of the oblique,"
and poems about Amsterdam, Italian lessons, India and Japan, the Sculpture
Museum and the Hall of Mirrors rehearse the genre of dissatisfaction. The
dream narrative *suffers* this poet to memorialize his losses, to conjugate
the downward history of Europe with the backward anamnesis of identity:

. . . As my eyes close, nearby
Something unwinds and breaks.
Perhaps the Discus Thrower has let fly
Or Laocoön stepped from his snakes
Like old clothes. The scene changes . . .

> But a white eyeless shape
> Is gesturing deep in my dream.
> I turn back to you for companionship . . .
>
> Well, I shall wake you now,
> Smiling myself to hide my fear . . .
>
> I judge it now in your slow eyes
> Which meet mine, fill with things
> We do not name, then fill with the sunrise
> And close, because too much light stings,
> All the more when shed on these
> Our sleeps of stone, our wakenings.

It is in this metropolitan book (the title refers to Switzerland, where "they all come to die, fluent therein as in a fourth tongue"), that Merrill is able, to a degree because of the technical innovations already discussed and to a degree because of a larger confidence in his own powers as a *persona* in the poem, the latter the fruit of travel—is able and ready, then, to shift from history and myth, through dream, to an unmediated confrontation with his own life, his own voice. Even in the persistent emblem poems, the moralized centrepiece is transformed, as in "A Timepiece," from a made or found object (a broken bowl, a black-and-white cameo, a decorative bird) to a living person—here the poet's pregnant sister:

> . . . It was not *her* life she was heavy with . . .
> Let us each have some milk, my sister smiled
> Meaning to muffle with the taste
> Of unbuilt bone a striking in her breast,
> For soon by what it tells the clock is stilled.

And if in other object lessons, like "Thistledown," there is still the static indulgence—a pleasure quite properly earned, of course; there is nothing in Merrill's airs and graces which is merely willful or willed, but rather the sense that we are watching a virtuoso who will shift into his heartbreaking Mad Scene just as soon as he gets through what are "roulades of relinquishment" indeed:

> Ha! how the Scotch flower's spendthrift
> Stars drifted down
> Many to tarn or turf, but ever a canny one
> On the stem left—

if there is still the preening of a feathery tautology: "Bewildered what to want past the extravagant notion of wanting," there is also a new responsibility to what it is that it being so spangled. Even in the ornamental

"Charles" pieces, like the "Laboratory Poem" in which the queasy hero watches his mistress dissecting turtles to test their hearts on the kymograph, there is a new instance of plain-speaking:

> He thought of certain human hearts, their climb
> Through violence into exquisite disciplines
> Of which, as it now appeared, they all expired.

Here, as in "A Timepiece," Merrill has found a way (it is mostly a prose way, a twist of the living idiom which combines the Jamesian with journalese) of adjusting his lust for the self-enclosed and the self-referring to metaphors of life far more appropriate than his old, ominous emblems of Time, Love and Doom. The patinated narcissism has been literally roughed up, and the resulting corrugation of surface corresponds, of course, to a new agitation of the depths. There is a rightness about the conceit of a heart which by its very "discipline" destroys itself, as there is in the image of the gravid woman "thrusting fullness from her, like a death"—more than a rightness, there is an *interest* in being told such things: the poet has *made over* his experience to language at a level deeper than that at which one wants merely to write poems, or to have written them, "given to grand personifications." In consequence, his poems, even when they are merely allegorized *things*, show a gain in consequence. Many succeed further in condensing the duration of larger narrative forms into their careful rhythms; for example "Mirror," in which a looking-glass that has weathered the fortunes and defeats of a family speaks:

> . . . as if a fish
> Had broken the perfect silver of my reflectiveness,
> I have lapses. I suspect
> Looks from behind, where nothing is, cool gazes
> Through the blind flaws of my mind. As days,
> As decades lengthen, this vision
> Spreads and blackens. I do not know whose it is,
> But I think it watches for my last silver
> To blister, flake, float leaf by leaf, each milling
> Downward dumb conceit, to a standstill . . .

Here even Merrill's ingenious rhyme on unaccented syllables and feminine words has a new justification beyond ingenuity, as if the moribund mirror itself enforced the "faulty" correspondence of "silver" and "standstill," "gazes" and "days." It is very close, this kind of technical iconography, where the self impersonates in speech its own decaying surface, to a direct image, or rather a discourse without images but rather of process—the poet speaking, as he will often henceforth do, in his own person, assuming his own past, acknowledging in the actions and rejected actions of the present his designs upon the future. In one of the brightest poems in the book, "The Doodler," designs on the future are precisely what the poet observes as he watches his unconscious spin itself out before his eyes, reflecting as he does on an aetiology of representation:

> . . . Far, far behind already is that aeon
> Of pin-heads, bodies each a ragged weevil,
> Slit mouthed and spider-legged, with eyes like gravel,
> Wavering under trees of purple crayon.
>
> Shapes never realized, were you dogs or chairs?
> That page is brittle now, if not long burned.
> This morning's little boy stands (I have learned
> To do feet) gazing down a flight of stairs.
>
> And when A. calls to tell me he enjoyed
> The evening, I begin again. Again
> Emerge, O sunbursts, garlands, creatures, men,
> Ever more lifelike out of the white void!

That is a characteristic Merrill invocation—riddling, chatty, sincere—of his own secret powers, the energy addressed showing a development away from mere embellishment ("sunbursts, garlands," the substance of *First Poems*) toward a responsible creative life ("creatures, men, / even more lifelike out of the white void!"). There is a humility now in his "designs" ("I have learned to do feet"). The accountability of the form tends to screen what is dangerous and abashing in these revelations (his mirror's last word is "I am amenable"—it might have been Petronius'). But the submission to such powers is not only expressed, it is welcomed, and the book's last poem, "A Dedication"—to the same Hans to whom the first and title poem was addressed—puts it with unheard-of frankness, or at least with a frankness unheard before in Merrill's poems:

> *These are the moments, if ever, an angel steps*
> *Into the mind, as kings into the dress*
> *Of a poor goatherd, for their acts of charity.*
> There are moments when speech is but a mouth pressed
> Lightly and humbly against the angel's hand.

The lines I distinguish by roman type are moving in every sense, for they surely define a poetics unavailable to this writer hitherto. Henceforth, it will be such moments that justify, even as they jeopardize, Merrill's powers.

In 1962 Merrill published a shorter but also more consistent volume of poems named this time not for a country but for the street in

Connecticut where he had set up house, *Water Street*; not only is there a domestic impulse in most of these poems, and a residential resonance to many of their names: "An Urban Convalescence," "Scenes of Child-hood," "The Lawn Fête," "A Tenancy," "A Vision of the Garden"—but the very division of impulse suggested in the book's title, the opposition between that which abides and that which flows, haunts the poet through-out this sober, disabused group of poems. Even the "technical" emblem poems, like "The Parrot Fish" and "To a Butterfly" are concerned, as in the latter case, with getting down to the single vision:

> Goodness, how tired one grows
> Just looking through a prism:
> Allegory, symbolism.
> I've tried, Lord knows,
>
> To keep from seeing double,
> Blushed for whenever I did . . .
>
> I am not yet
> Proof against rigmarole . . .
> The day you hover without any
> Tincture of soul,
>
> Red monarch, swallowtail,
> Will be the day my own
> Wiles gather dust. Each will have flown
> The other's jail.

And the consciousness of failure—these wiles are anything but dusty— seems not only to be ever at the poet's elbow, but to be a kind of consolation as well. Love is attended to as loss and separation, and wisdom is knowing it:

> For a decade love has rained down
> On our two hearts, instructing them
> In a strange bareness, that of weathered stone.
> Thinking how bare our hearts have grown
> I do not know if I feel pride or shame.

These are no longer the poems of paste and sequins or even of genuine gems: the pressure is off which would make this coal into diamonds. The poems are consequently longer, looser, they echo to the sound of a man talking less to make himself heard than to permit what he *has* to say (the compulsion is his own) to be overheard:

> . . . Wires and pipes, snapped off at the roots, quiver.
> Well, that is what life does. I stare

> A moment longer, so. And presently
> The massive volume of the world
> Closes again.
> Upon that book I swear
> To abide by what it teaches:
> Gospels of ugliness and waste,
> Of towering voids, of soiled gusts,
> Of a shrieking to be faced
> Full into, eyes astream with cold—
> With cold?
> All right then. With self-knowledge . . .

If so many of these poems are about to make a habitation out of some pretty disorderly houses, it is because the poet has confessed "the dull need to make some kind of house / out of the life lived, out of the love spent." For the soul's snowbound weather ("out of the white void!") he must find analogies in the world—hence homely poems of blizzards ("A new day. Fresh snow.") and of summer's end ("days when lover and beloved know / that love is what they are and where they go."). Love, travel and the scenes of childhood offer the occasion, learning and sympathy determine the form. The Proust of *Water Street* is no longer a conceit for the peacock "trailing too much of himself," but the sick man seen:

> Your eyes grow wide and dark, eyes of a Jew,
>
> You make for one dim room without contour
> And station yourself there, beyond the pale
> Of cough or of gardenia, erect, pale.
> What happened is becoming literature.
>
> Feverish in time, if you suspend the task,
> An old, old woman shuffling in to draw
> Curtains, will read a line or two, withdraw.
> The world will have put on a thin gold mask.

In these clear stanzas ("What happened is becoming literature" is a remarkable line for a poet who, though he knew happiness was bound up with happenings, once could not permit anything in his finished pieces to "become") whether the inner rhyme word is always itself, in a different acceptation—"pale" vs. "pale," reflecting the kind of transformation that time effects in Proust—the novelist is now conceived as an agent of preservation as well, not like the peacock merely showing off or showing others up, not like Stendhal "making the best of love, the best there is," but as a man concerned to perpetuate the universe. The thin gold mask is

not a defence against reality, not a concealment from it; it is a funerary
enduement which will withstand and redeem the wreckage of a life.
Similarly the "Prism" in this book is understood not in the baroque
diction and faceted rhythms of a broken bowl's "lucid unities," but as the
standing refutation of old dreams:

> . . . Look:
> You dreamed of this:
> To fuse in borrowed fires, to drown
> In depths that were not there . . . Now and then
> It is given to see clearly. There
> Is what remains of you, a body
> Unshaven, flung on the sofa. Stains of egg
> Harden about the mouth, smoke still
> Rises between fingers or from nostrils.
> The eyes deflect the stars through years of vacancy.
> Your agitation at such moments
> Is all too human . . . Yet the gem
> Revolves in space, the vision shuttles off.
> A toneless waltz glints through the pea-sized funhouse.
> The day is breaking someone else's heart.

Of course the old wit is there—as in the last two lines, where the
refraction of light is given as a "toneless waltz" and the explosion of the
spectrum is defined, in terms of both narrator and prism, as "breaking
someone else's heart." But there is nothing starched and nothing self-
pitying about these poems—the note of the dandy has been dropped: they
are simply very unhappy and very attractive. The opening and closing
poems in this collection represent the deepest sounding, along with the
"Scenes from Childhood," which Merrill has been able to make of his
self-knowledge. If they are disillusioned, "the primal figures jerky and
blurred," they are never dim or dull: every skill the poet has, and I think
he has them all, has been turned into an instrument for coming to terms
with the self:

> . . . in this new room,
> Mine, with my things and thoughts, a view
> Of housetops, treetops, the walls bare.
> A changing light is deepening, is changing
> To a gilt ballroom chair a chair
> Bound to break under someone before long.
> I let the light change also me . . .

And the next step, in this progress of wisdom which seems to consist in
putting off every garment, every mask but one of the thinnest gold is to

release into the world a naked identity—"leaner veteran"—that will not only endure but persist:

> . . . I put the flowers where I need them most
> And then, not asking why they come,
> Invite the visitors to sit.
> If I am host at last
> It is of little more than my own past.
> May others be at home in it.

In 1965, Atheneum published Merrill's second novel, *The (Diblos) Notebook,* a tenuous but extending experiment with versions of "happiness bound up with happenings" which bears the same relation to his 1966 book of poems *Nights and Days* that *The Seraglio* showed to the earlier poems. The novel takes place (and takes very little else: its characters are as uncertain of their margins as the X'd-out though legible phrases of its languorous narrator) in the ruined but still adorable Greece of the previous travel pieces:

> . . . All through
> The countryside were old ideas
> Found lying open to the elements.
> Of the gods' houses only
> A minor premise here and there
> Would be balancing the heaven of fixed stars
> Upon a Doric capital. The rest
> Lay spilled, their flutted drums half sunk in cyclamen
> Or deep in water's biting clarity
> Which just barely upheld me
> The next week, when I sailed for home.

And *home* of course is the self-cannibalizing New York: "it is not even as though the new / buildings did very much for architecture." *The Notebook* seems to have afforded Merrill a freedom in his erotic gestures, an elation in his surrender to the physical world that not even the allotted bonds of *Water Street* insured. Witness the long and intricate poem "From the Cupola," which takes up the romance of Eros and Psyche where the poet had left it in his very first book:

> So, where he slept in the dark bed, she took
> A candle, wooed his profile with the kiss
> Of all things bodiless . . .

and inflects it through a series of verse forms and even prose passages (some appear to be from a forgotten work called *Psyche's Sisters* by one A. H. Clarendon, which the author disingenuously quotes in another poem altogether), combining a modern version of the myth rather like that of *The Immortal Husband* with a psychoanalytic tale of Psyche and her sisters Alice and Gertrude who live in a Greek Revival house on the Connecticut shore of Long Island Sound. Into this teasing and iridescent farrago, the poet himself intrudes, pricking the fable and the sisters' memories with the insistent reminder that he is making the whole thing up:

> Psyche, hush. This is me, James.
>   Writing lest he think
> Of the reasons why he writes—
> Boredom, fear, mixed vanities and shames;
>   Also love.
> From my phosphorescent ink
> Trickle faint unwordly lights
>
> Down your face. Come, we'll both rest.
>   Weeping? You must not.
> All our pyrotechnic flights
> Miss the sleeper in the pitch-dark breast.
>   He is love.
> He is everyone's blind spot.
> We see according to our lights . . .

and after the whole story is over, or at least overt, after Psyche has cleaned the windows of the cupola and at last seen, as Marivaux (surely the right mentor here) would say, clear into her heart, the poet breaks in again, reviewing all the props and personages of the story, even Psyche's lamp:

> The lamp I smell in every other line.
>
> Do you smell mine? From its rubbed brass a moth
> Hurtles in motes and tatters of itself
> —Be careful, tiny sister, drabbest sylph!—
> Against the hot glare, the consuming myth,
> Drops and is still. My hands move. An intense
> Slow-paced, erratic dance goes on below.
> I have received from whom I do not know
> These letters. Show me, light, if they make sense.

the psyche moth is the last version of selfhood, battering itself against the "consuming myth," that Merrill allows in this long, funny, self-defeating poem. It offers glimpses of course of the old Merrill of the lacquer-work and decorative flourishes:

> My sisters' gold sedan's
> eyes have gone dim and dark   windows are sealed
>   For vision's sake two wipers wield
> the automatic coquetry of fans . . .

but released from the servitude of making sense by letting his senses make it. There is a new reality, or at least a new realism here, even in this fanciful and preposterous fable, a notation of experience quite beyond fooling; travel's spoils have effected a change of heart, and nothing is trivial because everything is interpreted, mediated, indulged by the five senses:

> *Dear ones* I say bending to kiss their faces
> *Trust me   One day you'll understand   Meanwhile*
> suppose we think of things to raise our spirits
> and leading the two easiest to beguile
>
> into the kitchen feed them shots of Bourbon
> Their brother who loves Brahams conceives a wish
> for gems from L'Africana played at volumes
> that make the dwarf palm shudder in its dish
>
> The pale one with your eyes restively flashing
> Takes in the dock the ashen Sound the sky
> The fingers of the eldest brush my features . . .

Merrill's self-conscious suspicion of his own learning ("Do you smell mine?") and his delight in novelistic complication (breaking up the narrative by interpolated quotations, discrepant verse forms, conversation) are more consequentially articulated, I think, in the other very long poem in this book, "The Thousand and Second Night." A kind of catch-all travel journal, Merrill's narrative puts Scheherazade on as easily as—it puts her off, say; and includes an attack of facial palsy, a visit to Hagia Sophia:

> You did not want to think of yourself for once,
> But you had held your head erect
> Too many years within such transcendental sculls
> As this one not to feel the usual, if no
> Longer flattering kinship. You'd let go
> Learning and faith as well, you too had wrecked
> Your precious sensibility. What else did you expect?

and to the Turkish bath; a prose memory of his grandmother's hand intervenes, whose shape was like the skyline of Istanbul, and then a terrifying bout of acidie in Athens:

> . . . The day I went up to the Parthenon
> Its humane splendor made me think *So what?* . . .
>
> Try, I suppose, we must, as even Valéry said,
> And said more grandly than I ever shall—

followed by a stern fragment of autobiography, which leads in turn to a dazzling examination of some dirty postcards that have turned up in a family legacy. Love, of course, follows logically, and is subjected to a going over, though here the speaker fails us:

> And now the long adventure
>
> Let that wait.
> I'm tired, it's late at night . . .

postponing his account until his return:

> Lost friends, my long ago
>
> Voyages, I bless you for sore
> Limbs and mouth kissed, face bronzed and lined,
> An earth held up, a text not wholly undermined
> By fluent passages of metaphor.

And the poem ends with a mocking exegesis of its own forms in a classroom parody, and a burst of feeling when the Sultan and his Scheherazade are parted—she now released and he enslaved. In a sense, the nights and days of this book's title are the dreams and experience of Merrill's life, opposed and ruefully—by lethargy, almost—united:

> She and her fictions soon were one.
> He slept through moonset, woke in blinding sun,
> Too late to question what the tale had meant.

The rest of the book is a virtual inventory of Merrill's dazzling repertoire: another "Charles" poem, an expatriate portrait, several family studies and scenes from childhood, emblem poems and dream sequences:

> Again last night I dreamed the dream called Laundry.
> In it the sheets and towels of a life we were going to share
> The milk-stiff bibs, the shroud, each rag to be ever
> Trampled or soiled, bled on or groped for blindly,
> Came swooning out of an enormous willow hamper
> Onto moon-marbly boards. We had just met . . .

Poems still about the movement and measure of water, like "The Current," and poems about possessions renounced, like "A Carpet Not Bought," indicate this poet's loyalty to his own mastered impulses. But beyond the variety and the complexity of Merrill's accumulated lusters, beyond the two long poems that are obviously the set-pieces of *Nights and Days*, there is the book's final poem that I take to be the poet's finest salute to his own continuing powers, indeed his hostage to their continuation: "Days of

1964." Named for those terrible late poems of Cavafy's—"Days of 1909," "Days of 1911," portraits of debauchery and transcending love—Merrill's long envoi has the true Alexandrian tone: in its certainty of place and circumstance—

> . . . Our neighborhood sun-cured if trembling still
> In pools of the night's rain . . .
> Across the street that led to the center of town
> A steep hill kept one company part way
> Or could be climbed in twenty minutes
> For some literally breathtaking views,
> Framed by umbrella pines, of city and sea.
> Underfoot, cyclamen, autumn crocus grew
> Spangled as with fine sweat among the relics
> Of good times had by all. If not Olympus,
> An out-of-earshot, year-round hillside revel. . . .

and its charity and grace in characterization:

> . . . Her legs hurt. She wore brown, was fat, past fifty,
> And looked like a Palmyra matron
> Copied in lard and horsehair. How she loved
> You, me, loved us all, the bird, the cat!
> I think now she *was* love. She sighed and glistened
> All day with it, or pain, or both . . .

the poem moves through a shocking encounter with this mythological factotum ("I think now she was love"), half gossip and half goddess disguised as a temple prostitute—for its subject is possession by the god:

> the erotic mask
> worn the world over by illusion
> to weddings of itself and simple need—

and returns, as "by a commodious vicus of recirculation" to a confrontation of love in the narrator's own life:

> I hoped it would climb when it needed to the heights
> Even of degradation, as I for one
> Seemed, those days, to be always climbing
> Into a world of wild
> Flowers, feasting, tears—or was I falling, legs
> Buckling, heights, depths,
> Into a pool of each night's rain?
> But you were everywhere beside me, masked
> As who was not, in laughter, pain and love.

Such a poem dramatizes the astonishing truth that this poet, the most decorative and glamor-clogged America had so far produced, has made himself, by a surrender to reality and its necessary illusions, a master of his experience and of his own nature.

"THE FIRE SCREEN"

Not an end in themselves but an ongoing ("a nature / which existed to be overthrown"), not pride of place but the modesty of replacement ("tones one forgets / even as one is changed for life by them"): continuing powers! To them is made the apostrophe, to them is offered the hope of what we prosaically call, in a poet's career, his *transitional* work. The hinge (as the word *hinge* once meant a hesitation, a hanging between) holding together the familiar, the accomplished, the *done for* on one side of the door ("certain things die only with oneself"), and on the other the hankered-after, the heterogenous ("to greet the perfect stranger")—that is the function and the emblem of James Merrill's new book. A look, in fact, at the characteristically emblematic title and its provenance will serve to show what we are up against, what we are squeezed between. In a poem of Proustian recall entitled "Mornings in a New House" (continuing the series of domestic studies, nesting grounds for divorce, disorderly houses held open in all six of Merrill's books of poems, in both his novels), "a cold man" wakes at dawn and once the fire is lit and the frosted window thawed, the worst is over:

> . . . Now between
> His person and that tamed uprush
> (which to recall alone can make him flush)
> Habit arranges the fire screen.

The first acceptation, then, is the one on the wrong side of the hinge: the fire screen is that grid of decorative devices ("all framework and embroidery") which protects against the blaze or at least the glow (even the fire, here, is "that *tamed* uprush"). Evidently uneasy about so much lamplight and crewel-work, Merrill adds a curious prose footnote to the phrase "fire screen", a revisionary impulse "days later" which suggests he missed his way, took the wrong road: "Fire screen—screen *of* fire. The Valkyrie's baffle, pulsing at trance pitch, godgiven, elemental . . . some such meaning might have caught, only I settled . . . Oh well. Our white heats lead us on no less than words do. Both have been devices in their day." A second acceptation, then, of the fire screen: not the comfortable household convenience, but the flaming curtain, the destructive element. And crucially, the realization—wry, chastened, ultimately cheering—that we are "led on" alternatively and equally by our white heats and our mere words. Brunhilde's trance is as much of a convention, a device, Merrill reassures himself, as Praed's trimeter. Both will be invoked and utilized in this book—we are *led on* in both senses: the sense of infatuation and the sense of futurity.

If a poet has mastered his own nature; if he has, like the sea, in his surrender to constraint found his continuing, what becomes of his poetry— poetry which he himself has taught us to take as the record of a struggle, as the terms of that surrender? Often enough—too often, as in the case of Browning, the case of Tennyson, though less outrageously there—nothing at all *becomes* of his poetry, he goes on writing it, he opens a museum of manners, a smiling public man indeed, or even a frowning one. The task, for the poet in this dilemma, will be to discover what lies beyond himself, what extends outside the literally charmed circle of his accomplishment by which he is merely entranced, what is on the other side of the fire screen.

With all his urbanity on the ready like a revolver, Merrill will proceed into new territory then, as resolved to mistrust the trance—"god-given, elemental"—as to transcend the merely mastered. Chief among the preoccupations in this new book, thus, will be harping upon, the harking back to pure personality: the calcined, clarified contour of identity when the accidents of period and place are consumed. "The Friend of the Fourth Decade," "Words for Maria," "Kostas Tympakianakis" are scorched portraits, attempts to reach that region of the self where, as the Friend himself writes, "individual and type are one." *L'individu seul est esclave; l'espèce est libre* is what Buffon wrote about falcons, and in the hawklike profiles of Merrill's sitters we recognize the bondage and the freedom both, recognize and salute. "Who could have imagined such a life as mine?" asks Kostas Tympakianakis at the end of his monologue. Why, no one *needs* imagine, Merrill's strict poems reply, not here, among the lineaments of reality.

For such a poet, at such a point in his making ("scene upon scene's immersion and emergence / rinsed of the word"), not only certain selves but certain sites will catch fire. Mostly Greek places for Merrill, landscapes reduced to "this or that novel mode of being together / without conjunctions." Harsh, bare, yet these "coastlines of white printless coves [are] already strewn with offbeat echolalia." Like Gide in the desert, Merrill finds in these waste places of the heart's landscape the most *inexhaustible* locus for his celebration. As he puts it at the end of "To My

Greek," a poem inextricably dedicated to a language and a personality, "the barest word be what I say in you."

Corrective, deprecatory, incredibly entertaining, another half of the book is offered up to framework and embroidery—what Merrill may call "settling for the obvious," though so subtle is the crewel-work and so restless the self-consciousness ("The meter grows misleading, / given my characters . . . I have no such hero, / no fearful deeds—unless / we count their quiet performance / by Time or Tenderness") that even the most diverted reader is not likely to be unaware of the depths he has been diverted from. When the Valkyrie's baffle proves to be merely portentous, Merrill turns, indeed returns, to his "household opera":

> The love scene (often cut). The potion. The tableau:
> Sleepers folded in a magic fire,
> Tongues flickering up from humdrum incident . . .

In a wonderful sonnet sequence called "Matinées" from which this other fire screen comes, in the filigree indulgence of a ballad of other lives called "The Summer People," in poems of emblem and recall beyond the wildest dreams of cleverness, Merrill counterpoints and orchestrates what I have called his transition. These civilities, these reticences ballast that other impulse so searing as to be suspect: the impulse which in one poem titled after Yeats (a constantly invoked figure here, even when he is gently mocked) is called "More Enterprise"—the impulse to reduce to anonymity, which in poetry is to be reduced to riches.

"BRAVING THE ELEMENTS"

A few seasons ago, I spoke of Merrill's previous book *The Fire Screen* as "poems not an end in themselves but an ongoing." Here, in considerable splendor, is what they went on to, the new poems which are indeed an end in themselves, a consummation, marriage and holocaust both, for they seek—and extensively, patulously, find—that point endured by the mystics and dared by the surrealists, that point which affords access to *reality*, to Being understood as existence without contradictions or conditions, where up and down, before and after, are no longr to be construed as opposites, where opposition is not construed at all. These, then, are poems of ecstatic apprehension, in which the dialectics of an identity, a biography, are renounced in favor and fervor of those great converging energies which bear the utterance to a pitch, a register where there is no longer what Shelley called the burr of self that sticks to one so, but that transparency which *renders* the world—others, weather, landscape, love: this poetry is, in every sense and with all the weight the phrase will bear, a *burning glass*.

Anything but accidental then, that the book begins with the asseveration "Everything changes, nothing does"; sustains this version in the center somewhere with the equivalent sense, "nothing lasts and nothing ends"; and concludes—in one of Merrill's many instrumentalities, the poem-as-lens, the self-as-the-*medium*-of-others—with the astonishing overtones of "Syrinx," in which the compass-rose becomes the final wisdom of transformation:

Nought

Waste   Eased

Sought

In a recent interview, Merrill wraps it up (*it* being just this poise of perception where the responsibility of form is not contested by the personal, the perversity of *wanting*): "How one tries—not just in writing—to escape from these opposites, from there being two sides to every question." Merrill tries, Merrill succeeds, by every means at his disposal, and he disposes of those means, dissolves them subsequently in the service of illumination: "centimeters deep yawns the abyss," he observes, and is therefore entitled to observe each centimeter with an exactitude ordinarily reserved for distances. Of course there are distances too—huge views, up mountains and down bank vaults, the landscapes of Greece and New Mexico, the *paysages d'âme* of a lover, a son, a master. And there are those explorations of the past, of memory and hallucination, of dreams and dramas ("the tempest used to be my cup of tea") which in Merrill's own earlier poems were merely memorial, merely elegiac. They have been transformed, transmuted, under tremendous pressure, like coal into crystal, so that it is no longer possible to say what was fantasy, what was flesh: it is all one ecstasy now, in Merrill, one modality:

I tremble, still

A thinking reed. Who puts his mouth to me

Draws out the scale of love and dread—

O ramify, sole antidote!

And the crystals do branch out. I used to reproach this poet, or at least to approach him warily, for being, as I called it, bejewelled. Cloudy emeralds, star sapphires, glaucous pearls were on every page, studding the desolations like tears. No longer: everything has been clarified, consumed, and one looks through the brilliant poems to the experience they render, they render *possible* by their intensity of purpose, their diamond-hard joy; nothing is decoration or decor now in Merrill's poetry, for the poet has discovered the link between what is cosmetic and what is cosmic. His poems are orders of experience from which he has won the right to be the *deus absconditus*, present everywhere in his works, and only there:

> . . . at once
> Transfiguring, transfigured. A voice grunts
> MATTER YOU MERELY DO I AM
>
> Which lies on snow in dark ideogram
> —Or as a later commentary words it,
> *One-night's-meats-another-morning's-mass-*
> *Against-inhuman-odds-I-celebrate.*

RICHARD SÁEZ

James Merrill's
Oedipal Fire

When James Merrill's "18 West 11th
Street" appeared in the *New York Review of Books* in the Spring of 1972, it
must have puzzled readers. A hermetic poem by America's most elegant
and apolitical poet about a politically explosive topic in the very politically committed review! The address is the house accidentally blown up in
March, 1971, by Weathermen who were using it as a headquarters for
constructing anti-personnel bombs: explosives with nails taped to their
exterior so as to score their points more piercingly. Amongst them was
Cathy Wilkerson, a daughter of the wealthy financier who owned the
elegant address. Unlike some of the others, she escaped the blast. She was
seen—bleeding and naked—fleeing from the burning building, and her
long-sought image haunted the headlines for months. But why had Merrill—
who has disclaimed contemporary events and even the present tense as
too hot to be handled by lyrical poetry—written about the house? In one
of his most memorable and frequently anthologized earlier poems, "The
Broken Home" (*Nights and Days*, 1966), as he remembers painfully his
traumas as the child of a wealthy financier, he defends his apolitical work
and his commitment to writing only about his private past and the
creative act. That was, of course, the point about "18 West 11th Street."
Cathy Wilkerson and James Merrill had more than an address in common.
Still, even for readers familiar with the poet's work, the poem remained
obscure.

    Merrill read it for the first time in New York at the New School

---

From *Parnassus* 1, vol. 3, (Fall/Winter 1974). Copyright © 1974 by *Parnassus*. "*18 West
11th Street,*" from *Braving the Elements*, © 1972 by James Merrill, is reprinted by permission
of Atheneum Publishers.

during the summer of 1972. He prefaced his reading by saying that although it was not his habit to write about contemporary events, he felt entitled to write about the demolished building since he had been born there. When one got over the extraordinary circumstance of fate—to have enmeshed one of America's most distinguished poets with one of her most psychologically and politically dramatic events—"18 West 11th Street" immediately lost some of its hermeticism. Merrill had not sought the headlines; in bold type the headlines had sought him. And he had not abandoned his usual themes: the poem is about his past, and it contrasts his own creative endeavors with the revolutionary activity of the Weathermen. But at the end of the reading, much of the poem remained veiled. One remembered from earlier poems a few details which teased with the promise of some light: in "An Urban Convalescence" (*Water Street*, 1962) the poet imagines one of his former homes collapsing, and in "The Broken Home" (*Nights and Days*, 1966), while meditating on his mother, he depicts thirties suffragettes hurling invectives at political leaders: "*War mongerer! Pig! Give us the vote.*" It was apparent that "18 West 11th Street" should be read in the light of the style, themes, and structures developed throughout Merrill's poetic career.

With almost masochistic glee Paul Valéry lamented the poet's lack of a musician's precision tools: "no tuning forks, no metronomes, no inventors of scales or theoreticians of harmony." The poet must "borrow language" from which he creates his own mode of expression. The studious craft of James Merrill's mode is increasingly evident. Within the past two years he has published his most perfectly achieved volume of poems. *Braving the Elements*, (1972); several subsequent poems which indicate he has entered a mature and sustained phase of his career; and *The Yellow Pages*, (1974)—a volume of previously uncollected early and late poems (1947–1968) "thrust aside" over the years in the compilation of his several published volumes. In effect, by showing us the rejected poems—"yellowed, brittle with reproach"—he has helped define his achieved style. "18 West 11th Street" is written in a personal idiom which shows Merrill's debt to the language of the French symbolist and English metaphysical poets.

Both the poems of *The Yellow Pages* and those of even his most recent volumes rely heavily on the traditional forms, meter, and rhyme of English prosody. One of the elements which makes the "selected" poems more successful is that Merrill understands Mallarmé's lesson to Degas: "Poems are made not with ideas but words." He has stated frequently enough in interviews, novels, footnotes to his poems, and in the poems themselves that for him word must *elicit* word. Indeed, Merrill's poems move and fulfill themselves as the words—chiseled and molded by the poet's extraordinary intuition and feeling—evoke and whisper their hidden resources: feelings and states of being only suggested in the poem but intuited precisely by the reader. Merrill would again agree with Valéry that poetry becomes, "musicalized, resonant, and, as it were, harmonically related." As we shall see in "18 West 11th Street" and some of the later poems, Merrill would also agree with Pound in seeing some of these musicalized poems as "a network of tentacular roots" which reach "down to the deepest terrors and desires."

"Willowware Cup" (*Braving the Elements*) is a perfect example of the style. The poem is a meditation on dimestore "chinaware" from which Merrill wrests *crazingly* complex associations. The words he uses to describe the cup evoke as mysterious presences as any Yeats imagined to dwell in the English language, and the parts are intricately blended in a way to make incision or excerpts impossible:

> Mass hysteria, wave after breaking wave
> Blueblooded Cantonese upon these shores
>
> Left the gene pool Lux-opaque and smoking
> With dimestore mutants. One turned up today.
>
> Plum in bloom, pagoda, bluebirds, plume of willow—
> Almost the replica of a prewar pattern—
>
> The same boat bearing the gnat-sized lovers away,
> The old bridge now bent double where her father signals
>
> Feebly, as from flypaper, minding less and less.
> Two smaller retainers with lanterns light him home.
>
> Is that a scroll he carries? He must by now be immensely
> Wise, and have given up earthly attachments, and all that.
>
> Soon, of these May mornings, rising in mist, he will ask
> Only to blend—like ink in flesh, blue anchor
>
> Needled upon drunkenness while its destroyer
> Full steam departs, the stigma throbbing, intricate—
>
> Only to blend into a crazing texture.
> You are far away. The leaves tell what they tell.
>
> But this lone, chipped vessel, if it fills,
> Fills for you with something warm and clear.
>
> Around its inner horizon the old odd designs
> Crowd as before, and seem to concentrate on you.

> They represent, I fancy, a version of heaven
> In its day more trouble to mend than to replace:
>
> Steep roofs aslant, minutely tiled;
> Tilted honeycombs, thunderhead blue.

From the imitation pattern on the cup the poet *invents* a legend. His story of the lovers' departure from the father does not arise inevitably from the pattern, but as Merrill becomes lost in his reverie, the words, rising like mist from earthly attachments, return him to the flesh: "like ink in flesh, blue anchor." The fading of the pattern on the cup modulates on the word "blend," through a counterpoint of "mist" and "steam," into a tattoo worn probably by a past lover: another scene of departure. Just as the destroyer of the tattoo has been anticipated in the initial evocation of mass violence, the poem is also conscious of earthly passionate fulfillment: "hysteria," "gene," "bloom," and "stigma" (in its botanical sense of the pollen-receiving pistil). Then all focuses on the friend, as distant now as prewar China. At this juncture of two literal levels of meaning, a point on which most of Merrill's poetry is balanced, the poem can speak about the original Chinese pattern *and* the friend: a paradisiacal bliss lost in the absence of cultivated uniqueness. Finally, the lost version of heaven is abstracted beyond plate and friend into pure design and color:

> Steep roofs aslant, minutely tiled;
> Tilted honeycombs, thunderhead blue.

The poem presents a metaphysical vision in which diverse physical realities are seen against—and, thereby, seen through—a disembodied pattern. The implied metaphor between a noumenal-phenomenal dichotomy and expensive china and its cheap imitation is purposefully bizarre, as is the relationship between the tattoo and the dinnerware pattern. But this wrested comparison is typical of Merrill (more usually present in puns like "crazing" or "stigma"). The violent yoking, as artfully intentional as the catachreses of seventeenth century metaphysical poetry, helps to reveal a reality far away from earthly attachments.

This metaphysical element, the triune legend of father and lovers, the *medium* of heat in "mists" and "steam," and the interplay between legend and pattern are aspects of Merrill's mature thematic concerns to which I shall return in discussing "18 West 11th Street." Before leaving a consideration of his style, I would like to compare the subtle harmonies of "Willowware Cup" with an earlier poem collected for the first time in *The Yellow Pages*. "Early Settlers" (1958) describes the failure of a pioneer couple. In the final quatrains the couple are seen spent and withdrawn, warming their winter with a fire:

Evenings, the air thins. One of them must kneel
Fumbling the skein of fumes till a dead branch
Puts brilliant leafage forth, whose buffets draw
From their drawn skins the same loud, senseless pulse.

A life is something not invented yet,
A square of linen worked in colored wools
To stand between its maker and that drumming,
Twitching, gibbering source of light and pain

They turn to, hand in hand, themselves becoming
Gnarled, then ashen, upon some hearth not seen
But tended in impassive silence by
A leathery god or two, crouched there for warmth.

The metaphor of an individual life as a fire screen upon which the vital source of Life fulfills itself is the most compelling element in the poem. The further leap which turns the couple into a source of fuel for a celestial fire screen seems forced and artificial. As so frequently in *The Yellow Pages*, it is a leap performed by an acrobatic poetic fancy rather than an arabesque unfolding quite naturally from poised language. In a later poem, "Mornings in a New House" (*The Fire Screen*, 1969), Merrill returns to the image of a fire screen. But that poem should be seen as an aspect of his phenomenology of fire: not only the heat present in the "steam" and "mists" of "Willowware Cup" and the fire screens of these poems but also the fire which destroys 18 West 11th Street.

In his novel *The Diblos Notebook*, Merrill reflects a difficult aspect of his poetry by creating what he calls "a composite literary hero: Perseus, Oedipus, Odysseus, Joseph (Mann), Hamlet, Don Q., Shelley, Houdini"; the French phenomenologist of poetic symbols, Gaston Bachelard, has taught us (mostly in *The Psychoanalysis of Fire*) that a relationship is to be found between the Oedipus complex and the Prometheus complex in a passionate desire "to know as much as our fathers, more than our fathers." Bachelard associates the imagery of fire used to describe the aroused male principle and the sexual shapes of the alchemist's tools with the intuition of fire as "the desire to change, to speed up the passage of time, to bring all of life to its conclusion, to its hereafter." Merrill often presents his poetic activity as a way of speeding up life to its "hereafter" and fire as the medium of change. In the earliest volumes and in *The Yellow Pages*, Merrill characteristically reflects the symbol in aesthetic objects—the gilder's or the potter's art and the "thin gold mask" in "For Proust" (*Water Street*)—in order to distance and intensify the psychic-aesthetic process. "Poem of a Summer's End" (*Water Street*) presents two lovers traveling in Umbria who, at the end of a decade of love, are at the point of intimacy

which is both fulfillment and point of departure in a tensionless knowledge of each other:

> Weaker each sunrise reddens that slow maze
> So freely entered. Now come days
> When lover and beloved know
> That love is what they are and where they go.
>
> Each learns to read at length the other's gaze.

It is a moment Merrill returns to frequently. In this poem it is manifested
as an Umbrian façade fired for an instant by the setting sun:

> The time for making love is done.
> A far off, sulphur-pale façade
> Gleams and goes out. It is as though by one
> Flash of lightning all things made
> Had glimpsed their maker's heart, read and obeyed.

The façade seems to be a flat plate glazed into aesthetic timelessness by a
celestial furnace while it also leads into the church and the shrines with
which the rest of the poem is concerned: the "hereafter" of the lovers'
inward mirroring gaze also holds God's holy fire.

These images of love, knowledge, creativity, and fire grow variously
in symbolic density throughout Merrill's poetry. As with the "mist" and
"steam" of "Willowware Cup," he also decorously or humorously displaces
fire in painted red nails or the inebriate flushes of Dionysus. In recent
poems, he seems to prefer the later stages of bio-geological life processes:
creativity is represented in precious gems, crystal prisms, geological rock,
and metals cooled into luminosity. As so often in Merrill, one is reminded
of Proust when he speaks of the mind as a mineral deposit of life
containing a potential work of art. The cooling of his symbols may reflect
Merrill's growing mastery, but the phenomenological force of fire remains.
In so recent a poem as "After the Fire" (*Braving the Elements*), an ancient
muse figure is described as an "oven-rosy witch" whose fire the poet
embraces in the closing verse: "and I / Am kneeling pressed to her old
burning frame."

"Dream About Clothes" (*Braving the Elements*) is more illustrative
of Merrill's "composite hero." There fire appears as the "dry hell / Of
volatile synthetic solvents," and the literal clothes being taken to the dry
cleaners are those of a man who resembles the poet's father as described in
his biographical novel, *The Seraglio*:

> In some, the man they made
> Penetrates the sunlit fitting room,

> Once more deciding among bolts of dark.
> The tailor kneels to take his measure.
> Soon a finished suit will be laid out
> By his valet, for him to change into.
> Change of clothes? The very clothes of change!
> Unchecked blazers women flutter round,
> Green coverts, midnight blues . . .
> My left hand a pincushion, I dispose,
> Til morning, of whole closets full of clues.

The oedipal hero of this dry nocturnal meditation asks:

> What ought I in fact to do with them?
> Give away suits worn six, eight times?
> Take them to the shrink until they fit?

But in refurbishing the psychic clothes of the poem, the poet turns from the Freudian exorcism of his early novel to a more consuming passion in a final invocation to "Art":

> Tell me something, Art.
> You know what it's like
> Awake in your dry hell
> Of volatile synthetic solvents.
> Won't you help us brave the elements
> Once more, of terror, anger, love?

Perhaps Merrill's most revealing metamorphosis of Promethean fire is into the linguistic process of "Lost in Translation" (*The New Yorker*, 6 April 1974). Here he remembers piecing together a puzzle with his multilingual governess, which evokes the more recent memory of a German translation by Rilke of Valéry's "*Palme*." Although he cannot find the translation, he imagines what is lost and retained in it:

> Yet I can't
> Just be imagining. I've seen it. Know
> How much of the sun-ripe original
> Felicity Rilke made himself forego
> (Who loved French words—verger, mûr, parfumer)
> In order to render its underlying sense.

For a poem in which the piecing together of a puzzle at every juncture responds to the fitting of words into a poetic pattern, the progress from a meditation on what is lost in literary translation to the transformation of life into literature is quite natural: "But nothing's lost. Or else: all is translation / And every bit of us is lost in it."

"Lost in Translation" is about Merrill's poetry in even more telling ways. Like the *oeuvre* itself, the legend of the puzzle—seen through the almost predominant pattern of its design—represents an "Eternal Triangle": a page (whom the governess imagines to be a son) torn between service to his sire or his sire's wife. (It is no surprise when the page's missing feet are found under the table with the child's own.) And the shapes of the individual pieces of the puzzle have—like the symbolist's words—their own significance:

> Many take
> Shapes known already—the craftsman's repertoire
> Nice in its limitation—from other puzzles:
> Witch on broomstick, ostrich, hourglass,
> Even (surely not just in retrospect)
> An inchling, innocently branching palm.

But nowhere does Merrill speak quite so precisely about his own craft— the individual poems and the totality of his work—as in the description by a medium of a "hand-sawn" individual piece of the puzzle:

> But hidden here is a freak fragment
> Of a pattern complex in appearance only.
> What it seems to show is superficial
> Next to that long-term lamination
> Of hazard and craft, the karma that has
> Made it matter in the first place.
> Plywood. Piece of a puzzle.

The puzzle exists in Merrill's poetry. The whole is composed of intricately related parts, and it rewards explication even though once it has been puzzled out there may be little to do but dismantle it like the puzzle in "Lost in Translation." Its emphasis on "lamination" and "craft" returns us to a discussion of the forms of his poetry.

James Merrill has evolved his phenomenology of fire within three quite distinct generic forms which he handles with equal mastery: long narratives in traditional ballad stanzas, emblematic lyrics, and multi-sectioned meditations on time and the aesthetic process—the genre to which "18 West 11th Street" belongs. Each form aims at aesthetic possession. The worlds of the long ballad narratives—the dwindling aristocracy of an eastern summer resort in "The Summer People" (*The Fire Screen*, 1969) and a child's wish-fulfillment dream of kidnap in "Days of 1935" (*Braving the Elements*)—are framed in mock-heroic caricature:

> That summer was the model
> For several in a row—

High-water marks of humor
And humankindness, no

Discord at cards, at picnics,
Charades or musicales.
Their faces bright with pleasure might
Not have displeased Frans Hals.

("The Summer People")

The brief lyrics hold the world in monadic emblems cut and polished so precisely as to reflect the lights of Merrill's entire work. (They are abstract enough to reflect as well any lights the readers might bring.) Their monadic quality isolates much of Merrill's phenomenology of fire.

"Mornings in a New House" emblazons the oedipal fire in a lyric which is Yeatsian both in quality and psychological overtones. A man awakens in a house to find the fire lit; a frozen window thaws, screening the claws of brightness. The poem then turns inward to contemplate his and his mother's childhood:

The worst is over. Now between
His person and that tamed uprush
(Which to recall alone can make him flush)
Habit arranges the fire screen.

Crewel-work. His mother as a child
Stitched giant birds and flowery trees
To dwarf a house, *her* mother's—see the chimney's
Puff of dull yarn! Still vaguely chilled,

Guessing how even then her eight
Years had foreknown him, nursed him, all,
Sewn his first dress, sung to him, let him fall,
Howled when his face chipped like a plate,

He stands there wondering until red
Infraradiance, wave on wave,
So enters each plume-petal's crazy weave,
Each worsted brick of the homestead,

That once more, deep indoors blood's drawn,
The tiny needlewoman cries,
And to some faintest creaking shut of eyes
His pleasure and the doll's are one.

Unlike the metaphor in "Early Settlers," this fire screen could support many interpretations. Perhaps the most obvious is the theme we have been tracing: crafted poetry informs psychic fire for both poet and reader, simultaneously re-animating life and comfortably distancing from its consuming heat. A whole complex of tenses as well as tension is unraveled in the crewel-work of the mother, and oedipal and promethean fire fuse in the violent eroticism: the sheathing of claws, the chipped doll's face, the drawing of blood, the mother's cries and the erotically-toned climax of pleasure as mother, doll, and son seem to have become one. The distancing of time backward toward the doll makes consummation possible.

In "Emerald" the distancing of time and possession is forward, and the disquieting oedipal eroticism of "The Fire Screen" is chillingly pressed into the brilliant and exquisite world of precious stone. The poem describes the poet's visit to his mother after the death of her second husband. Together they visit the vault where her valuables are kept. She offers him an emerald ring given to her by his father on the date of his birth and suggests he take it for his future wife, but the poet refuses:

> I do not tell her, it would sound theatrical,
> *Indeed this green room's mine, my very life.*
> *We are each other's; there will be no wife;*
> *The little feet that patter here are metrical.*

The two are immersed in a green light, and the poet implores her to keep the ring. The poem also describes the poet's pleasure at surviving with his mother her two husbands: "*We* were alive." It is poignantly conscious of death in a description of the mother's precautions against skin cancer— "Malignant atomies which an electric needle / Unfreckles from her soft white skin each fall"—and her appearance in the vault rummaging amongst her husband's "Will" and "Deed" as a "girl-bride jeweled in his grave." In the vault she is alive: "Her face gone queerly lit, fair, young, / Like faces of our dear ones who have died." While "Above ground, who can remember / Her as she once was?" Beneath the pressure of earth, the speeded life of cells and the fired poetic imagination work toward a harmonious radiance. The poem closes with a ritual gesture and a poetic promise:

> But onto her worn knuckle slip the ring.
> Wear it for me, I silently entreat,
> Until—until the time comes. Our eyes meet.
> The world beneath the world is brightening.

"Lorelei" (*The Fire Screen*) embraces both past and future and perfects Merrill's habit of distilling the people of different times and places into the golden mask of one persona.

The stones of kind and friend
Stretch off into a trembling, sweatlike haze.

They may not after all be stepping-stones
But you have followed them. Each strands you, then

Does not. Not yet. Not here.
Is it a crossing? Is there no way back?

Soft gleams lap the base of the one behind you
On which a black girl sings and combs her hair.

It's she who some day (when your stone is in place)
Will see that much further into the golden vagueness

Forever about to clear. Love with his chisel
Deepens the lines begun upon your face.

Family and friends are the two primary sources of Merrill's poetic characters. "Lorelei" visualizes their temporal passage as one blends into the
next. The expressive ambiguity "strands"—isolates or entwines—encourages
the sense of an infinite series of receding mirror images in which past is
contained by present into future infinity.

We are closer to "18 West 11th Street" in Merrill's long discursive
lyrics. These poems reveal his phenomenology of fire and coalesce his
biographical and aesthetic themes. Like the odes of the Romantic poets,
they share several thematic and stylistic traits which are consistent and
strong enough to give them the character of a personal genre. Each poem
begins after a physical or emotional crisis has enervated the poet, effecting
something like Proust's intensified sensibility after an asthmatic attack. A
delicate but incisive sensuous perception leads from the present to related
scenes in the past. There is a sense, and frequently the specified presence,
of a crowd (a silent chorus watching the scene); and just as the different
places and times in these poems are distilled into their aesthetic moment
and structure, the crowd is narrowed toward a solitude. Movement is more
in the rhythm of ritual dance—measured, repeated steps with darkly
significant variations—than narrative action; fire—in any of its many
forms—is more the protagonist than the poet who observes and meditates;
and eroticism is closer to the core than to the surface. When the focus has
narrowed sufficiently to burn through the poet's self-absorption, remaining
under the thin gauze of ashes is the poem: a cooling artifice which
coalesces and refigures the past.

Merrill's gradual mastery of this genre accompanies the subtle refinement of the forms and music of his poems. Several of the long lyrics
anticipate "18 West 11th Street" in presenting erotic trauma and violent

conflict between generations. In one of the earliest, "An Urban Convalescence," the scene of a demolished building leads the poet to imagine the
destruction of a former home. Through demonic, erotic, and subtle light
imagery, the poet does to his home in verse what the Weathermen
accomplished with their brutal weapons. "The Broken Home" (*Nights and
Days*) is quite explicit in its erotic concerns. During an evening walk, the
window-framed sight of parents and their child evokes the poet's own
childhood. His memory explodes the golden and static renaissance portrait
in the window into a darkly shaded canvas of manneristic tension. The
memory of his father is dissected and frozen in rigid meter and rhyme:

> My father, who had flown in World War I,
> Might have continued to invest his life
> In cloud banks well above Wall Street and wife.
> But the race was run below, and the point was to win. . . .
>
> Each thirteenth year he married. When he died
> There were already several chilled wives
> In sable orbit—rings, cars, permanent waves.
> We'd felt him warming up for a green bride.

In verses we have seen, the mother's alienation takes cover in the image
of suffragettes attacking the public figures of male authority, but there is
nothing displaced about the poet's description of his own childhood
trauma of erotic revelation:

> One afternoon, red, satyr-thighed
> Michael, the Irish setter, head
> Passionately lowered, led
> The child I was to a shut door. Inside,
>
> Blinds beat sun from the bed.
> The green-gold room throbbed like a bruise.
> Under a sheet, clad in taboos
> Lay whom we sought, her hair undone, outspread,
>
> And of a blackness found, if ever now, in old
> Engravings where the acid bit.
>
> I must have needed to touch it
> Or the whiteness—was she dead?
> Her eyes flew open, startled strange and cold.
> The dog slumped to the floor. She reached for me. I fled.

Variation in the meter, precipitousness in the flow from verse to verse,
and a slightly looser rhyme allow the bite, the hurt, the passion of the
experience to come through. Finally the poem cools in a familiar pattern:
in the *presence* of the home the past is creatively restructured.

"The Friend of the Fourth Decade" emphasizes not so much the recapture of time through poetic distillation as its destruction, and, for the first time, associates the process with guilt. Like the infinitely receding mirror image of "Lorelei" and the fire screen of "Mornings in a New House," "The Friend of the Fourth Decade" evolves from an emblematic image. In a baptism not of fire but of "holy water from the tap," poet and friend remove stamps from postcards which are left "rinsed of the word." Bereaved of individuality they become a visual metaphor for verse— anonymous 3 × 5 scenes. When the friend announces a trip and, later, sends a postcard from a country where "Individual and type are one," metaphor and reality have become one; the friend has joined the poet's collection of postcards. We witness the violence and guilt of this reduction to measured scenes in the "danger" of the country from which the friend writes.

> "Here," he wrote on the back,

> "individual and type are one.
> Do as I please, I *am* the simpleton

> Whose last exploit is to have been exploited
> Neck and crop.

Despite the guilt, typical of Merrill and the metaphysical tradition in which he writes, all of these poems conclude with a sense of resolution and even joy.

The intimation of psychic violence in the poetic activity of "The Friend of the Fourth Decade" is fully explored in the surprisingly narrative development of "18 West 11th Street." The poem begins with the children of the age of Aquarius "perfecting a device / . . . Of incommunication" in the basement. Suddenly, to this scene of Merrill's childhood in a broken home, the "prodigal / Sunset" returns, in the present, Merrill's most uneasy tense. His presence has a disorienting effect, and the poem suddenly explodes into a series of invectives against the mindless and vain love-hate violence of the Weathermen. Having established—through a pun on "premises"—the identity of the setting as both the poet's childhood home and the scene of Weathermen violence, the poem moves into a complicated rhythmic alternation between invertible scenes of the son's volatile past and the present poetic oasis of debris. The poet's home is recalled as it was: the funereal floral pattern of a carpet which nightly collected the ashes of metropolitan smokers, an erotically-tuned piano and the framed scene of ghostly presences above it. As the spectre of the past rises from the ruins, one realizes it had foreshadowed the present. Then, the chords of the piano modulate into the salt chords of surf, and several verses recall the Caribbean home of the Wilkersons (where the parents were vacationing at the time of the explosion). Headlines of the blast return us to the scene of ruin in "the March dawn." In visually stunning images, Merrill evokes the extinguished ruins, the floodlights of the bomb squad, the fire hoses and the defoliated trees. Again a return to the past of a hermetic but haunting scene of departure: two men and a woman, deeply and tragically involved, reach toward and through each other. In the final return to the March, 1971 scene there is a new tone of transfixed, if not transpired, purgation in which Cathy Wilkerson (as she was reported to have done by neighbors) makes a ghostly appearance. "18 West 11th Street" is so central to Merrill's most serious concerns and so consummately expressive of his recent style that before explication the complete poem should be quoted:

> In what at least
> Seemed anger the Aquarians in the basement
> Had been perfecting a device
>
> For making sense to us
> If only briefly and on pain
> Of incommunication ever after.
>
> Now look who's here. Our prodigal
> Sunset. Just passing through from Isfahan.
> Filled by him the glass
>
> Disorients. The swallow-flights
> Go word by numbskull word
> —Rebellion . . . Pentagon . . . Black Studies—
>
> Crashing into irreality,
> Plumage and parasites
> Plus who knows what of the reptilian,
> Till wit turns on the artificial lights
> Or heaven changes. The maid,
> Silent, pale as any victim,
>
> Comes in, identifies;
> Yet brings new silver, gives rise to the joint,
> The presidency's ritual eclipse.
>
> Take. Eat. His body to our lips. The point
> was anger, brother? Love? Dear premises
> Vainly exploded, vainly dwelt upon.
>
> Item: the carpet.
> Identical bouquets on black, rose-dusted
> Face in fifty funeral parlors,

Scentless and shaven, wall-to-wall
Extravagance without variety . . .
That morning's buzzing vacuum be fed

By ash of metropolitan evening's
Smoker inveterate between hot bouts
Of gloating over scrollwork,

The piano (three-legged by then like a thing in a riddle)
Fingered itself provocatively. Tones
Jangling whose tuner slept, moon's camphor mist

On the parterre compounding
Chromatic muddles which the limpid trot
Flew to construe. Up from camellias

Sent them by your great-great-grandfather,
Ghosts in dwarf sateen and miniver
Flitted once more askew

Through *Les Sylphides*. The fire was dead. Each summer,
While onto white keys miles from here
Warm salt chords kept breaking, snapping the strings,

The carpet—its days numbered—
Hatched another generation
Of strong-jawed, light-besotted saboteurs.

A mastermind
Kept track above the mantel. The cold caught,
One birthday in its shallows, racked

The weak frame, glazed with sleet
Overstuffed aunt and walnut uncle. Book
You could not read. Some utterly

Longed-for present meeting other eyes'
Blue arsenal of homemade elegies,
Duds every one. The deed

Diffused. Your breakfast *Mirror* put
Late to bed, a fever
Flashing through the veins of linotype:

NIX ON PEACE BID PROPHET STONED
FIVE FEARED DEAD IN BOMBED DWELLING
—Bulletin-pocked columns, molten font

Features would rise from, nose for news
Atwitch atchoo, God bless you!
Brought to your senses (five feared? not one bit)

Who walking home took in
The ruin. The young linden opposite
Shocked leafless, Item: the March dawn.

Shards of a blackened witness still in place.
The charred ice-sculpture garden
Beams fell upon. The cold blue searching beams.

Then all you sought
No longer, B came bearing. An arrangement
In time known simply as That June—

Fat snifter filled with morbidest
Possibly meat-eating flowers,
So hairy-stemmed, red-muscled, not to be pressed.

Pinhead notions underwater, yours,
Quicksilvered them afresh.
You let pass certain telltale prints

Left upon her in the interim
By that winter's person, where he touched her.
Still in her life now, was he, feeling the dim

Projection of your movie on his sheet?
Feeling how you reach past B towards him,
Brothers in grievance? But who grieves!

The night she left ("One day you'll understand")
You stood under the fruitless tree. The streetlight
Cast false green fires about, a tragic

Carpet of shadows of blossoms, shadows of leaves.
You understood. You would not seek rebirth
As a Dalmation stud or Tiny Tim.

Discolorations from within, dry film
Run backwards, parching, scorching, to consume
Whatever filled you to the brim,

Fierce tongue, black
Fumes massing forth once more on
Waterstilts that fail them. The

Commissioner unswears his oath. Sea serpent
Hoses recoil, the siren drowns in choking
Wind. The crowd has thinned to a coven

Rigorously chosen from so many called. Our
Instant trance. The girl's
Appearance now among us, as foreseen

Naked, frail but fox-eyed, head to toe
(Having passed through the mirror)
Adorned with heavy shreds of ribbon

Sluggish to bleed. She stirs, she moans the name
Adam. And is *gone*. By her own
Broom swept clean, god, stop, behind this

Drunken backdrop of debris, airquake,
Flame in bloom—a pigeon's throat
Lifting, the puddle

Healed. To let:
Cream paint, brown ivy, brickflush. Eye
Of the old journalist unwavering

Through gauze. Forty-odd years gone by.
Toy blocks. Church bells. Original vacancy.
O deepening spring.

The characteristics shared by Merrill's metaphysical lyrics are refined and complected in "18 West 11th Street." Here past blends impercep-
tibly into the present within the texture of his verses. For example, the
second transition from the demolished site to the past is accomplished by
allowing the description of the bomb squad's "cold blue searching beams"
to suggest a metaphor for introspection and memory. In the final transition from the tragically involved human triad to the scene of ruin, an
outburst of anger is transformed by metaphoric language into the smoul-
dering fire, and the scene is changed:

Discolorations from within, dry film
Run backwards, parching, scorching, to consume
Whatever filled you to the brim,

Fierce tongue, black
Fumes massing forth once more on
Waterstilts that fail them.

The ironically-voiced *lingo* of the Weathermen—"brother? Love?"—is echoed
in the description of the remembered triad: "Feeling how you reached past
B towards him, / Brothers in grievance?" And, finally, the Dionysiac madness of Cathy Wilkerson and her "light-besotted saboteurs" is, as we shall
see, embodied in Merrill's own voice. Within this closely woven texture, a
metaphysical relationship between the different generations residing on
West 11th Street is revealed in three of the most archetypal human myths:
the prodigal son, original sin, Oedipus. In a poem about the conflict of
generations, "18 West 11th Street," like the House of Thebes, becomes an

emblem for some unavoidable matrix of fate which involves both poet and revolutionary.

There is an eloquent counterpoint in the poem between radical vocabulary ("word by numbskull word / Rebellion . . . Pentagon . . . Black Studies") and poised poetic language. The initial stanzas tease the reader with the similarity between constructing a bomb and the poetic process: "perfecting a device / . . . Of incommunication ever after." "Incommunication" simultaneously brings to mind the reticence of much of Merrill's poetry and the parental excommunication which the child of a wealthy financier who had chosen poetry or radicalism as his life style would suffer. The poem continues to allude to the poetic process in many ways: the sleeping tuner, the construing of chromatic muddles, the arsenal of homemade elegies, the diffused deed, the charred ice-sculpture garden, the drunken backdrop of debris, and the pigeon's throat lifting. They are all focused in the last stanza into the poet's most moving evocation of his career:

> Forty-odd years gone by
> Toy blocks. Church bells. Original vacancy.
> O deepening spring.

In selecting the adjective "Toy," Merrill explores and detonates the psychic resources of words. This affecting reference to his craft, this pun within an intimated rhyme deepens the generic resolution in *joy*. "Toy" embraces both childhood and the mature note of universal pathos and loss at the core of the poem.

And just as the initial despair of the long lyrics deepens in "18 West 11th Street" into an awareness of the unchanging condition of the divinely but vainly gifted poet (only a puddle reflecting the backdrop of debris is healed), the crowd here is initiated and shares the poet's vision. Having seen a recoiling evil freeze over burnt-out life (as it does at the nadir of Dante's *Inferno*) and heard the song of the siren, this crowd intensifies into a "Rigorously chosen" coven whose gaze can still burn through the hermetic freeze. It knows that the destroyer of the West 11th Street home is not the aesthetic fire which glazes *objets d'art* nor the incidental anger of a confused generation but is deeply rooted in the human condition. Adam happened to be the name Cathy Wilkerson was heard to mutter before her escape, but the "Original vacancy" of the poem's conclusion is not merely the scene of departure from the poet's childhood. It is man's timeless exclusion from his unforgotten home.

Both the prodigal son and original sin strike a note of paternal betrayal. But "18 West 11th Street" is written in triple time: tercets, musical triads, and human triolism and a triple "composite" myth. In the first meditation on the past, the "three legged . . . thing in a riddle" almost names Oedipus, and the image is set to the suggestive and erotic tune of a piano provocatively fingering itself. The second meditation on the past describes two men reaching through a woman toward each other. As an alternative to the distilling of private passion into polished poetic images and forms—which Merrill does so well—he also displaces it in highly-stylized literary personae. (Note also the Eros and Psyche mask of "From the Cupola" in *Nights and Days*.) One scene from his long narrative of a child's fantasy kidnap, "Days of 1935" (*Braving the Elements*), comes to mind in connection with the veiled triad of "18 West 11th Street." Floyd and Jean are the Bonnie and Clyde-like kidnappers. When the son and Floyd are sleeping on the floor together because Jean is ill, Floyd passionately embraces the boy in his sleep. Of course, on second thought the analogy fails, but it is accurate to see the two as highly stylized and extreme forms of an "Eternal Triangle." Finally, the most forceful oedipal element in "18 West 11th Street" is the entangled relationship between Cathy Wilkerson's radicalism and James Merrill's poetry. Antigone and Oedipus were both born into the House of Thebes, and Cathy Wilkerson's destruction of her paternal home and James Merrill's pained elegies for his are acts of fate as well as their active wills. What had "Seemed anger" in the second verse is reticulated with such a wealth of biographical, histori- cal, psychological, and archetypal insights in the course of the poem as to be totally transformed. Indeed, in the concluding tercet nature itself is deflected from its amoral cyclical course to be glazed—not with the gilding, yellowing dust of earlier and lesser achieved poems but—with a patina of human destiny: "O *deepening* Spring." It is this awareness in "18 West 11th Street" which combines the calorism of fire and the animism of poetry with a tragic intensity greater than any previous poem by Merrill.

Merrill and Cathy Wilkerson standing as they do in mirrors at the two ends of "18 West 11th Street" almost have the effect of bracing the poem within the closed series of infinitely receding mirror reflections presented in "Lorelei." But in "Having passed through the mirror" at the poem's conclusion, Cathy Wilkerson seems to symbolize the psychic effect of the explosion on James Merrill and his poetry. The constant rhythm behind the complex thematic developments in "18 West 11th Street" is percus- sive: disorientations, explosions, ruptures, shocks and quakes. It is as if in shocking leafless the pattern-making linden opposite the house, the explosion has also shocked Merrill from the long, consecutive lines of his earlier poetry. His measures here are uneven and shorter; his thought more driving. Although these new elements are coerced by communion with "who knows what of the reptilian," disorientation is not decline in poetic merit. Rather, Merrill seems to have reached back through Cathy Wilkerson to Rimbaud for a final lesson from the symbolists: "the poet makes himself a *seer* by a long and reasoned derangement of all his senses."

"Yánnina" (*Saturday Review*, December 1972), a recent poem which associates the Turkish tyrant, Ali Pasha, with the poet's father ("Ali, my father—both are dead."), indicates Merrill may continue delineating father surrogates in his poetry. But the subtle tension of temporal sequence in "18 West 11th Street"—most evident in a cascade of participal phrases—promises some significant changes in the texture of his poetry. The facility with technique in his earlier volumes—some of the most perfectly measured meters, balanced rhymes, and syntaxed prosody in contemporary American poetry—has evolved into the expressive freedoms of occasional metrical irregularities, dissonant rhymes, and strained and elided syntax. But the irregularities are held in absolute if elliptical orbit by the ghost of an already-perfected classical style. The light of Apollonian fire has cooled, and the rhythm is more frenzied, more Dionysiac. In this most recent poetry rather than an extraterrestrial animus—the artifice of eternity—we hear more frequently the voice of the elements themselves: minerals, landscape, nature. In "Under Libra: Weights and Measures" (*Braving the Elements*), instead of past and present biographical time resolved into the poet's artifice, several characters evaporate off an indistinguishable southwestern landscape. Like a Cézanne painting, the legend is almost submerged in the textures of the canvas. "The Black Mesa" (*Braving the Elements*) is written in the voice of the plateau. In "McKane's Falls" (*Poetry*, September, 1973), the protagonists and landscape blend wittily and pictorially into each other. At its conclusion, the waterfall itself rather than the poet assumes the voice of the poem:

> Now you've seen through me, sang the cataract,
> A fraying force, but unafraid,
> Plunge through my bath of plus and minus both,
> Acid and base,
> The mind that mirrors and the hands that act.
> Enter this inmostspace
>
> Its lean illuminations decompose.

It is as if Merrill has found in nature a second informing vision for his world. In a footnote to "Mornings in a New House," Merrill lamented that he had not been led by words from the fire screen through the "screen of fire" to the scene on the inside baffle plate. His poetry seems now to have traveled that route and located itself dead center.

Phenomenologically, fire has rarely been considered a part of nature. Rather it is man's divinely inspired instrument for transforming nature to his own purposes. In nature itself, as in Merrill's later poetry, the heat of biological life is buried, pressured and frozen into mineral form. Were future semiologists to compare the "deep structure" shared by the progression of life from the flushed heat of living organisms to the cool brilliance of precious stones and the trajectory of aesthetic processes, James Merrill's poetry could well be their "mastermind."

When *Braving the Elements* won the Bollingen Poetry Prize for James Merrill, the New York *Times* published an ill-informed editorial criticizing the foundation for making the award in troubled times to a genteel and private poet. It is true Merrill has avoided confessional poetry and topical or fashionable subjects. But for readers who understand Merrill's highly-informed language, the poems of *Braving the Elements* deal more memorably and more incisively with liberation, radical violence, kidnapping, space travel, the assassination of political leaders, and the effect of mass-media on the English language than any poetry written in America today. More importantly, Merrill is the finest poet translating the tradition of French symbolism into the English language. On the European continent, the predominant force in contemporary poetry is still the symbolist movement. In the English speaking world other currents have deflected that potent language because Yeats found few successors sufficiently gifted in the style. Merrill is fluent in it. And if we are to understand lyrical poetry in the etymological sense of rootedness in musical expression, Merrill is one of its few preeminent masters.

DAVID KALSTONE

Transparent Things

It would be interesting to know at what point Merrill saw a larger pattern emerging in his work—the point at which conscious shaping caught up with what unplanned or unconscious experience had thrown his way. In retrospect a reader can see that *Braving the Elements* (1972) gathers behind it the titles—with full metaphorical force—of Merrill's previous books. In *The Country of a Thousand Years of Peace, Water Street, Nights and Days* and *The Fire Screen*, he had referred to the four elements braved in the book which followed them. (*Divine Comedies* extends it one realm further.) The books do present experience under different aspects, almost as under different zodiacal signs. And *The Fire Screen* is, among other things—and preeminently—the book of love. It reads like a sonnet sequence following the curve of a love affair to its close. Like important sonnet sequences, the implied narrative calls into play a range of anxieties not strictly connected to love, in Merrill's case challenging some of the balanced views of *Nights and Days*.

"The Friend of the Fourth Decade" is the launching point for this book—the poet at forty, setting one part of himself in dialogue with another. What is being tested here is the whole commitment to memory, to personal history, to a house and settling down—the very material to which Merrill entrusted himself after *Water Street*. The "friend" is an alter ego who comes to visit—really to confront—his poet-host, after a long absence. In the opening scene, against the settled atmosphere of his host's house, the friend is shot through with the setting sun so that he appears to be "Any man with ears aglow, / . . . gazing inward, mute." The temptation the friend represents is crystallized in a dream at the close of the poem. "Behind a door marked DANGER . . ."

> Swaddlings of his whole civilization,
> Prayers, accounts, long priceless scroll,
>
> Whip, hawk, prow, queen, down to some last
> Lost comedy, all that fine writing
>
> Rigid with rains and suns,
> Are being gingerly unwound.
>
> There. Now the mirror. Feel the patient's heart
> Pounding—oh please, this once—
>
> Till nothing moves but to a drum.
> See his eyes darkening in bewilderment—
>
> No, in joy—and his lips part
> To greet the perfect stranger.

The friend has taught him a mesmerizing game in which saved-up postcards, a whole history of personal attachments, are soaked while the ink dissolves. The views remain, but the messages disappear, "rinsed of the word." When the poet tries it himself, watching his mother's "Dearest Son" unfurl in the water, the message remains legible. "The memories it stirred did not elude me."

"The Friend of the Fourth Decade" tests a dream of escape, a drama extended and detailed by the poems set in Greece which follow it in *The Fire Screen*. In some sense the book is like Elizabeth Bishop's *Questions of Travel*, a deepening encounter with another language and a more elemental culture, in which the speaker becomes, from poem to poem, more identified with his new world, cleansed of the assumptions of the old. In "To My Greek," the Greek language, encountered as if it were a demon lover, or a siren, becomes a radiant, concrete release from the subtleties of the "mother tongue" and the burden of "Latin's rusted treasure." A newcomer to Greek, he is forced to be simple, even silly. With Merrill the experience is characteristically amplified. He treats it as a temptation to become "rinsed of the word" and to humble himself speechless in the presence of "the perfect stranger." Both the transcendental and the self-destructive overtones of that phrase from "The Friend of the Fourth Decade," where the "perfect stranger" is also Death, haunt this book.

The initiation into Greece is inseparable from the exhilaration and the mystery of a love affair. It was anticipated in "Days of 1964," the wonderful Cavafid conclusion to *Nights and Days*, and is allowed to run its course in *The Fire Screen*. In "The Envoys" Merrill finds a series of emblems for the sense of adventure and risk experienced in the lover's presence. In three narrative panels, he introduces creatures the lover momentarily traps and tames, binds and then frees: a scurrying lizard, a frightened kitten and a beetle threaded and whirled around his head:

> You knotted the frail harness, spoke,
> Revolved. Eureka! Round your head
> Whirred a living emerald satellite.

The experience is absorbed as a "modulation into a brighter key / Of terror we survive to play."

> Teach me, lizard, kitten, scarabee—
> Gemmed coffer opening on the dram
> Of everlasting life he represents,
>
> His brittle pharoahs in the vale of Hence
> Will hear who you are, who I am,
> And how you bound him close and set him free.

What he shares with the creatures is a moment at the gates of some other world, not insisted on, but imagined as if he were enjoying the danger. All the Greek poems, not only the love poems, benefit from that expansion of feeling. In a dramatic monologue whose tripping couplets are meant to suggest the energetic singsong of a simple Greek speaker, "Kostas Tympakianakis," Merrill seems almost literally to take up the speaker's invitation: "You'll see a different cosmos through the eyes of a Greek." He adopts the violence, the pride, the clear-eyed tone of the Greek. He accepts the welcome challenge, "Use my name," slips on the offered identity, but registers the gap between them in Kostas's final line: "Who could have imagined such a life as mine?" It is a small but telling rebuke of the poet's imagination always ticking away, its pressures momentarily relieved by taking on the voice of another. *The Fire Screen* contains several poems given over to the pleasures of evoking particular figures, humble like Kostas or sophisticated like Maria, the "muse of my off-days." It sees Greek peasant life through others' eyes ("David's Night at Veliès") or addresses itself to shared moments of happiness, as in "16.ix.65," with "evening's four and twenty candles" and the four friends who return from the beach "with honey on our drunken feet."

But at the core of the Greek section of this book are the love poems, some of them full of lyric intensity, others sharp and painful, like the dramatic soliloquy or fragment "Part of the Vigil," which is, in a sense, the turning point of the affair, a surreal exploration of the images in the lover's heart:

> What
> If all you knew of me were down there, leaking
> Fluids at once abubble, pierced by fierce
> Impulsions of unfeeling, life, limb turning
> To burning cubes, to devil's dice, to ash—
> What if my effigy were down there? What,
> Dear god, if it were not!
> If it were nowhere in your heart!
> Here I turned back.

The lover's image is to "Blaze on" in the poet's own "saved skin." But the poems which follow register both the end of the affair and the folly of thinking of the Greek experience as an escape or oblivion. "Another August," "A Fever" and "Flying to Byzantium" are among the most powerful poems in the book. With "Mornings in a New House," as he imagines a dwelling half way back toward cooler American landscapes, the whole experience modulates into a new key, absorbed, retrospective, fading into myth.

It is appropriate in Merrill's work that recovery should be imagined in terms of a "new house" (or a repainted one in the more comic and detached version of "After the Fire"). "Mornings in a New House" has him, "a cold man" who "hardly cares," slowly brought to life by a fire laid at dawn. Once again the new house is the available image to set against exposure. "The worst is over," the fire a tamed recall of the shattered (or spent?) affair. Against its "tamed uprush . . . Habit arranges the fire screen." The details of the screen, embroidered by his mother, place the entire lapsed passion into a withering perspective:

> Crewel-work. His mother as a child
> Stitched giant birds and flowery trees
> To dwarf a house, *her* mother's—see the chimney's
> Puff of dull yarn! Still vaguely chilled,
>
> Guessing how even then her eight
> Years had foreknown him, nursed him, all,
> Sewn his first dress, sung to him, let him fall,
> Howled when his face chipped like a plate,
>
> He stands there wondering until red
> Infraradiance, wave on wave,
> So enters each plume-petal's crazy weave,
> Each worsted brick of the homestead,

> That once more, deep indoors, blood's drawn,
> The tiny needlewoman cries,
> And to some faintest creaking shut of eyes
> His pleasure and the doll's are one.

It is hard to disentangle the impulses which contribute to this poem—harder even because the poet has added a footnote taking some of it back, imagining passion as itself a defense, not a danger, like the screen of fire that protects Brünnhilde in Wagner's opera. But, in the poem proper, the fire screen is devised against the damages of love. It bears, in a sense, the whole retrospective power of his writing, the ability of memory and art to absorb and rearrange experience. What marks this off from earlier moments in Merrill's poetry is the long perspective which the poem opens up, receding past his immediate pain, past his own childhood of "The Broken Home," to his mother who stitched the screen as a device involving *her* mother.

After all the carefully noted impulses in *The Fire Screen* to leave the mother behind—the attempts to rinse away her handwriting in "Friend of the Fourth Decade"; even the efforts to be free of Latin languages, the "mother tongue"—the poet returns to her in a new way. The "new house" of this poem is interwoven with the house his mother had sewn, *her* mother's house, dwarfed by giant birds and flowery trees. The discovery of these entwined destinies "deep indoors" draws blood. There is something like the remorse of "Childlessness" in what happens. The resources of art are seen as self-protective, even vengeful, a miniaturization of human powers, like the moment in the earlier poem when the annihilated village—teeming generations in dwarfed versions—is loaded aboard sampans and set adrift. But in "Mornings in a New House" the experience is without guilt and is shared in its brittle complexity. Waves of warmth and anger carry him inward to an identification with the "tiny needlewoman" mother, to share the childish pleasure and fear which even then would shape her feelings for the child *she* would one day have. With "some faintest creaking shut of eyes" they both become toys in a larger pattern, at once foreshortened and part of their shared, terrifying but ungrudging humanity. I think what is most notable in this poem is that Merrill, however rueful and pained, has emerged from the erotic fire into a newly defined and felt natural perspective—one which becomes visible and palpable at length in many of the poems of his next book, *Braving the Elements*.

II

I have talked about the double action we must watch in Merrill's poems, the way he twins a witty surface with the poet's power to discover the veined patterns of his life. We must pay special attention to his puns and his settings; they open alternative perspectives against which to read the time-bound and random incidents of daily life. In *Braving the Elements* (1972) and *Divine Comedies* (1976), he has become a master of this idiosyncratic method, something one might call—with apologies—symbolic autobiography, Merrill's way of making apparently ordinary detail transparent to deeper configurations.

This is quite clear in "After the Fire" and "Log," which move us from the world of *The Fire Screen* to that of *Braving the Elements*. The brisk narrative of "After the Fire" brings back the Greek housekeeper Kyria Kleo, whom in "Days of 1964" he had seen wearing "the erotic mask / Worn the world over by illusion / To weddings of itself and simple need." Now, in the new key of "After the Fire," the Athens house has been repainted after a mysterious blaze. Under its "quiet sensible light gray," the house hides his old love affairs as it hides those of Kleo and her rumpled son Noti, their erotic escapades buried and part of the past. The mood of *Braving the Elements* is the mood of the opening invocation, "Log": banked flames of passion, burning and diminution, a life "consumed with that which it was nourished by." The muse discovered "After the Fire" is Kleo's mother, the half-crazed crone. In the yiayia's presence, the candles which gutter before old lovers' ghosts are replaced:

> The snuffed-out candle-ends grow tall and shine,
> Dead flames encircle us, which cannot harm,
> The table's spread, she croons, and I
> Am kneeling pressed to her old burning frame.

The comic crone turns before our eyes into a sybilline figure, mistress of the now harmless flames of passionate memory. She is, in a sense, the informing spirit of the book, for what is new about *Braving the Elements* is the way it opens to long—in some cases, geological—perspectives, the kind of prehistoric, penetrating wisdom which dwarfs and absorbs moments of intense present pain. The book contains, once again, love poems and poems involving the Oedipal trials of childhood. But these familiar sources of anxiety are in *Braving the Elements* transposed to a different key, resolved as by the all-embracing parenthesis of dream.

For example, family triangles make mysterious appearances in "18 West 11th Street," but as part of a poem in which several generations are run through a New York house, almost as in a strip of film. The house is one in which Merrill spent the first years of his childhood. With one of those attempts history makes to try and rival fiction, this was also the house accidentally destroyed in 1971 by Weathermen who were using it as a center for making bombs in the absence of the owners, parents of one of the revolutionaries. Richard Sáez, in a penetrating reading of the poem, points to the unlikely and eloquent connection it makes between "Cathy Wilkerson's destruction of her paternal home and James Merrill's pained elegies for his." The parallels, Sáez asserts, "are acts of fate as well as their active wills," as poet and radicals enact in their mutually incompatibile fashions, but with equal intensity, the conflict of generations. " '18 West 11th Street,' like the House of Thebes, becomes an emblem for some unavoidable matrix of fate which involves both poet and revolutionary." Inexcapably linked to one another, the generations are themselves dissolved in the mirrors of the house and the long stretches of time, each generation finding its own means to suffer and to rebel. Sáez is right to single out the close of the poem as having a special new power in Merrill's work:

> Forty-odd years gone by,
> Toy blocks. Church bells. Original vacancy.
> O deepening spring.

Sáez points out—that "the 'Original vacancy' of the poem's conclusion is not merely the scene of departure from the poet's childhood. It is man's timeless exclusion from his unforgotten home." Yes, but the phrase also looks forward and seems to say "To Let." With the church bells and "toy blocks" the cityscape seems both distanced and renewed. Of course, the toy blocks are also the children's devices against their parents, whether as poems or explosives. And they are assumed into the ongoing beauty of the exclamation. "O deepening spring." Here Sáez is particularly acute: "In the concluding tercet nature itself is deflected from its amoral cyclical course to be glazed—not with the gilding, yellowing dust of earlier and lesser achieved poems but—with a patina of human destiny."

That same sense of unfolding destiny informs "Up and Down," a poem whose ingredients are familiar in Merrill's work, but never in so rich a combination. In an earlier book this might well have been two separate poems: one, "Snow King Chair Lift," reflecting the brief exhilarating rising arc of a love affair; the other, "The Emerald," an extraordinary and sympathetic encounter with his mother. But one thing Merrill does in his work is move toward larger and larger units of composition, not only long poems, but combinations of different forms, like the free juxtapositions of prose and more or less formal verse units in "The Thousand and Second Night" and "From the Cupola." The two sections of "Up and Down" limn out, together, an emotional landscape which neither of them could singly suggest.

On the surface it is a poem of contrasts: rising in a ski lift with a lover, descending into a bank vault with the mother; the ostensible freedom of one experience, while in the other, "palatial bronze gates shut like jaws." Yet the exhilaration of the ski lift—it begins in dramatic present tenses—is what is relegated finally to a cherished snapshot and to the past tense: "We gazed our little fills at boundlessness." The line almost bursts with its contradictions: unslaked appetite, or appetite only fulfilled and teased by "gazing our little fills." The lovers have not quite reached the condition of the Shakespearean "pitiful thrivers in their gazing spent"; they are more buoyant, but with a redirected and only momentary pleasure. "The Emerald," on the other hand, begins in brisk easy narrative pasts and moves toward a moment in the very present which the ski-lift section had forsaken. More important, whatever the surface contrasts between the two sections, there is an irresistible connection between the discoveries made by each. Or rather, the feelings of the opening poem enable the son to understand what happens to the mother in the closing poem. In the vault an unexpected secret jumps to light:

> Rustle of tissue, a sprung
> Lid. Her face gone queerly lit, fair, young,
> Like faces of our dear ones who have died.
>
> No rhinestone now, no dilute amethyst,
> But of the first water, linking star to pang,
> Teardrop to fire, my father's kisses hang
> In lipless concentration round her wrist.

The effect resembles the moment of thunder and lightning on the chair-lift in Part I, but here things are seen in a prolonged transforming light, the queer deathlike glow when the "mudbrown" coffin of a box is opened. It is as if the glimpse of "boundlessness" in Part I can only be extended and refined in the eternal light of underground. The poet and his mother are seen as part of a performance in the "green room" which the emerald suggests. Before his eyes she grows both youthful and like the dead. Surviving two husbands, she can still be transfixed by memory, transformed by the bracelet. "My father's kisses hang / In lipless concentration round her wrist." Contraries are reconciled: "star to pang, / Teardrop to fire." She is bride, widow and mother all at once, and something like the eternally preserved Mesopotamian consorts, "girl-bride jewelled in his grave."

Against this background mother and son have the unspoken reconciliation discussed earlier in this chapter. He slips onto her finger the emerald she had intended for his bride, the very ring his father gave her when the poet was born. All these elements compose an increasingly luminous frieze: "The world beneath the world is brightening." It is one of those moments assumed, as many are in *Braving the Elements*, into an ongoing process of time, and experienced not elegiacally but with a sense of promise. That deepening emotional landscape is most strongly suggested in the new physical surroundings of *Braving the Elements*. A series of difficult poems takes place in the Far West. Pieces like "Under Libra" and "In Nine Sleep Valley" are love poems played out against dwarfing panoramas and the geological erosions of a nonhuman world.

> Geode, the troll's melon
> Rind of crystals velvet smoke meat blue
> Formed far away under fantastic
> Pressures, then cloven in two
> By the taciturn rock shop man, twins now forever
>
> Will they hunger for each other
> When one goes north and one goes east?
>
> I expect minerals never do,
> Enough for them was a feast
> Of flaws, the molten start and glacial sleep,
> The parting kiss.
>
> Still face to face in halfmoonlight
> Sparkling comes easy to the Gemini.
>
> Centimeters deep yawns the abyss.

In "Under Libra" ancient stones are introduced into the poet's house ostensibly as doorstops and paperweights, but really as reminders of another scale of living. He goes "in the small hours from room to room / Stumbling onto their drugged stubborn sleep." These talismans overshadow desire; they place it in a perspective where past and future edge out the present. The solid human protagonists of the poem are dissolved before our eyes:

> . . . Ten years from next morning, pen in hand,
>
> Looking through saltwater, through flames,
> Enkindlings of an absent *I* and *you*.
> Live, spitting pronouns, sparks that flew

And were translated into windiest
Esperanto, zero tongue of powers
Diplomatic around 1 a.m.'s

Undripping centerpiece, the Swan . . .
Days were coming when the real thing
No longer shrugged a wing.

Some of the poems are pure ventriloquism. "The Black Mesa"
speaks; so do "Banks of a Stream Where Creatures Bathe." They seem to
embody a consensus of human voices, mythically inured to experience.
History, the details of private lives—everything repeats itself in the long
views these poems take. Hearing the poet take on these roles is like
talking to survivors. "The Black Mesa," addressing the low flatland,
musters for a moment the tone of an eager roué, but finally lapses back
into a weary geological view of his experience, outwaiting all competitors
and invaders: "I steal past him who next reclaims you, keep / Our hushed
appointments, grain by grain . . . / Dust of my dust, when will it all be
plain?" The effect is to make expressions of human tenderness mere
instances of the larger erosions and destinies which outlast them.

"Syrinx" is the most successful of such poems. She is, of course, an
established mythological figure, brightly familiar from Marvell: "And Pan
did after Syrinx speed / Not as a nymph, but for a reed." Merrill takes up
her fragile link to the nature from which she was abstracted, "a thinking
reed." Just who is she in this version? She addresses the poet as if she were
his muse and his lover. She is sophisticated enough to know about
slipware and to quote Pascal; also, to make puns about fashion and the
Pan-pipe's traditional shape: "Among the wreckage, bent in Christian
weeds, / Illiterate—X my mark—I tremble, still / A thinking reed."

"Bent in Christian weeds" makes it sound as if she were used to
dresses by Chanel, and "Illiterate—X my mark" walks a tightrope of
ingenuity and feeling. As unlikely as her witty denial of literacy may be,
Syrinx keeps shucking off the claims of words as if they were merely
garments. The most outrageous example is the incorporation of the musical scale: "Who puts his mouth to me / Draws out the scale of love and
dread— / O ramify, sole antidote!" The musician's breath or the lover's
kiss, and then the high tragedienne's apostrophe, which, on a second
glance, taking in the enjambment ("d— / O"), we see disintegrate
magically into the musical scale. This is precisely the action the poem
repeats over and over: a human gesture, then the witty afflatus and effort
of words which slip back before our eyes into analytic formulas, the
do-re-mi of the scale, or the particles of a mathematical formula which

expresses metastasis. Syrinx seems caught between human demands and ingenuity, which make her "tremble, still" and, on the other hand, her sense of being a worn part of a growing and disintegrating world:

> Foxglove
> Each year, cloud, hornet, fatal growths
>
> Proliferating by metastasis
> Rooted their total in the gliding stream.

Over and over the cleverness of the poem is matched by a hypnotic natural intonation, no more than in the astonishing close; as Syrinx slides back into her "scarred case,"

> Whose silvery breath-tarnished tones
> No longer rivet bone and star in place
>
> Or keep from shriveling, leather round a stone,
> The sunbather's precocious apricot
>
> Or stop the four winds racing overhead
> 　　　　Nought
> Waste　　　　　　　Eased
> 　　　　Sought

Those last four words clothe the cardinal points in notions of human aspiration and loss, which we may understand in varying combinations and intensities, depending on the order in which we read them. But ultimately they slip back into the toneless ideogram of the ongoing winds. How odd human words and feelings seem, depicted in this particular way. The lozenge of four words is tinged by, but ultimately surpasses, individual feelings.

HELEN VENDLER

James Merrill

"BRAVING THE ELEMENTS"

The time eventually comes, in a good poet's career, when readers actively long for his books: to know that someone out there is writing down your century, your generation, your language, your life—under whatever terms of difference—makes you wish for news of yourself, for those authentic tidings of invisible things, as Wordsworth called them, that only come in the interpretation of life voiced by poetry. With an impatience that picks up *The New Yorker* to see if there is a new poem, that goes to poetry readings to glean another sheaf, Merrill's readers have been assembling this book of poems in their minds in order to possess it before it emerges between covers.

Merrill has become one of our indispensable poets, earning that final unquestioned role of a sibling in our family, so that it no longer matters what exactly he does or what ups and downs he shows; since we take the latest news from his quarter as another entry in our common journal, we trust him, we accept wrong turnings as readily as right ones, certain that he knows his own way and will find it.

In *Braving the Elements* Merrill has found a use, finally, for all his many talents. His surreptitious fondness for narrative, which issued rather badly in his early novel *The Seraglio* (1957) and his later sketch for a novel *The (Diblos) Notebook* (1965), has now found a clear medium in his wonderful short narrative lyrics; his almost unnaturally exquisite gift for euphony has become unobtrusive but no less exquisite, in fact more so; his

---

ironic and wayward humor has been allowed to appear in poetry as well as in prose; his single best subject—love—has found a way of expressing itself masked and unmasked at once, instead of hiding almost mummified in swathings of secrecy. Secrecy and obliquity were Merrill's worst obstacles in his early verses; though his tone was usually clear, the occasion of the tone was impossibly veiled: who are these people? what relation are they in? what has just happened to provoke this response? what is the outcome? —all these questions led to the murkiest answers, if to any answers at all.

The trouble was not reticence: after all, without once mentioning his personal griefs in the odes, Keats made us know them almost by heart. But in Merrill's earliest poetry he stood at several removes from his own experience, or, to put it another way, he still called poems by titles like "The Black Swan," "Kite Poem," "The Parrot," "Periwinkles," "Marsyas," and "The Power Station." The confusing thing about these "objective" poems was the cloudy weight of displaced feeling they bore, all out of proportion to their ostensible subjects. Clots of pain or brittle arabesques of suffering equally hovered unexplained; chaotic dreams assumed their own authority; catastrophes and resolutions alike veered uneasily between social staccato and pregnant pause; and the "intellectuality" for which the poems were sometimes praised was more a matter of labyrinthine syntax than of penetrating thought. But always, in spite of these lapses, a beautiful and radiant cadence rippled its way through Merrill's pages: his verse, like a brook, tumbled over the obstructions set by his rather frigid subjects and had a concurrent voice of its own, infinitely clearer and surer of itself than the poems in themselves seemed to warrant.

In a way, no beginning is more promising, since bad poets usually begin full of subjects but lacking contour; good poets begin all contour looking for a content. When content remains dim, euphonies are useless; but when talent for content grows to equal talent for contour, the union of Truth and Beauty that is all we ask of poems can take place. Merrill's Nights and Days (1966) ended with a fine presaging "narrative" poem called (after Cavafy) "Days of 1964," and this new volume continues the form with "Days of 1971" as well as other poems ("After the Fire," "Strato in Plaster," "Up and Down," "Days of 1935," and so on).

These, Merrill's best new ventures, are autobiographical without being "confessional": they show none of that urgency to reveal the untellable or unspeakable that we associate with the poetry we call "confessional." These poems are gripping because they are quiet and conversational: it is as though a curtain had been drawn aside, and we were permitted a glimpse of the life inside the house, a life that goes on unconscious of us, with the narrator so perfectly an actor in his own drama that his presence as narrator is rendered transparent, invisible.

The unpredictability of life seems to flicker capriciously in some of these pieces; in others, the equal predictability of life shines in a contemplated steadiness. Among the first sort, the unpredictable ones, "After the Fire" remains entirely present long after it has been heard or read, and it can serve as an example of the form Merrill has brought to a high perfection. There has been a fire in the house that Merrill lived in with his lover in Greece, and from America he has ordered repairs: now he returns to Greece to find everything changed.

> Everything changes; nothing does. I am back,
> The doorbell rings, my heart leaps out of habit,
> But it is only Kleo—how thin, how old!—
> Trying to smile, lips chill as the fallen dusk.

Kleo was the servant; her old mother has "gone off the deep end" and calls out to the whole neighborhood that Kleo's son is "a *Degenerate!* a *Thieving / Faggot!* just as Kleo is a *Whore!*"

> I press Kleo's cold hand and wonder
> What could the poor yiayia have done
> To deserve this terrible gift of hindsight . . .

In fact, Kleo *was* once a "a buxom armful," and her son Panayioti "cruised the Naval Hospital." The mixture of the dismaying, the nostalgic, and the funny mounts with Merrill's visit to Kleo's house, where the forty-year-old son greets him with outrageous warmth in outrageous French, all the time wearing Merrill's bathrobe and slippers. Merrill's gaze takes in other relics from the fire, and he suddenly realizes the truth:

> It strikes me now, as happily it did not
> The insurance company, that P caused the fire.

The fire destroyed forever the house as it was when Merrill lived there with "love-blinded gaze": the love affair, like the original color of the walls, is "hidden now forever but not lost / Beneath this quiet sensible light gray." Interrupting this almost unstable mixture of loss and survival, the grotesque and the painful, the old senile grandmother shrieks out, in a sudden access of rationality,

> "It's Tzimi! He's returned!"
> —And with that she returns to human form,
> The snuffed-out candle-ends grow tall and shine,
> Dead flames encircle us, which cannot harm,

> The table's spread, she croons, and I
> Am kneeling pressed to her old burning frame.

These poems are a potpourri of all the odors of the past, or rather vials for those essential oils which, as Emily Dickinson said, are wrung. Nothing is simple any longer: the rapt words of love in "The Fire Screen" (1969), vows, claims, even farewells ("I love you still, I love you") subside into a detachment touched by judgment but touched also still by love. The life which first saw itself bound and hemmed in and which fled to Greece, light, sensation, and love now begins to shrink back into a semblance of its first dimensions, the efflorescence gone but resurrected in a fidelity straited with irony but yet not ironic. Somehow Merrill still arranges to see Strato, his Greek:

> Strato, each year's poem
> Says goodbye to you.
> Again, though, we've come through
> Without losing temper or face.

The painful grace Merrill finds to modulate the whole bizarre experience with Strato-as-chauffeur in "Days of 1971" can be appreciated only as the whole poem spins its way through its ten "sonnets." At ease, with social aplomb, Merrill narrates the journey from Paris through France and Italy to Greece, affection and self-knowledge, tenderness and ridicule all mixing to illustrate what Merrill calls "Proust's Law":

> a) What least thing our self-love longs for most
> Others instinctively withhold;
>
> b) Only when time has slain desire
> Is his wish granted to a smiling ghost
> Neither harmed nor warmed, now, by the fire.

That smiling ghost writes this book, and curiously he is nevertheless Merrill's most substantial incarnation. He stands in these poems at the point where Yeats could say, "Dear shadows, now you know it all." As if in spectral fulfillment, old portions of life rise up to be concluded: in Merrill's novel The Seraglio the mother of the protagonist has given up wearing her jewels: "the jewels waited in a vault for Francis's bride." Now, as the elements of life assert themselves, Merrill has fled Byzantium and its exotica, and there is no bride: the strongbox in the vault yields up (in the poem "Up and Down") an emerald ring, and the mother addresses her son:

> "He gave
> Me this when you were born. Here, take it for—

For when you marry. For your bride. It's yours."
A den of greenest light, it grows, shrinks, glows,
Hermetic stanza bedded in the prose
Of the last thirty semiprecious years.

I do not tell her, it would sound theatrical,
Indeed this green room's mine, my very life.
We are each other's; there will be no wife;
The little feet that patter here are metrical.
But onto her worn knuckle slip the ring.
Wear it for me, I silently entreat,
Until—until the time comes. Our eyes meet.
The world beneath the world is brightening.

As the social comedy of the obsequious bank attendants yields to the green-lit troth in the vault, we acquiesce, compelled, in the mixed media of life.

Merrill has arrived at an instantly recognizable personal voice— even its awkwardnesses are genuine. He refuses to give up either side of his language—the pure concentrate of distilled essence, present since his beginnings, and the more recent importation of casual talk, even down to slang and four-letter words. The forms Merrill has used before—dream, myth, ballad, sacred objects—re-emerge on these pages with greater or lesser success. For all its pathos (a rich neglected little boy fantasizing his own Lindbergh-like kidnapping by surrogate-parent criminals he falls in love with), I cannot really admire "Days of 1935," since, like most literary ballads, it wavers uncertainly between its own sophistication and the naiveté of its predecessors. On the other hand, Merrill's best mythical poem yet closes the collection. Called "Syrinx," it arises as a variation on the Pascalian notion that man is a "thinking reed." Pascal meant the metaphor as a sign of human frailty; Merrill uses it to remind us of the human capacity for art. In Ovid, the nymph Syrinx, pursued by Pan, was changed into a reed, from which Pan made his pipe; here, the reed-flute is played upon by the great god Pain:

> . . . he reaches for me, then
>
> Leaves me cold, the great god Pain,
> Letting me slide back into my scarred case
>
> Whose silvery breath-tarnished tones
> No longer rivet bone and star in place
>
> Or keep from shriveling, leather round a stone,
> The sunbather's precocious apricot

Or stop the four winds racing overhead
                    Nought
        Waste   Eased
                    Sought

It is not for nothing that Merrill has read Herbert: Herbert, I think, would recognize the punning names and formation of these yearning, despairing winds; Merrill's sexual apricot, ripe and shriveled at once, is not far from Herbert's heart: "Who would have thought my shrivel'd heart / Could have recover'd greennesse?" It is hard to know where Merrill will go from here—whether he will set himself to a Proustian remembering and give us more vignettes of the past, or whether some new convulsion of life will wreck the fine equilibrium by which, in this book, the four racing winds are held and viewed.

"DIVINE COMEDIES"

Since he published his *First Poems*, James Merrill's energies have been divided between successive books of increasingly brilliant lyric poems (the most recent, *Braving the Elements*, in 1972) and attempts in larger fictional forms—two plays (1955 and 1960) and two novels (1957 and 1965). The flashes and glimpses of "plot" in some of the lyrics—especially the longer poems—reminded Merrill's readers that he wanted more than the usual proportion of dailiness and detail in his lyrics, while preserving a language far from the plainness of journalistic poetry, a language full of arabesques, fancifulness, play of wit, and oblique metaphor. And yet the novels were not the solution, as Merrill himself apparently sensed.

In his new collection, where most of the poems have a narrative emphasis, Merrill succeeds in expressing his sensibility in a style deliberately invoking Scheherazade's tireless skein of talk: the long poem, "The Book of Ephraim," which takes up two-thirds of this volume, is described as "The Book of a Thousand and One Evenings." In explaining how he came to write this novelistic poem, Merrill recapitulates his struggle with fiction:

> I yearned for the kind of unseasoned telling found
> In legends, fairy tales, a tone licked clean
> Over the centuries by mild old tongues,
> Grandam to cub, serene, anonymous.
> Lacking that voice, the in its fashion brilliant
> Nouveau roman (including one I wrote)
> Struck me as an orphaned form.

He once more tried his hand at writing a novel, but it lost itself in "word-painting":

> The more I struggled to be plain, the more
> Mannerism hobbled me. What for?
> Since it had never truly fit, why wear
> The shoe of prose?

His narrative forms in verse allow Merrill the waywardness, the distractions, the eddies of thought impossible in legends or in the spare *nouveau roman*, and enable the creation of both the long tale and of a new sort of lyric, triumphantly present here in two faultless poems, sure to be anthologized, "Lost in Translation" and "Yannina."

    Divine Comedies marks a departure in Merrill's work. He has always been a poet of Eros, but in an unwritten novel, about "the incarnation and withdrawal of / A god," "the forces joined / By Eros" come briefly together and then disperse:

> Exeunt severally the forces joined
> By Eros—Eros in whose mouth the least
> Dull fact had shone of old, a wetted pebble.

And Merrill's servant in Greece, whose name (Kleo) he had never seen written, turns out to be named not Cleopatra, as he had thought, but Clio; she is not the presiding surrogate for Eros but the incarnation of the Muse of history, Merrill's new patroness:

> "Kleo" we still assume is the royal feline
> Who seduced Caesar, not the drab old muse
> Who did. Yet in the end it's Clio I compose
> A face to kiss, who clings to me in tears.
> What she has thought about us all God knows.

If the divinity of youth was Eros, the divinity of middle age is Clio; if the metaphor for being thirty was embrace, the metaphor for being fifty is companionship; and if the presence in the mind was once love, it is now death.

    Quickened by the thought of death, which so resists the rational intelligence, the imaginations of poets react and react and react, pressing back (to use Stevens' phrase) with all the inventions, illusions, conjectures, wiles, seductions, and protests of which they are capable. Nothing so compels poets to complication: and if what they conjure up to talk to them from the dark is a voice recognizably their own but bearing a different name, they (and their readers) are peculiarly consoled by the reflected Word. So Milton found his own best voice speaking back at him under the names of Phoebus Apollo and St. Peter; so Dante fell into colloquy with his elder self, Vergil; so Yeats invented his "mysterious instructors" who dictated to him and his wife his elaborate system of history and the afterlife; and so James Merrill, in his divine comedies, communicates with an affable familiar ghost named Ephraim, first evoked at the Ouija board in Stonington twenty years ago, and a frequent visitor since.

In his 1970 volume, *The Country of a Thousand Years of Peace* (literally Switzerland, but since Merrill's friend Hans Lodeizen had died there, also metaphorically the country of the dead), Merrill published his first Ouija poem, in which a candid, if ineptly expressed, stanza offers the motive for listening to "voices from the other world":

> Once looked at lit
> By the cold reflections of the dead
> Risen extinct but irresistible,
> Our lives have never seemed more full, more real,
> Nor the full moon more quick to chill.

These lines give at least some notion of the origins of "The Book of Ephraim." It is a poem in twenty-six sections, each beginning with a different letter of the alphabet, from A to Z, exhausting the twenty-six capital letters of the Ouija board. And yet, for all its ninety pages, the Book is not finished, scarcely even begun, its dramatic personae—living, dead, and invented—hardly glimpsed, and only partially listed, its tale of an unfinished novel still untold, its gaily inventive theology linking this world to the otherworld barely delineated.

Merrill casually and mockingly praises his own "net of loose talk tightening to verse" through his surrogates among the dead. Ephraim ("A Greek Jew / Born AD 8 at XANTHOS"), who communicates of course in the caps of the Ouija board, tells Merrill,

> . . . POPE SAYS THAT WHILE BITS
> STILL WANT POLISHING THE WHOLES A RITZ
> BIG AS A DIAMOND.

Instead of Vergilian solemnity, this guide to the otherworld uses social chitchat:

> U ARE SO QUICK MES CHERS I FEEL WE HAVE
> SKIPPING THE DULL CLASSROOM DONE IT ALL
> AT THE SALON LEVEL.

For rationalists reading the poem, Merrill includes a good deal of self-protective irony, even incorporating in the tale a visit to his ex-shrink, who proclaims the evocation of Ephraim and the other Ouija "guests" from the other world a *folie à deux* between Merrill and his friend David Jackson. But once the "machinery"—not here the sylphs and nymphs of *The Rape of the Lock*, but the ghosts of dead friends and other revenants—is accepted as a mode of imagination, what then can be said of the import of this strange poem?

It is centrally a hymn to history and a meditation on memory—personal history and personal memory, which are, for this poet at least, the muse's materials. The host receives his visible and invisible guests, convinced that Heaven—the invisible sphere—is "the surround of the living," that the poet's paradise is nothing other than all those beings whom he has known and has imagined. Through Ephraim,

> We, all we knew, dreamed, felt and had forgotten,
> Flesh made word, became . . . a set of
> Quasi-grammatical constructions . . .
>   Hadn't—from books, from living—
> The profusion dawned on us, of "languages"
> Any one of which, to who could read it,
> Lit up the system it conceived?—bird-flight,
> Hallucinogen, chorale and horoscope:
> Each its own world, hypnotic, many-sided
> Facet of the universal gem.

These "facets of the universal gem" shine throughout "The Book of Ephraim," which aims at being a poem of a thousand and one reflecting surfaces. The irregularities and accidents of life are summed up in the fiction of reincarnation which animates the book's theology: people pass in and out of life as the bodies in which their spirits are incarnated die of heart attacks, in fires, or by less violent means; spirits get placed in unsuitable bodies; and in the crowded world of the afterlife a constant influx of souls makes for an agitated scene. Merrill's father, dead and between lives, gets through on the board:

> Then CEM gets through,
> High-spirited, incredulous—he'd tried
> The Board without success when Nana died.
> Are we in India? Some goddam fool
> Hindoo is sending him to Sunday School.
> He loved his wives, his other children, me;
> Looks forward to his next life.

The next life of Charles Merrill, announces Ephraim, is in Kew:

> YR FATHER JM he goes on (we're back
> In the hotel room) WAS BORN YESTERDAY

> To a greengrocer: name, address in Kew
> Spelt out.

This social comedy between otherworld and this world is one tone of "The Book of Ephraim": another is reminiscence of a simpler ego:

> Götterdämmerung. From a long ago
> Matinee—the flooded Rhine, Valhalla
> In flames, my thirteenth birthday—one spark floating
> Through the darkened house had come to rest
> Upon a mind so pitifully green
> As only now, years later, to ignite . . .
> The heartstrings' leitmotif outsoared the fire.

Still another tone juxtaposes the eternal confrontation of youth and age, Eros and entropy, Prometheus and the eroding Parthenon:

> Leave to the sonneteer eternal youth.
> His views revised, an older man would say
> He was "content to live it all again."
> Let this year's girl meanwhile resume her pose,
> The failing sun its hellbent azimuth.
> Let stolen thunder dwindle out to sea.
> Dusk eat into the marble-pleated gown.

Merrill's company of the dead comes in late exchange for the abandoned dream of the immortal couple, echoed through the book in Wagnerian terms, in Tristan's "höchste Lust," and in Brünnhilde's choice of love over Valhalla: "Nie Liebe liesse ich nie, mir nähmen nie sie die Liebe." These sublimities remain, icons unattainable but not disallowed, at the edges of this deliberately social and tempered poetry. Wanting consuming passions, Merrill says, he has found only refining ones.

Merrill's lines, in their exquisite tones, are often painful to read. Though they keep their beautiful poise on the brink of sense and feeling, and aim here at the autumnal, or the ironic, they keep echoes, undimmed, of the past: Merrill is not yet, and I think will never be, a poet free of sensuality, love, and youth, actual or remembered. Enshrined with Brünnhilde in the section (Q, of course) of Quotations in "The Book of Ephraim" is Spenser's transcendent dream of the Garden of Adonis, where in "immortal blis . . . Franckly each paramour his leman knowes," in an equable and unfallen counterpart of Wagner's doomed couples.

"The Book of Ephraim," for the most part, refuses the postures thought appropriate to age—stoicism, resignation, disbelief, patience, or cynicism. The mild conviviality of Merrill's unearthly symposium is boyish in its welcome to comedy, sympathy, and nostalgia at once; and the poet's naive enthusiasm for "learning" from Ephraim the ins and outs of behavior and fate in the otherworld is so different from Dante's and Yeats's gloomy reverence for their guides that we are moved to delight by the refraction of these "divine comedies" from their more religious antecedents.

On the other hand, "The Book of Ephraim" is not really a comic poem. When Merrill and Jackson protest Ephraim's offhand tone about death, and say "Must *everything* be witty?" Ephraim answers, in a phrase that could be applied to the whole poem,

> AH MY DEARS
> I AM NOT LAUGHING   I WILL SIMPLY NOT SHED TEARS.

If life is "a death's head to be faced," it is also, in this poem, the repository of counterpointed treasures.

The claim of this long poem to moral significance rests in the way it balances two entirely opposite truths about middle age. One is the truth of perceived fate, as it declares itself in the simplest of sentences: *This is who I am; This is where I live; This is the person I live with; My father is dead; I will not fall in love again.* The other is the truth of received experience, as it glitters in a cloud of witnesses—all the things seen, the people met, the places traveled to, the books read, the faces loved, the lines written, the events lived through, the events imagined, the past absorbed—the past not only of personal life but of cultural history as well. The glowing dialectic of restriction of present life and expansion of experienced soul animates these pages into a visionary balancing of scales, now one pan up, now the other. Merrill's imagination has always been mercurial, airy, and darting, but here the counterweight of death adds a constant pull toward grief.

"The Book of Ephraim" might seem to risk the accusation of triviality, in its apparent refusal to take large issues seriously:

> Life like the periodical not yet
> Defunct kept hitting the stands. We seldom failed
> To leaf through each new issue—war, election,
> Starlet; write, scratch out; eat steak au poivre,
> Chat with Ephraim.

But under this briskness lies a wasting ennui:

> The whole house needs repairs. Neither can bring
> Himself to say so. Hardly lingering,
> We've reached the point, where the tired Sound just washes
> Up to, then avoids our feet.

In this repetitive routine, Merrill is free to admit all the flotsam and jetsam floating in his mind, and to let us judge that mind as we will.

Because Merrill is a poet whose devotion goes to the Absolute under the form of the Beautiful, his range, like that of the Beautiful itself, is diverse: the Good and the True do not really participate in a spectrum of more and less in quite the same way. From bibelots to Beatrice, from embroidery to altarpiece, goes the scale, and Merrill's tone modulates along with its object. Like Proust and Nabokov, two other sensibilities more attached to the Beautiful than to the Scientific, the Philosophical, the Ethical, or the Ideological, Merrill avoids being polemical or commit-ted, in the ordinary sense of those words. By taking conversation—from lovers' exchange of vows to friends' sentences in intimacy—as the highest form of human expression (in contrast to the rhapsode's hymns, the orator's harangues, or the initiate's hermetic colloquies with the divine) Merrill becomes susceptible to charges of frivolity, at least from readers with a taste only for the solemn. But this espousal of the conversational as the ultimate in linguistic achievement is a moral choice, one which locates value in the human and everyday rather than in the transcendent.

It is no accident that Merrill appropriates for himself Keats's image of the chameleon poet, as delighted by an Iago as by an Imogen; he draws out a constantly changing veil of language like the endless scarves of silk from the illusionist's hands, now one color, now another, scattering light in rainbow transparency over and under his subject. And yet the severity of death fixes a new, unwavering color on the apparently boundless earlier sympathy with the attractions of experience:

> Already I take up
> Less emotional space than a snowdrop.
> . . . Young chameleon, I used to
> Ask how on earth one got sufficiently
> Imbued with otherness. And now I see.

Though the other poems in this collection share the conversational immediacy of "The Book of Ephraim," they also, in their persistent elegiac tone, seem to be fragments from a modern version of *The Prelude*. "Lost in Translation," of which the putative subject is Merrill's putting together, as a child, a complicated jigsaw puzzle with the aid of his governess, is really a gorgeous combination of Popean diversity of surface talk and Wordsworthian rumination on the past, and on the powers and lapses of memory. It is an easier poem than "Yannina," an elegy for Merrill's father set in the Turkish town of Yannina, once ruled by Ali Pasha, who becomes in the poem the surrogate for Charles Merrill. We see Ali flanked by "two loves, two versions of the Feminine": one the "pious matron" Frossíni, drowned at Ali's order for having refused compliance; the other Vassilikí, pictured with Ali sleeping in her lap. Byron (whose ottava rima Merrill here borrows and rings changes on) visited Ali, and found him "Very kind . . . indeed, a father." Merrill continues,

> Funny, that is how I think of Ali.
> On the one hand, the power and the gory
> Details, pigeon-blood rages and retali-
> Ations, gouts of fate that crust his story;
> And on the other, charm, the whimsically
> Meek brow, its motives all ab ulteriori,
> The flower-blue gaze twining to choke proportion,
> Having made one more pretty face's fortune . . .
>
> Ali, my father—both are dead.

Around this center vacillate feelings about the Oriental multiplicity of Yannina—its provincial promenade cluttered with sellers' booths, a magician's tent, loudspeaker music—and feelings about the two women, the wronged matron and the complaisant concubine. The scene on the promenade resembles the London Fair in *The Prelude*, but the human jumble of sight and sound, so inimical to the recoiling Wordsworthian sensibility which required solitude and massive forms, is the food of life to Merrill, who needs movement, color, the vulgar and the passionate together. As for the two women, one, the wronged Frossíni, has become a secular saint:

> And in the dark gray water sleeps
> One who said no to Ali. Kiosks all over town
> Sell that postcard, "Kyra Frossíni's Drown,"
> Showing her, eyeballs white as mothballs, trussed
> Beneath the bulging moon of Ali's lust.
> A devil (turban and moustache and sword)
> Chucks the pious matron overboard.

Frossíni's fate is half farce, half martyrdom; and "her story's aftertaste / Varies according to the listener," especially when her garish memorial postcard is placed against the skillful, still preserved, painting of Ali and Vassilikí—"almost a love-death, höchste Lust!" In the end, though, both versions of the feminine—"one virginal and tense, brief as a bubble, / One flesh and bone"—goes up in smoke, and the poem dips momentarily into ghoulish images of death.

> Where giant spits revolving try their rusty treble,
> Sheep's eyes pop, and death-wish ravens croak
> . . . At the island monastery, eyes

> Gouged long since to the gesso sockets will outstare
> This or that old timer on his knees.

The empty sockets would seem to betoken the end of Ali and his women, and of the blushing girls and radiant young men courting on the promenade as well:

> Where did it lead,
> The race, the radiance? To oblivion
> Dissembled by a sac of sparse black seed.

This is Merrill's most complicated retelling of his family history. But since living, of itself, perpetuates nothing, he turns, almost reluctantly, to his pain and his pen at home, far from Yannina, and invites us to enter with him, in fantasy, the magician's tent on the promenade where a woman can be sawed into two, then miraculously healed, a reassuring myth to set over against Frossíni's fate:

> A glittering death
> Is hefted, swung. The victim smiles consent.
> To a sharp intake of breath she comes apart . . .
> Then to a general exhalation heals
>
> Like anybody's life, bubble and smoke
> In afterthought.

Afterthought may, in comparison to life, be only "bubble and smoke," but afterthought is also the domain of art, where a dreamy eternity envelops Ali. In afterthought, the "elements converge":

> Glory of windless mornings that the barge
> (Two barges, one reflected, a quicksilver joke)
> Kept scissoring and mending as it steered
> The old man outward and away,
> Amber mouthpiece of a narghilé
> Buried in his by then snow white beard.

In this universe, the poet's reflective mind meets and internalizes all the Oriental opulence of Ali and his town, the prudishness and pathos of Frossíni, the luxuriousness of Vassilikí, and the recurrent chorus of the courting couples on the promenade: "What shall the heart learn, that already knows / Its place by water, and its time by sun?" It also accepts the ghastly permanence of the dead bodies visible in the monastery underground burial-place, and the dying animals turning on spits. But it believes that in writing it can make "some inmost face to shine / Maned with light, ember and anodyne, / Deep in a desktop burnished to its grain." The lights have vanished along the lake in Yannina, but

Weeks later, in this study gone opaque,
They are relit. See through me. See me through.

The pun, like most of Merrill's plays on words, is serious, and the elegy has gone as far as a poem can go in attempting to take into its stylized world of "bubble and smoke" the fleshly lusts of Ali and the theatrical immolation of Frossíni, the Vanity Fair of the world and the gruesome end of the sexual impulse. It is an odd, crowded, and baroque elegy, with a remarkable joining of filial and paternal spheres.

It remains to be seen how Merrill, whose inventiveness is to be trusted, will continue with such narrative poems and, perhaps, with more installments of "The Book of Ephraim." Mozart, according to Ephraim, has been currently reincarnated as a black rock star: it makes one want more news from that source.

"MIRABELL: BOOKS OF NUMBER"

James Merrill's *Mirabell: Books of Number*, which won the National Book Award for 1978, is the middle volume of a trilogy composed with the aid of a Ouija board. The Ouija board is a symbol system that offers potentially unlimited combinations of letters and numbers, affirmations and denials; it can stand, we might say, for language itself. The first installment of Merrill's trilogy, "The Book of Ephraim" (printed in *Divine Comedies*, in 1976), exhausted the letters of the board; it was composed in twenty-six sections labeled "A" through "Z." The current volume uses up the numbers of the board in ten books going from zero to nine. The final volume, to be called *Scripts for the Pageant*, is left with "Yes" and "No." The Ouija board is a shared system, used by the dead and the living, in which tradition, in the person of the dead, meets an individual talent—or, in this case, the joint talents of the poet and his friend David Jackson. Together, as JM and DJ, in their house at Stonington, where the action of *Mirabell* occurs, they transcribe the rapid gestures of a blue-willow cup that they use instead of a planchette. The messages from "the other side," all in the uppercase of the board, are edited by Merrill—compressed, made intelligible, made into poetry. The books of the trilogy consist of board messages interspersed with commentary and colloquy by the poet.

The pages of the books are typographically unnerving, as blocks of otherworldly uppercase—looking, as a friend remarked, like a computer printout—alternate with blocks of mortal lowercase. The uppercase, in the board's peculiar spelling—"before" becomes "B4," "you" becomes

"U"—is sometimes a ten-syllable line (when dead people talk), sometimes a fourteen-syllable line (when the spirits, who enact "a fall from metrical grace," take over). Human talk is always decasyllabic, in "this rough pentameter, our virtual birthright." From time to time, a lyric form, like a strain of music, appears. The talk of the dead and of the living alike tends to rhyme in couplets and quatrains, but that of the spirits does not rhyme. The spirits, who are here represented chiefly by one among them bearing the number 741, seem to be in part what Milton would have called the fallen angels, and are first conceived of as black batlike creatures. At the center of the third book, 741 metamorphoses into a peacock, and he is later given the name Mirabell, supposedly after the "strut and plumage" of Congreve's hero, but also after "Merrill." Mirabell, "a paragon of courtly gentleness," here replaces the earlier Ephraim as familiar spirit. Ephraim was chatty, conversational; he was comfortable in iambic pentameter, since he was human ("A Greek Jew / Born AD 8 at XANTHOS . . . / a favorite of TIBERIUS . . . Died / AD 36 on CAPRI throttled / By the imperial guard for having LOVED / THE MONSTER'S NEPHEW [sic] CALIGULA"). However, Ephraim spoke rather rarely, and his book is narrated mostly by Merrill. Mirabell, on the other hand, speaks in ungainly syllabics, and the poet's interpolated lines serve as connective tissue between Mirabell's speeches and the speeches of the dead. The dead, principally, are Wystan Auden and Maria Mitsotáki, a childless Greek friend of Merrill's, whom he celebrated in a lyric, "Words for Maria" (1969), and who died of cancer.

Mirabell is a poem about the dead in part because it is a poem of the single life and childlessness; since there is no question of posterity, life is composed of oneself and one's friends, the dead as much as the living. The four bound together round the Ouija board—JM, DJ, Wystan, Maria— are chosen for their lessons because of their childlessness. To Auden's question "Why the four of us?" Mirabell answers, "KEEP IN MIND THE CHILDLESSNESS WE SHARE THIS TURNS US / OUTWARD TO THE LESSONS & THE MYSTERIES." The scale of the poem is both domestic and cosmic. The domestic life includes day-by-day details of life in Greece and in Stonington, the visits of friends, the deaths of parents, an operation. The cosmic life, presided over in Manichean fashion by two gods—Chaos, the god of feeling, and an inexorable "God B" (for "biology")—is evolutionary, hierarchical, mythological, and intermittently purposive. God B's successive projects have included Atlantis, the centaurs, and Eden; he "is not only history but earth itself." The literary tradition in which the poem falls includes all works written by men to whom the angels speak outright: Dante, the four Apostles, Buddha, Mohammed, and, in later days, Milton, Blake, Victor Hugo, and Yeats. Merrill himself diffidently admits to doubts about "all this / warmed up Milton, Dante, Genesis," fearing "Allegory in whose gloom the whole / Horror of Popthink fastens on the soul"; he worries about being "cast / Into this paper Hell out of Doré / or Disney." On the other hand, the quintet of Merrill, Jackson, Auden, Maria Mitsotáki, and Mirabell is said to be an example of the "vital groupings of five," who do "V work"—the work of mind and heart (primarily poetry and music)—encouraged, according to Mirabell, by loves that do not envisage the production of bodies:

> LOVE OF ONE MAN FOR ANOTHER OR LOVE BETWEEN WOMEN
> IS A NEW DEVELOPMENT OF THE PAST 4000 YEARS
> ENCOURAGING SUCH MIND VALUES AS PRODUCE THE BLOSSOMS
> OF POETRY & MUSIC, THOSE 2 PRINCIPAL LIGHTS OF
> GOD BIOLOGY. LESSER ARTS NEEDED NO EXEGETES:
> ARCHITECTURE SCULPTURE THE MOSAICS & PAINTINGS THAT
> FLOWERD IN GREECE & PERSIA CELEBRATED THE BODY.
> POETRY MUSIC SONG INDWELL & CELEBRATE THE MIND . . .
> HEART IF U WILL.

Few painters or sculptors enter this life of the mind, Mirabell adds, since they, "LIKE ALL SO-CALLED NORMAL LOVERS," exist for no purpose other than to produce bodies. This Platonic myth is mocked by Mirabell's listeners: "Come now, admit that certain very great / Poets and musicians have been straight." But the claim, however whimsical, has been made, and the whole of Merrill's trilogy can be seen as a substitution of the virtues of mind and heart—culminating in music and poetry—for the civic and familial and martial virtues usually espoused by the epic.

We might hesitate to think of *Mirabell* in epic terms, since it learns at least as much from Pope and Byron as from Dante. But in its encylopedic instructions about the history of the cosmos and its cast of characters from Olympus (if we may so locate the spirits) and from Hades as well as from earth, its traits are epic ones. For all its rueful tone as it fears and doubts its own matter and method, it goes irrepressibly along, piecing together shards of myth from all cultures—Akhnaton rubs shoulders with Mohammed and centaurs, while Mother Nature, in conjunction with the Sultan God B, presides over all. The hymn to nature in the seventh book articulates the ebb and flow of loyalty—now to mind, now to nature—implicit in the whole poem. Fearful of the power of the senses, Merrill, like some modern metaphysical, asks what rational instruments they have robbed him of—"What have you done with / My books, my watch and compass, my slide-rule?"—but nature answers with her own fascination of texture, whether in constellations or in bodies, "those infinite / Spangled thinnesses whose weave gosling and cygnet / Have learned already in the shell."

When Merrill contemplates what he has done in writing this book, he complains to Auden that the result is maddening:

> It's all by someone else!
> In your voice, Wystan, or in Mirabell's.
> I want it mine, but cannot spare those twenty
> Years in a cool dark place that *Ephraim* took
> In order to be palatable wine.
> This book by contrast, immature, supine,
> Still kicks against its archetypal cradle.
> . . . I'd set
> My whole heart, after *Ephraim*, on returning
> To private life, to my own words. Instead,
> Here I go again, a vehicle
> In this cosmic carpool. Mirabell once said
> He taps my word banks. I'd be happier
> If *I* were tapping them. Or thought I were.

Auden replies in a magisterial defense of convention, tradition, and fable. On convention:

> THINK WHAT A MINOR
> PART THE SELF PLAYS IN A WORK OF ART
> COMPARED TO THOSE GREAT GIVENS   THE ROSEBRICK MANOR
> ALL TOPIARY FORMS & METRICAL
> MOAT ARIPPLE!

On tradition:

> AS FOR THE FAMILY ITSELF MY DEAR
> JUST GAPE UP AT THAT CORONETED FRIEZE:
> SWEET WILLIAMS & FATE-FLAVORED EMILIES
> THE DOUBTING THOMAS & THE DULCET ONE
> (HARDY MY BOY WHO ELSE? & CAMPION).

On the superiority of fable to facts:

> FACTS JM WERE ALL U KNEW TO WANT,
> WRETCHED RICKETY RECALCITRANT
> URCHINS   THE FEW WHO LIVE GROW UP TO BE
> IMPS OF THE ANTIMASQUE.

In fable, "A TABLE / IS SET & LAMPS LIT FOR THE FEASTING GODS." Auden concludes that, given time, facts themselves take on the livery of fable, and become material for art. The poem ends as Mirabell withdraws in favor of a stern-voiced angel Michael, speaking in long, irregular lines: he will be the next instructor, an unfallen rather than a fallen one, as Merrill proceeds into the *Paradiso* of his "Divine Comedies."

"Ephraim" is, on the whole, a cheerful book, constructed around a mythology of reincarnation: most people live on, over and over, even if in someone else's body. In *Mirabell*, Merrill and Jackson discover that their dead companions Auden and Maria will not be reincarnated, but will dissolve into their elements, having first been stripped of their earthly connections. The end of the book celebrates "Maria's Himmelfahrt" and Auden's. Goodbyes are said, of a careful lightness:

> How
> We'll miss you! We'd imagined—I know   CIAO

JM had imagined a thousand and one nights of conversation with these indispensable voices. But the Ouija board meets the law of dissolution, and in the last episode Auden and Maria seem to have disappeared, leaving behind only a snapshot—"Young, windblown / Maria with dark glasses and Gitane"—and a book "by Wystan / Face up . . . all week / Open to Miranda's villanelle." *Mirabell* is a book of long farewell to the parental figures of Auden and Maria, a book that holds on to the dead as long as possible. They are the people who call JM and DJ "MES ENFANTS" (Maria, known as "Maman") or "MY BOYS" (Auden). When these voices fall silent, there will be no one to whom the poet is a child. Though Merrill's mother is alive, she is deliberately left out of the trilogy, as "Ephraim" explains:

> All of which lights up, as scholarship
> Now and then does, a matter hitherto
> Overpainted—the absence from these pages
> Of my own mother. Because of course she's here
> Throughout, the breath drawn after every line,
> Essential to its making as to mine.

The deaths of David Jackson's parents preface the appearance of Mirabell. In the usual biological cycle, parents die after their children have become parents; the internalizing of the parental role, it is believed, enables the parents to be absorbed into the filial psyche. In the childless world of *Mirabell*, the disappearance of parents, or parental friends, is the disappearance of the parental and therefore of the filial; JM and DJ can no longer be "boys," but must put on the mortality of the survivor. However much the sweetness of posthumous conversation with Auden and Maria may be prolonged—with analyses of their character, examples of their wit, descriptions of their lives—the end of the exchange is envisaged from

Maria's first warning, at the end of Book 1: "I HAVE MORE TO LOSE." In Merrill's myth, Maria will become a plant, not a human being; the radiation she endured as a treatment for cancer reduced her human soul to the vegetative level. Auden will be "stripped, reduced to essences, joined to infinity," like one of his beloved minerals:

> What must at length be borne
> Is that the sacred bonds are chemical.

The "seminar" of the participants round the Ouija board is itself such a "stripping process," since Mirabell, Wystan, and Maria will gradually fade away. Merrill's work in creating the trilogy is a comparable "stripping":

> Art—
> The tale that all but shapes itself—survives
> By feeding on its personages' lives,
> The stripping process, sort of. What to say?
> Our lives led *to* this. It's the price we pay.

If the artist needs new resources in middle age, it is not because the old ones are exhausted. On the contrary, the old ones, accumulating exponentially, seem to forbid the acquisition of the new. At some point the writer begins his replay in slow motion of all the eclectic litter and learning that crowds his mind: unburdening himself, he discharges, in an art relatively random by contrast to that of his earlier years, portions of everything he knows. So the board throws up bits and pieces of Merrill's reading (as A *Vision* threw up Yeats's, as *History* threw up Lowell's), and one of the difficulties with the trilogy is that no one of us duplicates Merrill's reading bank, any more than we duplicate Blake's or Milton's. The jumble that is any fifty-year-old memory poses for a reader the problem of other minds; the encyclopedic modern poem, from the *Cantos* on, presses the question almost intolerably.

Though the allusive density of *Mirabell* makes the poem at first difficult, the test of such a poem is not in the first reading (though if there is not enough pleasure in that, the reader is lost for good), but in the reading that takes place once the scheme, the family relations, and the life histories in question have become natural and familiar. In this poem Merrill is enterprisingly (with some incidental wreckage) enlarging his theater of operations. He avoids for lines on end the effortless jeweled effects for which he has been known, and he has turned aside from lyrics of the personal life to narrative, to mythological and metaphysical "expla-nations" of a discursive order ruled not by "feeling" or by "beauty" but by "truth." He is writing in voices other than his own. These undertakings

are not wholly new: Merrill said as far back as 1962: "If I am host at last /
It is of little more than my own past. / May others be at home in it." But
the past of the earlier volumes was on the whole a selective one, careful of
its references, arranged in exquisite forms, and restricted to crises of
feeling. Two poems in *Nights and Days*, of 1966, appear to anticipate the
trilogy. In a sequence of reflections on love called "The Thousand and
Second Night," "the rough pentameter / Quatrains give way, you will
observe, to three / Interpolations, prose as well as verse," reflecting on
"mind, body, and soul (or memory)." The second instance is the inquiry
into the nature of Eros in a long sequence called "From the Cupola." The
poet adapts the myth of Eros and Psyche, and is himself both Psyche's
poet (like Keats) and Psyche herself, receiving letters from the unknown
Eros. Two caricatured evil sisters mock Psyche's claim to an invisible
lover, but Psyche's real anxiety derives not from their realist cynicism but,
rather, from her own distrust of love's distorting idealism. She is consoled
by her poet in Audenesque cadences:

> Psyche, hush. This is me, James
> Writing lest he think
> Of the reasons why he writes—
> Boredom, fear, mixed vanities and shames;
> Also love.
> From my phosphorescent ink
> Trickle faint unworldly lights.

By the end of *Mirabell* the faint unworldly lights have brightened
into the radiance of enlightenment. But in his pursuit of truth Merrill has
by no means forgotten his earlier homage to the senses. The daily life
described in *Mirabell*, which offers itself as one realized version of human
existence, is attentive to the senses, to friendship, to domesticity, to
art—all the elements found in Merrill's lyrics—as well as to the dead, for
whom the poet has had to invent his trilogy. "The dead," "Ephraim" tells
us, "are the surround of the living."

Merrill's argument for the senses denies the old propriety that
would distinguish the aesthetic from the sensual. (In this, he resembles
Keats rather than his other master, Auden.) A continuity between the
aesthetic and the sensual is at the heart of Merrill's work, from the earliest
lyrics on—as if it were inconceivable that a love of textures, shapes, lines,
light, and color should not also be a love of faces and bodies, even if "one
falls back, soiled, blurred." Merrill's primary intuition is that of the
absolute ravishment of the senses. As they combine and mingle, the
senses create, in the order of flesh, interrelations and reinforcings that are

like the elements of an artwork. Yet Merrill's interest in the translation of the data of the senses into the nonpictorial forms of verse and music poses difficulties. Language cannot imitate reality in any easily describable way; and the well-known pitfalls of testifying in verse to the more sensuous of the world's pleasures—pitfalls that are clearest in early Keats and Hopkins— argue against a too literal rendering of sensuality. Language, an abstract medium, is always in allegorical relation to perception and sensation.

In arguing that the sensual and the spiritual are indivisible, Merrill places his trust in the affections as a middle term. Faithlessness and infidelities are acts not of the flesh but of the spirit, and they occur when affection doubts or betrays its own powers. The certain loss of all "sacred bonds" underlies Merrill's verse. But as disbelief and death depopulate his real and imagined worlds, Merrill compensates by a poetry of exuberant mythology and a symposium of incarnate and discarnate voices. The eclectic banquet of youth is replaced in middle age by a Proustian feast of memory. In the fiction of *Mirabell*, the blessings of conversation replace the blessings of sensuality. The audible conversation of tongues—life's addendum to the sensual conversation of bodies—gives way to the inaudible ghostly converse of the dead and the disembodied, as language, letter by letter, assembles itself through the Ouija board. As narrator of, and Prospero to, the whole pageant, Merrill, though fictionally the child of the "father of forms and matter of fact mother" on "the other side," is the adult progenitor of all that happens. The providential and parental figures of Mirabell, Auden, and Maria are only the creatures of his creation.

We might ask whether Merrill's case, at least in the trilogy, is too special to be susceptible of translation into our own terms. Does this flood of transcriptions from another world, this massive treatise on "science" and "history," imply anything for us? Merrill's implicit protest against the censorship of feeling by our relentless ironic intellectualizing of life (he speaks here for all reflective people) takes the form of a defiant mythology— though, in a charming revenge exacted by the time we live in, the mythology must couch itself in "scientific" terms. The mysterious instructors told Merrill to write "Poems of Science." He went home and waited, but nothing happened, since his "word bank" was unfurnished with material. He resorted to potted science (Isaac Asimov, Lewis Thomas) and to remembered childhood myths, inventing macrocosmic and subatomic perspectives from which nothing can be hidden to the enlightened eye. Merrill's mythology attempts to ask what work we can find for that part of the mind hitherto occupied in inventing religious systems. Unlike Robert Lowell, who considered the really interesting people in history to be the emperors, the kings, and the politicians, Merrill thinks that the most attractive souls are those who thought up Edens and afterlifes, saints and satyrs.

It is surprising that Merrill, a poet of infinite finish, should come down so decisively in favor of large mythological outlines and of expository theology. Or perhaps it is not so surprising. The epic poetic of the trilogy demands the large, and even the prosaic. Whereas the lyric is discontinuous, and rejects the narrativity that (however much it may be submerged) links the successive events of drama and fiction, the epic goes beyond narrativity to an encyclopedic account of all things in heaven and earth. The instructors promise to return Merrill to his "chronicles of love and loss" after the trilogy is done, but he will not be the same poet who set down the first lines of "The Book of Ephraim"—the stretching and straining of this large effort cannot be forgotten in a contraction to lyric shapes.

The lessons of *Mirabell* are the unpopular ones of middle age. Most people, the poem tells us, are unevolved, and remain in an animal unawareness, in which they grow, couple, reproduce themselves, and die. Some souls evolve beyond this—into thought, vision, and art. (They are the souls "cloned" in the "Research Lab" of the spirits and sent into the world to do the "V work" of civilization—creating religions, symphonies, temples, cultures, poems.) There is no permanent culture; ours is one of successive attempts by God B to order chaos. The achievements of mind always seem to excel their material origins: hence the myth of inspiring Muses, mysterious instructors, visions, and oracles. The honey of generation is an opiate; the childless have freer access to the spiritual life. Everyone dies. The conversation of friends is precious. As parents and friends die, we dwell more and more on the dead. Our minds become a repository of all we have read, learned, been brought up on. We begin to think in larger terms—about history, about the survival of the planet, about genius.

But it is not for these or other worthy observations in their bald sense that we prize *Mirabell*. It is, rather, for the intimate and solid circumstantiality in which those truths are based. We know the death of parents not propositionally but circumstantially, in the long, particular narration of the death of David Jackson's parents, in "stupor, fear, incontinence," and their burial in a "raw trench." We know the loss of friends as Merrill accustoms us, through a hundred and seventy-eight pages, to the tender and solicitous raillery of Auden and Maria, and then, once we look forward to hearing them indefinitely, strikes the knell of their disappearance. We come to prize even the most frail creations of culture as Merrill's myths link the oldest constructions, like Atlantis and Eden, named rather than evoked, to the creation, metamorphosis, and humanizing of the bat-peacock Mirabell. First an inhuman other, Mirabell becomes, through "this world of courtesy"—the board of communication—someone who can love ("I HAVE COME TO LOVE U"), someone self-conscious and aesthetically reflective. In his becoming we see the coming-to-be of every conscious creature, through language and love:

> B4 OUR MEETINGS I WAS NOTHING   NO TIME PASSD   BUT NOW
> YR TOUCH LIKE A LAMP HAS SHOWN ME TO MYSELF & I AM
> ME: 741! I HAVE ENTERED A GREAT WORLD   I AM FILLED
> WITH IS IT MANNERS?

There are stretches of flats in the exposition of the mythology, yet its density shares with all systems—from Leviticus to *The Book of Mormon* and Melville's cetology—a sheer willingness to bore. The visionary mind has its own pedantries. Just as complicated poets, like Milton, have to learn to be simple, so Merrill, natively compact, has here decided to learn a discursive plainness.

Before the concluding speech of the archangel Michael, who announces the next act of the comedy, Merrill speaks in his own voice of the world's diversity, as he glances out to numberless brilliances of light over the water:

> The message hardly needs decoding, so
> Sheer the text, so innocent and fleet
> These overlapping pandemonia:
> Birdlife, leafplay, rockface, waterglow
> Lending us their being, till the given
> Moment comes to render what we owe.

Merrill has offered a self-definition through metaphor in the course of the poem: his metal is silver (Auden's is platinum), his element air, his mineral crystal, his color "cold lavender." In themselves, these specifications are definitive. By middle age, one knows what one is. If Merrill reminds us sometimes of Ariel, he is yet an Ariel making a deliberate gesture toward an enlarging of style in his refusal to be exclusively beautiful. By its admission of the learning, conversation, and random use of language that underlie the crystallizations of lyric, Merrill's poem pays homage to the riches of unordered literary experience:

> MAN'S TERMITE PALACE BEEHIVE ANTHILL PYRAMID JM
> IS LANGUAGE   USE IT   STIR THE THINKERS & DETER THE REST.

Language "of such a depth, shimmer, and force" is the "life raft" that carries the poet over the flood of sensation. *Mirabell* is more a diary, in fact, than a planned "system": each section encompasses whatever rises to the surface at a given moment of composition. The mind whose word banks and image banks are here tapped is not in any way a typical one. It is preternaturally knowing, and eclectically read; it strikes attitudes; it is fond but acutely critical; it likes puns perhaps more than it should; its relativism is both despairing and elated. It never lacks fit language—silky and astringent by turns, lustrous and decorative one moment, attenuated and scholastically drab the next, candid or esoteric as its author decides.

What is in the American mind these days—the detritus of past belief, a hodgepodge of Western science and culture, a firm belief in the worth of the private self and in the holiness of the heart's affections, a sense of time and space beyond the immediate—is here displayed for judgment. Somewhat less general in reference, perhaps, is Merrill's examination of what, as a personal aim, can replace self-reproduction in child-bearing. Once the biological purpose of life is even theoretically put aside as a justification of living, we must (theological justification having been abandoned long since) advocate something like Merrill's civilizing "V work." The Arnoldian doctrine of the saving remnant seems in this poem to have a new defender; but Merrill dwells, as Arnold does not, on the parallel necessity of private affection. Love and civilization here go hand in hand, the work of art and science refining life in public as the bonds of affection refine life in private. *Mirabell* is Merrill's hymn to the spiritual evolution that seems possible, if precarious, now that biological evolution has invented man; its dark undersong is Hiroshima in the realm of science, and subhuman stupidity in the realm of the private life.

What Merrill once said of Eugenio Montale—that his emotional refinement is "surprisingly permeable by quite ordinary objects: ladles, hens, pianos, half-read letters"—is true of Merrill himself. The claim of ordinary objects and ordinary events on lyric is a mark of the democratic sense in every modern poet of quality—from the priestlike Eliot down through the alchemizing Merrill—that the things of the world can lend a myth (as Crane said of the Brooklyn Bridge) to God. The tendency of modern American lyric poets to reclaim whole tracts of language and experience ceded in the nineteenth century to novels or nonfictional prose continues in Merrill. It is this tendency that has caused us to outstrip our parent stock in England. If to play so free with tradition one poet needs the Ouija board, and another, like Ginsberg, needs visions, and another, like Eliot, needs Buddhism, those who are not poets can only conclude that the work of creation proceeds by its own means.

STEPHEN YENSER

The Fullness of Time:
James Merrill's ''Book of Ephraim''

Until very recently we had somehow managed not to see, perhaps to his benefit, that we have been harboring among us a truly extraordinary poet. Even now, the numerous prizes and the growing reputation notwithstanding, it might not be too late to begin a discussion of James Merrill's work by playing advocate. Once his trilogy in progress has been completed, however, that role will surely seem nothing but a transparent ploy. Merrill is putting together one of the most ambitious, original, and variously brilliant works written by an American.

He has accomplished it in a remarkably short time. The first poem, *The Book of Ephraim*, appeared in *Divine Comedies* in 1976, three years after the publication of *Braving the Elements* and two years before *The Yellow Pages*, a selection of earlier uncollected work. The second poem, *Mirabell: Books of Number*, came out in 1978, and notes accompanying excerpts from *Scripts for the Pageant* now appearing in journals promise its publication this year. The first two books make it clear that the trilogy will be a unified work, with its successive parts building upon its earlier ones. But they also make it clear that each book will have its own integrity. *Ephraim* might well turn out to be the most easily detachable of the three, for in *Mirabell*, at the same time that he leads us to expect a third volume, Merrill implies that the second came as a surprise. In any case, because of its initial position, as well as because of its independent structure and its density, *Ephraim* should first be read as a separate work.

Running to about 2500 lines, and thus substantially less than

From *Canto* 2, vol. 3, (Spring 1980). Copyright © 1980 by *Canto*.

half the length of *Mirabell*, *Ephraim* is a good deal longer than *Notes toward a Supreme Fiction* and *Four Quartets*, with both of which it shares certain thematic concerns as well as a sustained and varied excellence. Not that it resembles either of those poems, or any other, very much. A sort of eccentric *Essay on Man*—of course any *Essay on Man* would have to be eccentric today—it also conjures up works as different from Pope's and from each other as *A Vision* and *Pale Fire*. As though turning Nabokov's *donnée* inside out, Merrill incorporates in his verse bits of a novel, the unfinished manuscript of which was left in a taxicab in Georgia and never recovered. Like the lost manuscript, although in a more straightforward fashion, the poem sets forth the experiences that Merrill and his friend, David Jackson, who live together, have had with the other world, especially with a spirit named Ephraim, whom they contacted in one of their first sessions with the ouija board over twenty years ago and with whom they have been in touch ever since. (Experience with the ouija board plays a part in Merrill's first novel, *The Seraglio*, published in 1957, and is the subject of a poem called "Voices from the Other World" in his second volume of poems, *The Country of a Thousand Years of Peace*, published in 1959.) Like Yeats's communicators, Ephraim provides information about the structure of the universe, but unlike them he has a subtle sense of humor, a predilection for aphorism, and, being at only stage six in an empyrean he imagines to consist mostly of nine stages, a less than complete understanding of the nature of things. This last is fortunate, no less for JM and DJ, as our mediums are known, than for the reader:

> —For as it happened I had been half trying
> To make sense of *A Vision*
> When our friend dropped his bombshell: POOR OLD YEATS
> STILL SIMPLIFYING

Ephraim speaks in the board's capitals, of course, and without punctuation (although Merrill mercifully uses a double space to indicate a full stop), with the result that his voice sounds to the inner ear more distinct from JM's than it might otherwise. The capitals also provide a clever means of disposition, for the poem is divided into twenty-six sections, each beginning with the appropriate letter of the alphabet. Throughout the poem the normative metre is iambic pentameter, occasionally rhymed, from which other verse forms emerge and into which they then dissolve: couplets, quatrains, sonnets, sonnet sequences, hendecasyllabics, *terza rima*, and other prosodic schemes swirl to the surface to form their own permanently transitory little systems. These are all interlocked by motif as well as by narrative so that the effect is largely musical, and it is hardly surprising to find Mahler, Stravinsky, Beethoven, Mozart, Bach, Haydn, Puccini, Verdi, Satie, and Wagner alluded to. Wagner's *Götterdämmerung* is in fact one of the main motifs in *Ephraim*, and the ease with which the poem can absorb such an influence indicates its extensiveness and depth.

But more of motif in a moment. First it will be helpful to summarize the situation—or rather situations, for there are three main plot lines woven together through *Ephraim*. The first of these arises from the relationship between DJ and JM on the one hand and Ephraim and the other world on the other. One night during the summer of 1955, a year after moving into their house in Stonington, Connecticut, DJ and JM sit down to try their hands at the ouija board, and after a few false starts—contacts with recently disembodied souls who have not yet learned how to use this sort of wireless—raise Ephraim, a Greek Jew "Born AD 8 at XANTHOS" who "Died / AD 36 on CAPRI," a minion of Tiberius and lover of Caligula. Clever, profound, sybaritic, and moral by turns, and golden haired, with *"eyes that amazing / blood-washed gold our headlights catch"* (so we learn from the recounting of the one unforgettable glimpse DJ gets of him when under hypnosis), Ephraim is thenceforth this poem's counterpart to Beatrice, instructing DJ and JM by séance in the ways of the soul after death. They learn that every person on earth is a "representative" of a spirit or "patron," who however has virtually no control over the representative's actions; that regardless of that last limitation, patrons are promoted from stage to heavenly stage partly on the basis of their representatives' representations; that, as in much Oriental philosophy, a soul can escape the wheel of life—and thus become a patron himself. They also talk on the party line to Stevens, Auden, and others who move in Ephraim's circles. Meanwhile, Ephraim, who can see anything within his mediums' ken that appears in a reflecting surface and who can hear as well as most of us, meets friends and relatives (both living and dead) of JM and DJ, listens to Mahler and Stravinsky for the first time, and accompanies the other members of the board on trips to the western U.S. and around the world.

The second plot line, in part a translation of the autobiographical narrative, is that of the novel, which JM summarizes and even extends in the poem. The action takes place in New Mexico, and the chief figures are Eros, a sensual spirit whose character is an exaggeration of one aspect of Ephraim; Sergei Markovich, a Russian emigré who bears a discreet resemblance to JM; the enigmatic Mrs. Rosamund Smith, later the Marchesa Santofior, owner of some property in New Mexico on which Sergei lives; Leo Cade, who served in Viet Nam, where he seems to have taken part in a murder or a gang rape of a young Vietnamese his outfit made out to be a spy, and who has returned to the U.S., where he falls under the spell of Eros and has experiences that recall both DJ (his vision under hypnosis) and JM (his return through hallucination to an earlier self); Leo's helpless wife Ellen; and Joanna, a middle-aged vamp with inscrutable motives and dark designs on the affections of Matt Prentiss, a character modeled on DJ's father. Definitely a subplot, the action in the novel gets extensive treatment only in sections J, N, S, T, X, and the ingenious D, for "Dramatis personae," where Merrill lists several of the novel's characters as well as a number of actual and apparently actual people who figure in the poem.

In the third place we have the story of the writing of this poem, always rendered in the present tense. This plot is less related to the first than an element in it, since it covers the last of the reported phrases of the association with Ephraim, and is closely allied with the second, partly because the history of the poem involves the tale of the lost novel. At this level, the action takes exactly one year, from January, 1974, when JM begins the poem in Stonington, through December, 1974, when, back in Stonington, he completes it. In the interim, he takes an autumn trip to Greece, where he and DJ have a second home, and returns to the States by way of Venice, where he chances upon a nephew, Wendell Pincus, who, owing to a certain reprehensible exchange of information between the ouija boarders and their familiar spirit, is the latter's representative. He is also the son of Betsy Pincus, purportedly the model for the figure of Ellen Prentiss Cade in the unfinishable novel.

But of course the novel *is* finished, in the form of the poem, for if the novel was a translation into fiction of scenes from real life, the poem is a sort of detranslation of the novel. In A, after admitting his weariness of "Our age's fancy narrative concoctions," of authors "Suckled by Woolf not Mann," JM goes ahead to explain:

> So my narrative
> Wanted to be limpid, unfragmented;
> My characters, conventional stock figures
> Afflicted to a minimal degree
> With personality and past experience—
> A witch, a hermit, innocent young lovers,
> The kinds of beings we recall from Grimm,
> Jung, Verdi, and the commedia dell'arte.
> That such a project was beyond me merely
> Incited further futile stabs at it.

Or so he claims. But although its narrative is not unfragmented, the poem is crowded with precisely the types listed here, not just because he retells much of the novel in verse, but also because his real people often fit into the categories named—as how could they not? The linking of Grimm, Jung, and Verdi startles us into remembering that conventional figures are conventional because they distill common experience. The real Maya Deren is as much a witch as the fictional Joanna, JM as much a hermit as Sergei, DJ and JM once as much innocent young lovers as Leo and Ellen. (Indeed Ephraim refers to them in C as "MY POOR / INNOCENTS.") It figures, then, that about three-quarters through the poem, in S, Merrill should recapitulate an incident that was to occur "three-quarters through the novel." Again, reflecting on the relationship between truth and fiction in T, he declines to pursue the subject further because what he would have had to say about it comes "too near the end of the unwritten book," and from one point of view the gist is that we must wait until later sections—especially V and X—for the continuation of the meditation.

One of the oldest and most fertile themes in Merrill's work, the interdependence of reality and fiction takes a dozen different shapes here. In A, JM describes his original quandary as to form:

> Also my subject matter
> Gave me pause—so intimate, so novel.
> Best after all to do it as a novel?
> Looking about me, I found characters
> Human and otherwise (if the distinction
> Meant anything in fiction).

Of course he found the "characters / Human and otherwise" in life as well as in fiction, if the distinction means anything in a realm just possibly overseen by those less human than otherwise:

> If we are characters
> As now and then strikes us, in some superplot
> Of Ephraim's, isn't our prerogative
> To run away with its author?
>   (K)

At one juncture in L, JM recalls that he and DJ, after one of the inevitable arguments, vowed never to repeat such " 'a scene / From real life' "; and in T he finds that a certain "foreshortening" of time in Proust, which he once took "for an unconvincing / Trick of the teller," now seems to be "truth instead / Babbling through his own astonishment." As he put it in an earlier poem, "Days of 1935" (*Braving the Elements*), "life was fiction in disguise." In V, tourists hurry "To sit out the storm in the presence of Giorgione's / *Tempesta*"—which is then described as "nothing less / Than earthly life in all its mystery." It is characteristic that, in S,

Stendhal should be referred to, in the context of a discussion of fictional characters, as "H BEYLE," his "real" name.

The poem's basic composition itself, including as it does verifiable autobiography, "Notes for the ill-starred novel," figures from others of Merrill's works, and characters and incidents apparently invented for *Ephraim*, interlaces the realms of reality and fiction. Moreover, since Merrill forces us to make a provisional distinction between novel and poem he is paradoxically able both to imply the literal nature of his poetic account and to remind us that it too might have its fictional elements. What are we to make, for example, of such a figure as Beatrice ("Betsy") Merrill Pincus? We are told in D that she was born in 1937 and is "JM's niece" as well as the "Model for Ellen Prentiss Cade." Inquiry made of those who should know, however, has disclosed no such conveniently named real person—and it does seem unlikely that, if she were real, Merrill would have confessed to her, let alone in public, that he and DJ were responsible, through their dealings with Ephraim, for the sort of soul that was slipped into the foetus in her womb during the sixth month of her pregnancy. Or *would* he? Where are we?

> Where were we? On unsteady ground. Earth, Heaven;
> Reality, Projection—half-stoned couples
> Doing the Chicken-and-the-Egg till dawn.
> Which came first? And would two never come
> Together, sleep then in each other's arms
> Above the stable rich with dung and hay?
>
> (M)

II

The deft persistence with which reality and fiction are woven together in *The Book of Ephraim* perhaps suggests the poem's density of texture. If it could be charted by a computer—and why not, since birdsong can now be graphed and pyramids x-rayed—the result would show something like a system of ley lines, lines of force supposedly traceable in England even today between ancient sacred sights which intersect in quantity at key points and lace the whole island together with their irregular mesh. Since *Ephraim* is so tightly reticulated that almost any passage in it might be considered both a point of intersection and a point of departure, there is no reason not to open a discussion of its designs *in medias res*; in fact, the nature of the middle of things makes it appropriate that we do so.

Near the center of *Ephraim*—in lines 51–52 of the even 100 lines of M—JM paraphrases for us his familiar spirit's explanation of a dream purportedly dreamed by Maya Deren, a friend of the poet and DJ until her death in 1961 and (as we have been told in D) the "doyenne of our / American experimental film": "This dream [Ephraim] blandly adds, is a low-budget / Remake—imagine—of the *Paradiso*." Now Dante's presence is felt throughout this poem, from the epigraph (drawn from the *Paradiso*, XV, 61–63), through a documented allusion in K, to the encounter in the Venetian twilight with a figure from the poet's past (related in *terza rima* as fluent as any since Shelley) in W. Hardly less pervasive is the influence of Maya Deren, who recorded her own fascination with occult deities in her book on Haitian voodoo, *Divine Horsemen*, which is excerpted in Q, and whose experiments in film have analogues in Merrill's experimental adaptation of certain cinematic techniques. At the end of L, for example, when JM recalls with Ephraim's coaching his death in the preceding life, the episode is done in reverse chronological order, as one might run film backward—and as indeed Merrill did run his own newsreel backward in an earlier poem, "18 West 11th Street" (*Braving the Elements*). Maya Deren, in short, holds up one of the many mirrors in this poem that reflect JM, and Ephraim's studiedly casual remark—though too much (or little) could be made too quickly of the relationship—applies to the "book" that bears his name as well as to Maya's dream.

This "dream," related in the first half of M, actually constitutes, according to Ephraim, an instance in which Maya's soul leaves her sleeping body and, in this permutation of the roles of Beatrice and Dante, escorted by him, attends an elegant *soirée* on the sixth stage ("chandeliers, white orchids, silver trays / Dense with bubbling glassfuls"), where a breathtaking transformation occurs. At first, Maya is the only one in the gathering not resplendent in evening dress—she is in fact in "mourning weeds"—but then:

> [Ephraim] leads
> Her to a spring, or source, oh wonder! in
> Whose shining depths her gown turns white, her jet
> To diamonds, and black veil to bridal snow.
> Her features are unchanged, yet her pale skin
> Is black, with glowing nostrils—a not yet
> Printed self . . . Then it is time to go.

Maya's glimpse of her future self, rendered in appropriately photographic terms, draws together several of the poem's major motifs: water, the mirror, and transformation or rebirth. The first of these motifs runs through *Ephraim* like (and often in the form of) a stream, sometimes in

evidence and sometimes not but never far away, so that the reader finds
himself in a position something like that of a visitor to Pope's famous
grotto, described by Peter Quennell, who is quoted (as a number of the
poem's seeming matrices are) in Q:

> Every surface sparkled or shimmered or gleamed with a smooth subaqueous
> lustre; and, while these coruscating details enchanted the eye, a delicate
> water-music had been arranged to please the ear; the 'little dripping murmur' of
> an underground spring—discovered by the workmen during their excavations—
> echoed through the cavern day and night . . . Pope intended . . . that the
> visitor, when at length he emerged, should feel that he had been reborn into a
> new existence.

    In other words, even as he lets the "workmen" anticipate his
critics, Merrill implicitly compares his own "folly" (or folie à deux, as his
analyst and he, with less conviction, view it in I) to that of Pope—whose
influence, recurrently apparent, JM explicitly notes in D, where it is
revealed that his own patron is one Kinton Ford (1810–1843), a hitherto
unknown editor of the Augustan poet's works. Both poem and cavern,
after all, remove us from the quotidian world, as Maya's "dream" removes
her—and sure enough, back in M, she wakes from her dream "in bliss."
Later, we learn in the second half of M, she makes her film "Ritual in
Transfigured Time," in which "The young white actress gowned and veiled
in black / Walks out into a calm, shining sea" and as she sinks "Feetfirst in
phosphorescent negative" becomes "a black bride." In treating in the last
part of M an actual film that is based on a dream, reported in the first
part, that is really a vision of paradise, Merrill sets his own work, with its
concern with the interface of reality and fiction—as Ephraim has DJ and
JM place the euonymous Maya in G—between two mirrors.
    If the spring in which Maya looks to find herself transformed as in
a magic glass is the same one that flows through Pope's grotto, it is also
the one that is identified with the "voice" of JM's genius, or the creative
power. Recalling Ephraim's dictée in C, JM says: "As it flowed on, his
stream-of-consciousness / deepened." The phrase "stream-of-consciousness"
itself suggests how closely allied the spirit and the poet's inspiration
are—how tempting is the analyst's argument that Ephraim is "only" a
projection—and just as the poem moves from underground depths to
glittering surface detail so Ephraim's profundity sometimes gives way to
superficiality: "Observe the easy, graceful way we swim," JM says in P,
"Back to his shallows." When the "novel" peters out in T: "Now along
crevices inch rivulets / At every turning balked." At the conclusion of T,
significantly juxtaposed with the end of that particular endeavor, there

occurs this marvelously startling paean to a power at once mundane and transcendent:

> When the urge
> Comes to make water, a thin brass-hot stream
> Sails out into the updraft, spattering
> One impotent old tree that shakes its claws.
> The droplets atomize, evaporate
> To dazzlement a blankness overdusts
> Pale blue, then paler blue. It stops at nothing.

Ephraim finally disappears in X, "Back underground he sinks, a stream," and JM wonders in what mood he will now face a new season, since he will be "without a guide," with "nothing along those lines—or these / Whose writing, if not justifies, so mirrors, / So embodies up to now some guiding force." Again, in S, he explains that he wanted the "neutral ground" of the lost novel on which to work out his theme, "so that (when the fall rains fell) would go / Flashing through me a perfected flow / Landscape and figures once removed."

The "guiding force" or "stream" takes the form also of "a Bach courante / Or brook that running slips into a shawl / Of crystal noise" (N), and as the metaphor insinuates the power it seeks to define is elusive. It is one thing for Ephraim or Dante's ancestor Cacciaguida, the heavenly soul who is the speaker of the lines quoted as an epigraph, to "look on the mirror in which, before you think, you express your thought," and quite another for the mortal poet to set about his task. Only too often the latter finds himself in this discouraging situation, described in a punning phrase in Z as the "Cost of living high":

> The fire we huddle with our drinks by
> Pops and snaps. Throughout the empty house
> (Tenants away until the New Year) taps
> Glumly trickling keep the pipes from freezing.

On the other hand, when imagination flows unchecked, when the poet really feels in touch with the source—well, let JM tell it, in the syllabic lines he refers to as "loose talk" in X:

> What I think I feel now, by its own nature
> Remains beyond my power to say outright,
> Short of grasping the naked current where it
> Flows through field and book, dog howling, the firelit
> Glances, the caresses, whatever draws us
> To, and insulates us from, the absolute . . .

The dilemma is familiar enough—we find it, for example, in Eliot's *Quartets*, with their "intolerable wrestle / With words and meanings" in an attempt to say what human kind could hardly bear anyway, and in Stevens's "Prologues to What Is Possible," where the unsayable syllable that lures the poet on "would shatter the boat" if it were caught up with—but not the more easily resolved for that.

The elusiveness of this "spring, or source" that manifests itself in the dog's howl as well as in the lover's caress and the poet's book both keeps us from seizing it and keeps us tracking it. If the course is a "naked current," that current is multiform, being for instance metaphorically electrical as well as fluid, as the preceding reference to insulation suggests. The *anagnorisis* of the novel takes place in New Mexico when, JM says in J, Joanna and Sergei

> "Recognize" each other, or I as author
> Recognize in them the plus and minus
> —Good and evil, let my reader say—
> Vital to the psychic current's flow.

By such means Merrill turns his water into fire, and in doing so, in converting the one current into what might seem to be its opposite, he at least exemplifies the power that it lies beyond his power to define. Time and again he equates the apparently beneficent element with the potentially dangerous one: in C, when Ephraim flows on in his "stream-of-consciousness" and leaves an issue "hanging fire"; in X, where in a rainstorm the clouds become "sable bulks awince / With fire"; in P, where the poet recalls hearing the Rhinemaidens in *Götterdämmerung*, "fettered in chain / Reaction," singing their refrain and thus causing a "spark" to alight on his mind ("so pitifully green" that it did not catch for years). A room in the Stonington house with "Walls of ready-mixed matte 'flame' (a witty / Shade, now *water*melon, now sun*burn*)," is where JM and DJ receive the flood of information—in which fiction is to fact as water is to fire (or as water is to electricity, since the one current conducts the other)—from another changeable, witty shade.

Besides that of the ambiguous current, this force also takes the form, perhaps more surprisingly, of *the* current, or the flow of time, as in A, where time "was running out like water," and in a difficult passage in T, where fire and water mix once more:

> "All that we dread by midnight we have burst
> Into a drifting, cooling soot of light,
> Each speck a voodoo bullet dodged in vain
> Or stopped with sangfroid—is the moment now?

> At sunrise? Yet the hangfire talks go on,
> Current events no sooner sped than din. . . ."

The speaker, who goes on with what Merrill later calls an "Unrelenting fluency" and who thus reminds us of Cacciaguida's gift and Ephraim's stream of consciousness, is an initially mysterious "figure in the mirror stealing looks"—who must be, as both the ambivalence of "stealing looks" and this section's letter indicate, Time himself, at the same time that he is literally a reflection of Sergei, the person spoken to in this passage.

Time, it turns out, often speaks in spoonerisms and related devices, as the figure in the mirror implies when he conflates the phrase "no sooner said than done" with the name of the popularizer of the rhetorical slip and comes up with " 'no sooner sped than din'." He also observes, in a purer example, that he and Sergei pick their ways toward one another through " 'grums of class,' " and—to return to the mainstream—he announces to Sergei that " 'You clothe my mowing as I don your flask'." In donning the mask of Sergei, that is, Time disguises his mowing as a flowing. This inevitable alliance, nay, identity with whom we are wont to consider the enemy, this complicity with the wrinkles we cannot iron out, is the subject of one of Cavafy's marginalia on Ruskin, which Merrill has quoted in a luminous review of Robert Liddell's book on the Greek poet: "When we say 'Time' we mean ourselves. Most abstractions are simply our pseudonyms. It is superfluous to say 'Time is scytheless and toothless.' We know it. We are time." (*The New York Review of Books*, 17 July 1975). When JM, hearing in R the shriek of the crowd at the Athens stadium, likens the noise to that of a "blade / On grindstone," he sets up the same equation, although he restores to Time his traditional implement. Time's remark to Sergei here in X that " 'One wand hashes the other'," even as it unmasks the optimistic adage, makes the point just as grimly and more specifically. The artist works hand in glove with Time, in other words, and yet the other hand of the latter, not caring what its partner is doing, wields the scythe.

Time and the imagination, although from one point of view apparently different names for the same absolute but fugitive force, have been provisionally opposed from the beginning. A passage in A that foreshadows T's confrontation contradicts another sanguine commonplace in describing JM's plight after the manuscript of the novel was lost or stolen:

> I alone was left
> To tell my story. For it seemed that Time—
> The grizzled washer of his hands appearing

> To say so in a spectrum-bezeled space
> Above hot water—Time would not . . .

The passage from *The Faerie Queene* (III. vi. 41–42) included in Q's garland of quotations epitomizes this eternal dilemma:

> But were it not, that Time their troubler is,
> All that in this delightful Gardin growes,
> Should happy be, and have immortal blis . . .

As JM says in another context in K, "There will be no way to fly back in time." Only Time himself, it appears, can be both the "grizzled washer of his hands" of all things and the capricious infant enigmatized by Heraclitus, also quoted (and translated) in Q:

> Alōn pais esti paizōn, pessevōn; paidos hē basilēiē.
> Time is a child, playing a board game: the kingdom of the child.

Nor is art exempt, as the havoc Time plays with venerable phrases in T perhaps suggests. In any case, even such a masterpiece as Giorgione's *Tempesta* is slyly said to be "timeless in its fashion."

But " 'One wand hashes the other'," and that the spoonerism cuts both ways is one point obliquely made in the treatment of Giorgione's famously riddling painting in X. Deriving many of his views from a recent eye-opening essay by Nancy Thompson de Grummond (in *L'Arte*, 5, no. 18–19, 20, 5–53) JM interprets *La Tempesta* as a rendering of the salient incidents in the legend of the life of St. Theodore, the patron saint (before St. Mark) of Venice. On this interpretation, the "young man in dark rose, leaning on his staff"—or wand—is St. Theodore the Recruit, after he has slain the dragon or serpent, thus at one stroke saving the town and rescuing his mother, and after the archangel Gabriel has changed the course of the stream that blocked an exit from the cave in which Theodore and his mother were imprisoned. The naked young woman nursing a baby, according to Grummond, is St. Theodore's mother, but at an earlier stage in her life—at that stage, in fact, when she was nursing the young Theodore. In the background is the storm from which the painting gets its traditional but spurious title and which alludes to the power that St. Theodore was thought to have over the elements—or, as Merrill more pointedly has it—over "electric storms."

As excavation at Pope's grotto revealed the presence of an underground stream, so x-rays of the painting have shown that Giorgione painted out, along with an earlier version of the woman, the image of the dragon—now referred to only by an emblem "above a distant portal" and an unobtrusive reptile in the foreground. (The "mute hermit slithers to his cleft": the sexual twist given the image makes it comport with the Oedipal overtones Merrill finds in the painting.) Giorgione's pentimento is much to Merrill's purpose:

> As for the victim, flood-green, flash-
> Violet coils translated into landscape
> Blocked the cave mouth, till Gabriel himself
> Condescended to divert the stream. . . .

There are two translations going on here, for if the painter changed the dragon to landscape, the poet turns him into a reptilian stream that absorbs some of the qualities of the electrical storm, and this conversion, especially when coupled with the blocking of the "cave mouth," suggests that we are dealing here with the old force primarily in its adversary aspect, that of time. In fact, in T, Time has pictured himself as a "slitherer" with scales of "coalfire-blue." Accordingly, St. Theodore and Gabriel (his diverting aide as Ephraim is JM's) are the figures emulated by the poet, whose own work, like Giorgione's (which affords a rare example of synchronicity in the Renaissance), seeks to overcome the temporal, or to turn the destructive flow of time into the creative flow of the imagination. Indeed the poem might have been called, after Maya Deren's film, "Ritual in Transfigured Time."

Merrill rings a number of changes on this theme. Here in X he invokes Wagner's Siegfried and "his worm / Slain among rhinestones," and on several occasions he refers fleetingly to Mercury, whose caduceus (or wand) includes two intertwined serpents. The dragon is really "relegated / To a motif above a distant portal" at the beginning of P, where the dollar sign is interpreted as a combination of "Snake and Tree of Life." More directly to the point, in Q, Merrill quotes John Michell's *The View over Atlantis* on the Lord of Lambton, an English folk hero:

> He put on a suit of armour set all over with sharp blades and stood on an island in the river. The dragon rushed upon him and tried to crush him in its coils, but the knives on the armour cut it into little pieces which were swept away by the current before the dragon could exercise its traditional power of reassembling its dismembered parts.

" 'One wand hashes the other'." The river in this case, if we see the poem as a whole in the light of this passage, *is* the poem, its flow sweeping along the numerous time segments that result from the narrative lines' continual interruption of one another. To belabor JM's passing pun in U, there are three "stories" in this structure, but none of them is toured all at once; on the contrary, we are frequently *de*toured, led by some unexpected stairway or passage concealed by a book case down or up a level, discovering as we go that certain features (mirrors, arrangements of flowers, furnaces, etc.) are repeated with slight variation, so that it is sometimes difficult to say which story we are in, especially since the tenses shift not according to historical time but according to narrative exigency. Imagination hashes chronology, and time's passage is acknowledged only to be transformed by the configuration of events.

It is not just time that is divided so; but then, according to the quotation from Cavafy, it is not just time that is time: at the beginning of T, Sergei looks into the mirror and sees Time's visage. But things are a good deal more intricate than that, for Sergei, as his name perhaps intimates (Sergei = Sir Gay?) is a figurative reflection of JM, who at the end of S has himself been addressing Sergei, who turns out to be a "cutting" from a real person. In S, musing over a cut geranium, JM recalls his fictional character's lineage, which can be traced to an old man who, years past, lived next door in Stonington. "When he was cut down" by the proverbial reaper, the poet "took slips of him," one of which became the houseman Ken in his poem "The Summer People" (*The Fire Screen*) and another of which "came up Russian":

> Here you are now, old self in a new form,
> Some of these roots look stronger, some have died.
> Tell me, tell me, as I turn to you,
> What every moment does, has done, will do—
> Questions one simply cannot face in person.

The figure JM "turns to" then in T—for the poem's characters are almost as volatile as its main current, and we will recall that Maya's source mirrors as it transforms—is Sergei, or Time in the guise of Sergei.

Much of the poem's infrastructure consists of such metamorphoses, as a glance at some of the different embodiments of the female principle ought to suggest. Repeatedly portrayed as "smoking" or "fuming" (J, S, T), Joanna is also a version of the adversary, a Jungian terrible mother, and is thought in X to be "the last gasp of [JM's] dragon." At the end of J, she "reminds" her creator of his stepmother, once the leading character in a real *tranche de vie* he entitles *The Other Woman*, but then in X she represents an aspect of his real mother when JM finds the latter present in Joanna's "fuming." The poet's mother, in turn, merges with St. Theodore's and suddenly seems to be "here / Throughout, the breath drawn after every line, / Essential to its making as to mine." One reason that she is "Essential" is implied in a passage in R in which JM questions Maya, over the board, about her Haitian goddess:

How about Erzulie? BUT SHE IS THE QUEEN
OF HEAVEN   Oh, not Mary?   Not Kuan Yin?
THEY ARE ALL ONE QUINTESSENCE   CHANEL NO
5 × 5 × 5 × 5 × 5

The relationship among the other women, in short, doubles and overlaps with that among those in heaven, and Joanna, St. Theodore's mother, JM's mother, Maya (whose dream transformed her in Erzulie's image), and Lucy Prentiss (Maya's "BOSS" is St. Lucy) are also among the "COUNT-LESS FACES" of the Queen of Heaven.

Mirroring images proliferate. If the poet's mother is "Here . . . in Maya's prodigality" (X), Maya is here in JM's, most notably in R's second sonnet. In the context of a memory of Maya's last days, JM asks himself whether he should revise section P or let it stand, and he finds that he is "divided"—a claim that has other meanings when we come to the recol-lection that he and DJ "tried to bear / The stroke *for* Maya." Her stroke divided her from him, to be sure, but it also divided him from that part of himself which, since he so loved her, *was* Maya. "What light there was" in the hospital ward "fell sideways from a mind / Half dark," he says and we see that the "mind" is either his or Maya's. The point is also made by a pun on "eye" in the description of his friend, by now an alter ego, just before her death: "The other eye, the one that saw, remained / Full of wit, affection, and despair."

Joanna is another "old self in a new form," for it is she who flies the ouija board into the novel, and her name, as we are told in T, is intended to connect her with St. John the Evangelist, the supposed author of the Book of Revelation and the brother of St. James. (James and John were known collectively as the Boanerges, the "Sons of Thunder," because of their impulsiveness. In Luke 9:54 they ask Jesus to call down fire on the heads of the Samaritans and have them consumed. Joanna first appears in a terrible thunderstorm, and JM, who through St. Theodore is associated with storms, asks that lightning strike in R and gets caught in his own cloudburst in V.) Because of these relationships with Joanna and Maya, themselves linked to the Queen of Heaven, it is no surprise to find JM imagining, when confronted with Ephraim's announcement that he and DJ will not be reborn together, "Dressing up as the Blessed Damozel / At Heaven's Bar to intervene" with the powers that govern reincarnation.

In fact, or rather by proxy, JM does more obviously dress himself up, if not in drag, in an unexpected costume to appear before a different kind of bar. Q provides the opportunity, in a quotation that purports to come from a book entitled *Time Was* by one A. H. Clarendon, a mythical authority whom Merrill has cited before, and that is really based on a hilarious anecodote about the flamboyant Brian Howard, recorded less vividly in Martin Green's *Children of the Sun*:

> One evening late in the war he was at the crowded bar of the then smart Pyramid Club, in uniform, and behaving quite outrageously. Among the observers an elderly American admiral had been growing more and more incensed. He now went over and tapped Teddie on the shoulder: "Lieutenant, you are a disgrace to the Service. I must insist on having your name and squadron." An awful silence fell. Teddie's newly-won wings glinted. He snapped shut his thin gold compact (from Hermès) and narrowed his eyes at the admiral. "My name," he said distinctly, "is Mrs. Smith."

And the name *is* Smith, just as it is also Theodore ("Teddie" is a "recruit") or JM. He might also be called Ephraim—since he is associated, by way of the compact and the wings, with the messenger of the gods—and Ephraim, that other mercurial envoy, who becomes Eros in the novel and whose counterpart in Maya Deren's experience is Erzulie, is of course in some sense JM.

We are told early in C that "several facts" in Ephraim's background "coincide" with those in JM's and in I that Ephraim's knowledge of history, geography, and languages is virtually coextensive with the combined knowledge of DJ and JM. It is perhaps no more than another coincidence that St. Ephraem (according to the *Penguin Dictionary of Saints*) was a poet who also "wrote commentaries on a considerable number of books of the Bible, and a personal 'Testament' which seems to have been added to by a later hand" and that "even as a theologian he wrote as a poet," but it is not a coincidence that would startle Tom, JM's analyst. Reading the lines in B in which JM says that "even the most fragmentary message" from Ephraim was "Twice as entertaining, twice as wise / As either of its mediums," Tom would probably say: Exactly so.

Tom's explanation of Ephraim, however, would be at least a fractional truth, if only because there is hardly a figure in the poem who is not just as intimately connected with JM—it is not for nothing that his familiar spirit, a Greek Jew with a converted Christian father born in Asia Minor, is a sort of Everyman—and it is with this reflection in mind that we must read the delicately shaded conclusion of Y, in which Merrill touches on some "spells of odd / Self-effacing balance" apparently induced by the writing of *Ephraim*:

> Better to stop
> While we still can. Already I take up
> Less emotional space than a snowdrop.
> My father in his last illness complained
> Of the effect of medication on

> His real self—today Bluebeard, tomorrow
> Babbitt. Young chameleon, I used to
> Ask how on earth one got sufficiently
> Imbued with otherness. And now I see.

As he remarks in X: "So Time has—but who needs that nom de plume? I've— / We've modulated," and the plural encompasses a host of characters.

In "The Critic as Artist," in a passage partly paraphrased in I, one of Wilde's *personae* contends that "the objective form is the most subjective in matter. Man is least himself when he talks in his own person. Give him a mask and he will tell the truth." One has no difficulty applying the observation. If we were to take Ephraim and these other figures simply as projections, however, we would be in danger of compounding Tom's mistake, or of committing an error analogous to that committed by Dante in the *Paradiso*, III (a comparatively unremarkable phrase of which gets quoted in K) when he mistakenly takes some faces lambent in the moonlight for reflections rather than real spirits. Merrill is no Narcissus—indeed he is also reflected in the figure of Wendell, who turns up as a portrait artist in W—and these other figures retain their individuality at the same time that to varying degrees they represent JM. The point is that, by availing himself of these different masks—which is really to say, by finding himself in these different people, real and fictional, "Good and evil"—Merrill, like Proust in Q, testifies to his "*désire de mener la vie de tout le monde*" and that, by leading that variegated life, he comes closer to bodying forth what R calls "The god's own truth, or fiction." Especially in the context of Wilde's insight, the last term seems an appositive rather than an alternative. So we are where we were, on unsteady ground.

III

The place is Venice, unsteady a ground as could be found, the time is the fall of 1974 (JM is en route from Athens, his "home away from home," to Stonington), and the weather is stormy. "Let lightning strike," JM has pleaded in R, when in the stifling Athens September he felt short on inspiration, but in that section "Stolen thunder dwindle[d] out to sea" and the response was instead the memory of Maya's stroke. Here, in V, within hailing distance of the Accademia, as JM walks across the bridge over the Grand Canal, and as we recall that Proust's manifold desire in Q included a "*désir . . . des tempetes*" and a "*désir de Venise*," lightning finally (in two senses of the phrase) "strikes the set":

Gust of sustaining timbers' creosote
Pungency the abrupt drench releases—
Cold hissing white—the old man of the Sea
Who, clung to now, must truthfully reply—

Bellying shirt, sheer windbag wrung to high
Relief, to needle-keen transparency—
Air and water blown glass-hard—their blind
Man's buff with unsurrendering gooseflesh

Streamlined from conception—crack! boom! flash!—
Glaze soaking inward as it came to mind
How anybody's monster breathing flames
Vitrified in metamorphosis

To monstrance clouded then like a blown fuse
If not a reliquary for St James'
Vision of life: how Venice, her least stone
Pure menace at the start, at length became

A window fiery mild, whose walked through frame
Everything else, at sunset, hinged upon—

and then we are in W. Wonderfully evocative of the sudden poststorm
calm as well as of the initially furious cloudburst, this passage is still
probably as difficult as anything in *Ephraim*, partly because of its chain
lightning puns, partly because of its quasi-Jamesian syntax, but primarily
because in it Merrill tries not only to cling to his shapeshifter (who
according to legend, prophesies truthfully if held through all his metamorphoses) but also, concentrating his general strategy, to become him.
Yesterday a young chameleon, today an older Proteus.

This symbolist passage is in the first place a small ritual in transfigured time, as Merrill's old man of the sea, the very principle of metamorphosis, having first changed from the poet into the recognizable "monster
breathing flames," briefly assumes the shape of a monstrance (which, since
it contains the host after transubstantiation, is to this passage what the
passage itself is to the poem) before becoming, in the poet's ironic glance
at his own virtuoso effort, a blown fuse and thus perhaps another recepta-
cle, a reliquary for the vestiges of a vision that is more James Merrill's
then Henry James's or the impetuous apostle's. Here Merrill condenses the
vision that energizes much of the poem. We are time, and time is change
(we are "Streamlined from conception"), but change is the essence of life
and thus sacred, and to recognize that is to see the monster turn to
monstrance—the difficulty being that that proposition, once made, tends
to fix itself and thus to blow like a fuse. "NOTHING LIVE IS MOTION-

LESS HERE," Ephraim says in Q, and what he seems to be saying of the *au-delà* holds true in its converse form of the here and now.

For these lines constitute in the second place a phase of the discovery of the identity of heaven and earth. The phrase "vision of life" itself, in its blurring of the ideal and the actual, tends in this direction, as does the religious terminology. In sense as well as euphony, V's opening catenation—"Venise, pavane, nirvana, vice, wrote Proust"—recalls M's linkage: "Paris—the Piraeus—Paradise." "A whole heavenly city" Venice is called earlier in V, and the appellation is not to be taken lightly. Almost as important to *Ephraim* as to the *Cantos*, in which it is one of the richest images of the "paradiso terrestre" Pound claimed to have tried to create, Venice is here not only a microcosm of a possibly moribund world but also an analogue of the good place. It is thus a version of Valhalla; and it is also, this "Palladian sculpture / Maze" (W) built on water, a convenient metaphor for any intricate work of art. So it is that we find the consummate artist, Proust, earlier in V, with his last suppers, "Passion," and attempt "Through superhuman counterpoint to work / The body's resurrection, sense by sense." Although he makes more use of the literally superhuman than the earlier visitor to Venice, Merrill's endeavor is the same. "Does it still appear / We'll get our senses somehow purified / Back?" he asks the "powers that be" in P; and while this poem declines to deal unequivocally with eschatology, it is at every point and counterpoint an argument for art's power to resurrect—to resurrect not only one's personal past but also the pasts of friends and the cultural past, to lead at least a significant part of the life of all the world. Hence the comparison of Proust to the god-man, and hence too "the sustaining timbers' creosote / Pungency." The sustaining timber is surely that of the bridge, which links Merrill to Proust, James, and Giorgione, and reality to fiction (JM meets Wendell on the bridge in W), rather than that of the cross, but the bridge also connects earth to heaven, and the pungency released here derives in part from the Greek roots of "creosote," which means "flesh" and "preserver." The poet's aim, as JM has it in I's transposition, is "Flesh made word." The episode in L in which JM resurrects his former self, Rufus, is emblematic of one part of the task Merrill has set himself.

He dramatically compresses the theme in Z. DJ and JM return one night to their Stonington house to find a "bedroom ransacked, lights on, loud / Tick of alarm, the mirror off its hook / Looking daggers at the ceiling fixture"; but this particular thief in the night—this "burglar . . . in the Enchanted Village" reminiscent of both the Troubler in the Garden and Hermes, patron of thieves ("Mercury dropping" JM has noted earlier in Z), as well as of Ephraim, who was perhaps responsible for the loss of the novel—seems to have taken nothing: "nothing's gone, or nothing we recall." Later, "Nothing we can recollect is missing." Why, precisely: Time steals to the extent that we fail to recollect, which proposition correlates with that represented by, say, Proust's undertaking—and which is another way of saying "We are Time."

The problem, which seen aright might be its own resolution, is not so much that even a Proust can only be partially successful in the end, although of course that is true to the degree that we suppose the criterion for success to be a triumph over time; it is rather that the artist-recruit enlists himself also in the service of time. It could hardly be otherwise, since as JM puts it at the beginning of the poem: "Time, it had transpired, was of the essence. / Time, the very attar of the Rose. . . ." And the Rose, we learn by tracing a few connections, is for one thing the rose of the world, evident in both Venice's "dull red mazes caked with slime / Bearing some scented drivel of undying / Love and regret" (V) and the lost novel's landscape, its "arroyos— / Each the abraded, vast, baked-rose detail / Of a primeval circulatory system" (S), as well as in the poet's "red flower" (or flow-er) "Not yet in the dread phrase cut-and-dried" (S). Specious etymology could discover the key phrase in the first name of the ubiquitous Mrs. Rosamund Smith, who is described in D as "Perennially youthful, worldly, rich, / And out of sight until the close" and who nonetheless reappears as Teddie in Q and, appropriately, as "the resourceful Mrs. Smith" in S (where a photo of her is torn into "pieces" and where she is also the eponym of "a showy hybrid" flower) before she returns anonymously in Z as "The ancient, ageless woman of the world," a sort of refined version of Stevens's "Fat girl." Rather like Spenser's "great Grandmother of all creatures bred . . . Unseene of any, yet of all beheld" as well as Ephraim, whose "presence" in H is "Everywhere felt" although he never shows his face—she has been here all along, in JM's mother, in Joanna, whose face is explicitly likened to that of the earth in J, in Maya, her "Touches of tart and maiden, muse and wife / Glowing forth once more from an *Etude / De Jeune Femme* no longer dimmed by time" (R). In fact, the title of Merrill's picture in memory is another shadow title for his poem—although Mahler's *Das Lied von der Erde*, mentioned in G, might be more in keeping, especially since "Ephraim" means "fruitful" in Hebrew and Mrs. Smith appears in D's description of the twilight of the novel (if not of the gods) as one who "will / Have wrinkled soon to purple fruitlessness."

Because *Ephraim* is through and through a song of the earth, it is also a vindication of "the test of time, which all things pass" (R), and in the final analysis the poet might be represented less fully by St. Theodore than by yet another James, Joyce, "the great wordsmith" (he is another member of that family too), "Forging a snake that swallows its own tail" (X). To incarnate the monster, as Merrill does in V and X, is not after all to slay it but to make it take a shape; and to make it swallow its tail, as Joyce does in *Finnegans Wake* or Wagner does in his *Ring*, is to keep time from swallowing its own tale. The ouroboros, the Gnostic symbol of time and life's continuity, reappears in diminished form in Z ("Zero hour": the year's cycle completes itself and the poem comes full circle), when the furnace fails and JM imagines, with characteristic wryness, that the furnace man might find "an easy-to-repair / Short circuit." It will either be that, he surmises, or "the failure long foreseen / As total, of our period machine." An alternative description of this poem, as well as of the world it celebrates, the "period machine" frankly gives time its due, and in its capacity as furnace it recalls the means of martyrdom of St. Theodore, who had to do the same. JM decides in Z *not* to burn the transcripts of the hours with Ephraim, and by extension the manuscript of this poem, but he entertains the idea:

> And that (unless it floated, spangled ash,
> Outward, upward, one lone carp aflash
> Languorously through its habitat
> For crumbs that once upon a . . .) would be that.

The word "time" is elided in this formulaic beginning not only because the poem in its end has in a sense overcome the temporal but also because, with the burning of these pages which praise it, time would give away that much more to the awful silence of eternity, represented here by the ellipses JM refers to in X as "black holes." From one point of view, then, and in the very process of recollection that foils the thief, the dragon cut up in Q reassembles itself in the poem, although in a transfigured form. In short, it is no coincidence that in X the dragon-slayer is a "young man in dark *rose*."

But—and how often Merrill's conjunctions force us to that conjunction—even as it is on earth and in the fullness of time that "a whole heavenly city" is created, the Rose of which time is the attar is also redolent of Dante's heavenly rose. One is reminded of Eliot's dictum in "Burnt Norton," "Only through time time is conquered," but to the degree that Eliot stresses the *apprehension* of "The point of intersection of the timeless / With time," the saint rather than the swordsman, the efforts of Yeats and Stevens better comport with those of Merrill. Ephraim, in Q, provides this poem's most candid, distinctive, and moving comments on the relationship between earth and heaven, worlds so joined in his view that JM (in F) no longer prays "For the remission of their synthesis":

& NOW ABOUT DEVOTION IT IS I AM FORCED TO BELIEVE THE MAIN IMPE-
TUS DEVOTION TO EACH OTHER TO WORK TO REPRODUCTION TO AN IDEAL IT
IS BOTH THE MOULD AND THE CLAY SO WE ARRIVE AT GOD OR A DEVOTION TO
ALL OR MANYS IDEAL OF THE CONTINUUM SO WE CREATE THE MOULDS OF
HEAVENLY PERFECTION & THE ONES ABOVE OF RARER & MORE EXPERT USEFUL-
NESS & AT LAST DEVOTION WITH THE COMBINED FORCES OF FALLING AND
WEARING WATER PREPARES A HIGHER MORE FINISHED WORLD OR HEAVEN

The entire poem eulogizes these various facets of "DEVOTION," and one
of its chief aims is precisely to help to "CREATE THE MOULDS OF
HEAVENLY PERFECTION" and even "THE ONES ABOVE." This idea
of a world that has the potential of creating the ideal it might become lies
at the heart of *Ephraim*, for it is this idea that ultimately justifies its union
of fiction and reality even as it renders futile and superfluous any speculation about the ontological status of Ephraim and his peers.

Just as the configurating *process* implicit in this concept distinguishes
this poem's universe from those of other works inevitably called up—from,
say, the terraced cosmos of the *Paradiso* or the Escher-like labyrinth of *Pale
Fire*—so the temperament disclosed by it distinguishes Merrill's "vision of
life" from that of such an obviously kindred spirit as Stevens. The former's
"devotion" (symbolized by the "heart-emblem" that Maya burns on to the
floor in G and embodied in the unselfish services rendered the natives of
Kenya by Isak Dinesen in O) is after all closer to "*l'amor che move il sole e
l'altre stelle*" than to the latter's abstracter "imagination." Still, Stevens is
a tutelary spirit here, as Merrill testifies in S, where he paraphrases
propositions in *Adagia* and "The Noble Rider and the Sound of Words":

> Stevens imagined the imagination
> And God as one; the imagination, also,
> As that which presses back, in parlous times,
> Against "the pressure of reality."
> Scholia discordant (who could say?)
> Yet coursing with heart's blood the moment read.

Even as the emphasis upon the heart's assent, the renunciation of even
the momentary pose of the savant, sets Merrill apart from his predecessor—
not that Stevens would have quarrelled with Yeats's summation, that man
cannot know truth but can embody it—these lines assert a strong affinity.

What attracts Merrill to Stevens's view of the divine power of the
imagination attracts him also to Jung, to whom he alludes in U: "Jung
says—or if he doesn't, all but does / That God and the unconscious are
one." The theme informs much of Jung's work, of course, but it seems
that Merrill has the "Answer to Job" in mind. In that long essay Jung
argues against what he considers the "opposition" in orthodox Christianity

between God and man, and while he stops short of denying man a certain individuality, the blessed poverty of the "limited ego," he finds it difficult to extricate him from "the One": "It is only through the Psyche that we can establish that God acts upon us, but we are unable to distinguish whether these actions emanate from God or from the unconscious. We cannot tell whether God and the unconscious are two different entities." To the extent that they are one, Ephraim's little lecture on the creation of the moulds of heavenly perfection and Jung's thesis dovetail, for according to Jung the crucial question is "whether man can climb up to a higher mortal level, to a higher plane of consciousness, in order to be equal to the superhuman powers" he possesses. If he fails to do so, man has neither excuse nor future, "for the dark god . . . has given him the power to empty out the apocalyptic vials of wrath upon his fellow creatures."

    Merrill has carefully situated and highlighted this grim side of his theme. R begins with the poet's injunction to himself:

> Rewrite P. It was to be the section
> Golden with end of summer light. Impossible
> So long, at least, as there's no end to summer.
> Late September is a choking furnace.

The graceful allusion is to what has come to be called "the golden section," the classical ratio and proportion discerned by Euclid and structurally implemented from time to time by artists, writers, and composers from Vergil through Bartok. In the *Elements*, the golden section is set forth in these terms: "A straight line is said to have been cut in extreme and mean ratio when, as the whole line is to the greater segment, so is the greater to the less" (Book 6, Prop. 3). In its simplest numerical terms, the ratio is 1:0.618. In this poem of twenty-six sections, the division would occur in the sixteenth section, P, and within P, which is 127 lines long, the division would occur at line 78. Without knowing whether Merrill did eventually rewrite P so that it would utilize the golden section, we can observe that there is a division in P at line 78 and that the passage that follows is in a sense "Golden with end of summer light," for it comprises a memory of attending *Götterdämmerung*, and it focuses on the climactic moment when Valhalla goes up in flames, the gods are destroyed, and the Rhine floods, enabling the Rhinemaidens to regain their golden ring at last. This memory of the final act of the *Ring* cycle has been inspired by Ephraim's comments on "the Cosmic Mind" to the effect that the existence of heaven depends upon that of the earth. Should we destroy ourselves by misusing the "Power" celebrated in P, "when the flood ebbed, or the fire burned low, / Heaven, the world no longer at its feet, / Itself would up and vanish." In the light of such information, the two mediums' earlier "swig of no-proof rhetoric"—the insouciant observation that they are content to "Let what would be, be" if an annihilated earth could "Melt like dew into the Cosmic Mind"—is precisely no proof at all. Just as man can create the moulds of heavenly perfection, so he can destroy them. In Jung's terms, there is "an antinomy in Deity itself," and the Deity acts through the unconscious.

Jung characterizes God in other pertinent terms: "we can [also] imagine God," he says, "as an eternally flowing current of vital energy that endlessly changes shape." The same as the one that "Flows through field and book," Jung's current further manifests itself in the "Unrelenting fluency" of time and in the flow of the imagination—for in this stream one hand washes the other—and it can be followed back to the "spring, or source" in Maya's dream. As the ultimate power, the "naked current" which is both inside and outside man, it is epitomized in Proteus and implied by all of Merrill's metamorphoses and mirrors, his diverse *personae*. These figures are all variations on what Jung calls "a few basic principles or archetypes" which collectively represent God and which, "like the psyche itself, or like matter, are unknowable as such." "All we can do," Jung argues, "is to construct models of them which we know to be inadequate, a fact which is confirmed again and again by religious statements." As he proceeds to make clear, however, the inadequacy of these models notwithstanding, our very construction of them serves a maieutic purpose, bringing the unconscious to the light of consciousness, incarnating God in man, creating the moulds of heavenly perfection. "The religious need longs for wholeness, and therefore lays hold of the images of wholeness offered by the unconscious, which, independently of the conscious mind, rise up from the depths of our psychic life." Merrill's metamorphic stream is just such an image, his "woman of the world" another, and it is the result of the coupling of exactly such a need with devotion that Ephraim speaks of in Q:

> U & YR GUESTS THESE TIMES WE SPEAK ARE WITHIN SIGHT OF & ALL CONNECTED TO EACH OTHER DEAD OR ALIVE NOW DO YOU UNDERSTAND WHAT HEAVEN IS IT IS THE SURROUND OF THE LIVING

Merrill's statement is not Dante's. It could not be, since as Jung says the mind "manipulates images and ideals which are dependent on human imagination and its temporal and local conditions, and which have therefore changed innumerable times in the course of their long history." At the same time, however, the implicit comparison at the center of this poem, which is where we are still, needs to be there. In their respective ways both the *Paradiso and The Book of Ephraim* concern themselves with (in Jung's terms) man's "limited ego" and "the One who dwells within him, whose form has no knowable boundaries, who encompasses him on all sides, fathomless as the abysms of the earth and vast as the sky."

IV

But where were we? Merrill answers his own earlier question at the same time that he answers one asked in the last lines of his poem by another who receives all manner of guests, everyone's patroness and hostess:

> And look, the stars have wound in filigree
> The ancient, ageless woman of the world.
> She's seen us. She is not particular—
> Everyone gets her injured, musical
> "Why do you no longer come to me?"
> To which there's no reply. For here we are.

Here on earth, evidently. And yet the filigree of starlight, which seems to presuppose a distant vantage point, would be appropriate dress for the Queen of Heaven. In any case, the scene combines heaven and earth, the "fanciful" and the "real," which are as inextricable as the unconscious and God. In other words, it is *because* Ephraim is primarily spirit that JM and DJ have "reached a / Stage through him that he will never himself reach" (X), for that stage is one in which reality and fiction merge. There is a passage in "Three Academic Pieces" in which Stevens says one thing that I think this poem means to show:

> We have been trying to get at a truth about poetry, to get at one of the principles that compose the theory of poetry. It comes to this, that poetry is a part of the structure of reality. If this has been demonstrated, it pretty much amounts to saying that the structure of poetry and the structure of reality are one or, in effect, that poetry and reality are one, or should be.

As the qualifications indicate, however, Stevens had his doubts, and Merrill for his part is far too wise, too aware of the susceptibility of dogma to rigor mortis, to formulate principles or to purge his work of ambiguities. Late in the poem, it is true, in X's conclusion, he conjoins "The world's poem" and "the poem's world" and proceeds to describe the universe in terms of his verse, even likening black holes, "Vanishing points," to his ellipses; but even there, by reference to "Gassy expansion and succinct collapse," he includes rather than reduces antipodes, and his concluding suspension points leave us somewhat up in the air in regard to poetry and reality, heaven and earth. Indeed they must do so if Merrill is to keep hold of his Proteus, Yeats's simple embodiment of truth, Jung's eternally flowing current. The canal in V is continually "Ruining another batch of images," and as Heinrich Zimmer tells us in Q:

> The powers have to be consulted again directly—again, again and again. Our primary task is to learn, not so much what they are said to have said, as how to approach them, evoke fresh speech from them, and understand that speech. In the face of such an assignment, we must all remain dilettantes, whether we like it or not.

Or as Rilke reminds us in Letters to Merline, the poet must always be willing to be a beginner. The trilogy in progress, the latest result of Merrill's willingness—more impressively apparent in every book he has published—is the finest achievement thus far of one of the subtlest and strongest poets we have had. There is an image in chapter twenty-seven of Middlemarch, adapted by Merrill in N and Y, of a candle held before an old mirror at night, with the result that random scratches form themselves into a halo about the reflected flame. Provided that the evil envisioned in P does not come to pass, when posterity looks back at the twentieth century, the light of Merrill's candle will surely lend the scratchings in the dark mirror of the age just such an "Illusion of coherence."

JOHN HOLLANDER

"Mirror"

The response to a call for the imagination's moral power is one thing, and I have wanted to suggest that it is never a simple matter. But it is the poem itself which shall now concern us, the poem which, in whatever its small or cool or tinted mode of glowing, stares sightlessly out at the reader from the page until some voice—although not its own, perhaps—is heard to say what Rilke heard in the presence of his stone poem of antiquity: *"Du muss dein Leben ändern,"* you must alter your life. This is not to say that poets cannot—in verses of some sort and, thereby, putatively as poets rather than generally as exhorting men—do the work that the journalist and the commentator, given the fading away of American literacy, are less and less able exaltedly to do. Sorrow and rage at injustice; or the chill that lasts after the pained smile has gone at ironies which seem now to inhere in events, rather than in the tropes of the writer and thinker—producing these is the bitter work of reportage. The British chaplain De Stogumber, in Shaw's *Saint Joan,* confesses that the burning he had encouraged has altered his life: "I had not seen it [cruelty] you know. That is the great thing . . . It was dreadful . . . but it saved me," to which the poetic ironist Cauchon must respond: "Must then a Christ perish in torment in every age to save those who have no imagination?" The relation between what Yeats called rhetoric and true poetry is in some ways like the relation between the experience of horror and true imagination in Shaw's great question, to which the answer is, alas, probably "Yes." But if we do in fact need both poetry and rhetoric, we should not confuse their functions. Poems do not urge, or propound programs of deportment, or criticize in detail those already

From *The Yale Review* (Winter 1981). Copyright © 1980 by *The Yale Review.*

propounded. The contemporary poem, like the Renaissance one, must ultimately do its teaching, and be enabled to alter our lives, by mythographic means, even at a late time of myth-making, when instead of moralizing Ovid, it adduces new mythologies in explanation of older ones.

But in order to hear the poem's command to do something about our lives, we must place ourselves directly before it, until there is no place in it that does not indeed see us. Let us start with a beautiful poem of looking and reflecting, written about twenty years ago by a poet only beginning to feel his powers. A dramatic monologue in half-evaded rhymed couplets (the second line, irregular in length, rhymes with the penultimate or antepenultimate syllable of the first one), the poem is also an emblem that reads itself for significance. James Merrill's "Mirror" is truly a speaking picture: the reflecting glass considers itself, and most importantly addresses its pragmatic counterpart, an open window opposite.

> I grow old under an intensity
> Of questioning looks. *Nonsense,*
> I try to say, *I cannot teach you children*
> *How to live.—If not you, who will?*
> Cries one of them aloud, grasping my gilded
> Frame till the world sways. *If not you, who will?*

—The question is not intended as a rhetorical one, but must inevitably remain just that. The mirror of art held up to nature is too wise to attempt an answer, but instead continues:

> Between their visits the table, its arrangement
> Of Bible, fern and Paisley, all past change,
> Does very nicely. If ever I feel curious
> As to what others endure,
> Across the parlor *you* provide examples,
> Wide open, sunny, of everything I am
> Not . . .

(and what a wicked enjambment for a mirror to employ in its treatment of what seems manifestly primary to its mere echoing answer)

> You embrace a whole world without once caring
> To set it in order. That takes thought. Out there
> Something is being picked. The red-and-white bandannas
> Go to my heart. A fine young man
> Rides by on horseback. Now the door shuts. Hester
> Confides in me her first unhappiness.
> This much, you see, would never have been fitted
> Together, but for me. Why then is it
> They more and more neglect me? Late one sleepless

> Midsummer night I strained to keep
> Five tapers from your breathing. *No,* the widowed
> Cousin said, *let them go out.* I did.
> The room brimmed with gray sound, all the instreaming
> Muslin of your dream . . .

As if to answer her own rhetorical question (and we must recognize the mirror now, I think, for what she is, gilded and elegant, an extremely wise old lady, a great Proustian aunt), the mirror remembers a death. And this is the one point in her meditation at which the continuing present tense of the verbs, synchronizing all she has seen in a reflected plane, gives way to preterites. At her most frighteningly magisterial she asserts, without undue insistence, that it was she and not the window who abandoned the mad effort of all daughters of memory to eternize human breath. We notice, too, how she remarks on "all the instreaming / Muslin of your dream . . ." *Your* dream: the window's dream is that plangent cliché of reverie, the inblown curtains enshrined in romantic paintings of meditative room interiors from Adolph von Menzel to Edward Hopper. The mirror hears the flapping of death in the darkness; she can read the emblems of consciousness that inhere even in the objects of conscious perception as no mere window can. And this is why, and the fact of death is why, they more and more neglect her.

> Years later now, two of the grown grandchildren
> Sit with novels face-down on the sill,
> Content to muse upon your tall transparence,
> Your clouds, brown fields, persimmon far
> And cypress near. One speaks. *How superficial
> Appearances are!* . . .

—Indeed! But the mirror's depths, her realities, are on, or at most, she knows, *in,* her surface; she, and the poem itself, shiver at the callow beauty of the young people's discovery, and when she takes up her musing for the last time, it is with a brilliant pun, what the French call a *rime riche* on the penultimate syllable of "superficial," at first almost coarsely answering the charge with a flash of *Dasein,* a gross presence, an angel of gleaming surfacing from literal depths. But then, having surfaced, it adds its light to the surface of shining discourse that is the mirror's triumph over mere openness of window, or candor of artificial light:

> *How superficial
> Appearances are!* Since then, as if a fish
> Had broken the perfect silver of my reflectiveness,
> I have lapses. I suspect

> Looks from behind, where nothing is, cool gazes
> Through the blind flaws of my mind. As days,
> As decades lengthen, this vision
> Spreads and blackens. I do not know whose it is,
> But I think it watches for my last silver
> To blister, flake, float leaf by life, each milling-
> Downward dumb conceit, to a standstill
> From which not even you strike any brilliant
> Chord in me, and to a faceless will,
> Echo of mine, I am amenable.

Where she—or, rather, perhaps, *it* again, for we are clearly talking of poetry itself—is most transparent, the poem is most blind. It can only reflect—this mirror of art and of our highest consciousness—when its transparency, its Emersonian eyeball, is itself illuminated from within its capacity to know, by a gleaming, a shining from behind. For poetry to be a mirror, after centuries of flaking and dimming belief in its truth, it must at the very least be its own lamp as well. The images, the patches of silvery fiction which project that light forward, fall not like leaves of romantic poetry into the broadcasting wind, but down into silent darkness. And when there is nothing to the mirror but the clear glass through which the nothingness of that dark can be read, the imagelessness of that deep truth is preserved even as the truth is presented. In the last darkness which will not be dawned upon, the mirror and the window alike are cold, smooth, unseen glass.

Merrill's mirror reveals itself first as a novelist's figure of wisdom (and why is it that in modern America one encounters more wise old women than wise old men?). Then, radiant beyond the Renaissance emblem of mimetic art, it becomes the modern poem, "the poem of the mind in the act of finding / What will suffice." It is the world mirrored in the most profound way: Hester, alone with her unhappiness and that consoling image that is the legacy of Milton's Eve, cannot but unwittingly confide in the mirror even when she is most alone. We cannot talk about our feelings—and this has been true in the case of all our poetry of love, from Sappho on—without talking about talking about them, without pointing out the peculiar ways in which we must use language in order to tell the truth. Merrill's poem remains shiny, clear, framed in a gilded, semiantique meter, not in order to be itself—even for Americans, bowed under the weight of history's injunctions to be ourselves, that is not, alas, enough—but in order to mean something. *"I cannot teach you children / How to live."* But the children's response is our own, and is the poet's own, as he was coming to knowledge of what would suffice. Modernism dictated the refusal to teach, but something at once younger and more grown-up hears the voices of the children. *"If not you, who will?"* It is that enabling climate in which Merrill's poem itself seems to grow older and wiser as we read it; from a modern poem about poetry—and therefore morally pure, unrotted by didactic intention as its surface seems unflecked by expository rhetoric—it emerges as a mirror of life after all. It is in order to reflect what the cheerful, mindless window can only helplessly reveal that the mirror *reflects upon* itself, upon its own mode of reflecting. Less solipsistic than the human children who consult it, the poem comes, by being about itself, to be about everything else outside it. *That* takes something more than thought. The romantics called it Imagination.

The lessons we learn are about time, space, and reflections. We are reminded of all the mythology which lies behind the speaking mirror—the looking glasses of both the nude lady who may be Vanitas or Venus, and the one who is surely truth; the mirror into which it is dangerous to gaze, lest, like Narcissus, we inadvertently heed the philosopher's injunction to know ourselves, and thereby lose everything; the strong, enabling mirror held up to the goddess by Amor, an emblem of her own power; the *esoptron* ("glass") of St. Paul, by which we perceive truth "darkly" (*en ainigmati*) in the riddle and puzzle by which all the half-reliable oracles speak; the mirror of modernism, an image of paradox, reversal, self-reference, and schematic mystery; the mirrors of Jean Cocteau's *Orphée*, all of which are easily unfrozen surfaces covering the many entrances to the poet's hell of self-absorption. But Merrill's poem is also mythopoetic, in that the mirror, the wise old presence, the almost novelistic domestication, and the confrontation with the unanswering window, leave the emblem forever transformed, materially augmented. That augmentation partially exists in the dimension of the work of reflection and memory which we do in our rereading and consideration of it. The images which, Shelley said, enable language to "unveil the permanent analogy of things" can "participate in the life of truth" by making the reader into a kind of poet as well.

Merrill's "Mirror" is by no means his best poem. He went on in subsequent books to move in a Proustian direction which was quite original, and in *Water Street* and afterwards he assimilated the impulses of narrative autobiography to a commanding and continuing mythopoeia. His way has been that of the mirror, not the window. His mature poetry inhabits part of that region of emblematic tale-telling which Elizabeth Bishop for some decades before her death, and Robert Penn Warren more recently, have inhabited for their major poetry. I do not refer, of course, to what has been called "confessional," that shrill and pitiful mode of contemporary verse which, neither window nor mirror, most resembles the sound of breaking glass. We can hear it, but learn nothing from it except that some disaster has occurred and that our lives are full of woe, which it seems shocking to need poetry for to inform us. The first part of Merrill's most recent trilogy mythologizes what is in fact the Spirit of Involuntary Memory as a psychic "control" of a ouija board. This is partially to say that the long, astonishing poem called "The Book of Ephraim" is, in almost every way, in lieu of a novel. But the mirror poem revealed a door, a hallway, down which American poetry of the next two decades would walk, not with the purpose of leaving the house and doing something outside of it, nor indeed on a nervous stroll marked by glances out of the windows in distaste. It was a walk taken indoors in an endless house, continually being added to and restored in some of its older parts, neglected to the point of near-ruin in others. But to explore it, and to map it, was to map heaven and hell, now and then, all the overlays which enable us to read the raw sense of the physical map of life itself

J. D. McCLATCHY

Monsters Wrapped in Silk: "The Country of a Thousand Years of Peace"

Eight years elapsed between James Merrill's *First Poems* (1951) and the publication of *The Country of a Thousand Years of Peace*, the longest interval between any two of his poetry collections. During that time Merrill made two important moves. One, his change of residence from New York City to Stonington, a traditional Connecticut seacoast village, was a kind of strategic withdrawal and resettlement that had decisive repercussions on his work, though not until *Water Street* (1962) does a more domestic focus prevail. The other move, an elaborate and prolonged trip around the world, is more immediately apparent in *The Country of a Thousand Years of Peace*. The literal extravagance of Merrill's travels is reflected in two ways. In an obvious sense, the volume is decked out with a good deal of local color. Without ever being merely diaristic, he takes advantage of the convention that a travel poem is to make observations. He can count on a reader's unfamiliarity with and interest in a foreign curiosity or custom. The exotic locales of many of these poems—Japan, India, Greece, Switzerland, Holland, France—are an indication not only of a more cosmopolitan viewpoint, but also of Merrill's increased respect for the genius of places. The settings of *First Poems* are usually the stanzas of the poems themselves, or the associations their symbols have staked out, or the compass of the poet's own imagination. These new, more varied and specific settings are

From *Contemporary Poetry* 4, vol. 4, (Fall 1982). Copyright © 1982 by J. D. McClatchy.

a recognition of a world outside the boundaries of verse and the self, and of the poet's ability to explore it—a recognition, that is, of *history*, of events located in space and unfolding in time, of significance emerging from process rather than embodied in a product. In much the same way, this book, instead of confining itself to a limited, recurring set of self-conscious symbols and subliminal anxieties, deliberately takes up a range of experiences that lie beyond the ego recording them—hallucinations, ouija board transmissions, revenants, altered states, dreamwork and rituals, the whole welter of the preconscious life that is also a "starry land/ Under the world," as the title poem describes its mythic country of death. These two impulses in *The Country of a Thousand Years of Peace*—a recognition of history, and the cultivation of the unconscious—will, in later books, each be developed in more intricate ways, and together be combined into Merrill's attention to involuntary memories and archetypal characterizations of his past. Here, they remain impulses rather than habits.

Seeking to account for the advance this book marks over *First Poems*, Richard Howard argued that the "patinated narcissism has been literally roughed up, and the resulting corrugation of surface corresponds, of course, to a new agitation of the depths." Howard is right to stress the connection between the book's adjusted technique and its more adventuresome subject matter, but wrong to suggest that this results from a kind of stylistic decomposition. There is less Art than in *First Poems*, but more artfulness. It is true that the poems are projected on a smaller scale than most of his *First Poems*, and their very concision—to say nothing of their sometimes willful obliquity—may leave some readers with the impression that the book as a whole is more thematically skittish and less formally ambitious than its predecessor. Certainly this book does specialize in that sort of poem Merrill himself calls, in a review he wrote at the time of someone else's work, "a small, perfect poem—whose subject matter may even be calculated not to engage a reader overmuch; something leanly modeled, its elements composed and juxtaposed to give a sense of much ground covered in mysterious ways." The direct proportion between smallness and perfection duly noted, it bears repeating that *The Country of a Thousand Years of Peace* does represent an advance. An earned mastery of technique is in charge: the mazy syntax, the more expertly fractioned rhythms, the greater variety and convincing flexibility of verse schemes. Sometimes these techniques are subtle enough to distract attention from their own ingenuity—the leisurely runs of blank verse, for instance, or a sonnet in discrete couplets, or his occasional use of apocopated schemes where the rhymes are present but never insistent. There is also more sparkle and salt in this book, the free-wheeling play of mind that comes with technical control. There is a greater ease in generalizing. This is not a question of his having created slots in a poem through which messages can be slipped, but of having learned to allow his nimble intelligence to indulge its conceptual tendencies by means of aphorism and pithy aside. In "Midas Among Goldenrod," the hay-fevered hero's mouth "Shuts and opens like a ventriloquist's dummy/Eloquent with opinions it does not really believe." The "Italian Lesson" turns to Roman promenades "Where each cool eye plays moth/To flames largely its own." And in one especially sly witticism, the geography of Europe is outlined by re-enacting the rape of Europa, who is left—"The god at last indifferent," as in Yeats's sonnet—"no longer chaste but continent." The book's intellectual prowess is also noticeable in grander, more virtuosic ways. Several times, for instance—"The Octopus" and "The Lovers" are the most striking cases—a poem's overly abstract issues or too intimate *donnée* are handled by a single extended simile, the magnet of the initial comparison drawing to itself filings of phrase and detail. "The Lovers" begins: "They met in loving like the hands of one/Who. . . ." The rest of the poem works out the terms of the analogy and never returns to its point of departure—does not need to, the simpler image having explained the complex emotion.

But this artful control seems to bring with it, almost inevitably for a poet as mercurial as Merrill, a certain restlessness, sometimes spirited, sometimes coy. To its advantage, the book is teased, not hauled, into thought, and at the same time can entertain uncertainties, mysteries, doubts, without any irritable reaching after fact or reason. But occasionally a poem's very elegance and equanimity serve to disguise the obscurity of its subject or treatment. It is difficult to say how "About the Phoenix" moves from one florid or puzzling point to another; it is difficult to say what "A View of the Burning" is about at all. Part of the difficulty here results from a quite conscious decision by the poet to favor a chiaroscuro that dissolves a poem's structural plan into figural textures. Or, when plotting his more overtly narrative poems—"The Day of the Eclipse" or the waggish "A Narrow Escape" are convenient examples—he tends to focus on a moment before or after the action's climax, so that revelations are implied or displaced, and the emotional force of the poem depends on a reader's sense of anticipation or presumed relief. Insofar as this is a deliberate method to avoid any topical or moralizing pretensions—as, in later books, he often shies from the pitch of the sublime or from autobiography's call to candor—it is not unlike Borges's musing, in his essay "The Wall and the Books," that "music, states of happiness, mythology, faces belabored by time, certain twilights and certain places try to tell us something, or have said something we should have missed, or are about to say something; this imminence of a revelation which does not occur is, perhaps, the aesthetic phenomenon." Such a wise but wary passivity, while not exactly an abdication of the poet's responsibility to both shape and interpret his material, depends too much on what has been excluded from the poem, on what is *not* taken on or worked out.

Part of the difficulty *The Country of a Thousand Years of Peace* presents to a reader undoubtedly stems from the kind of material it engages—material that, despite the poetic skills used to render it, is elusive. "The Cruise," an otherwise charming anecdote, can be read as an allegory of the entire book's endeavor and problem. Having passed a less than imaginary iceberg whose hidden menace reminds them of "That law of which nine-tenths is a possession/By powers we do not ourselves possess," the ship's passengers are shopping in a port of call, and shown "Monsters in crystal" that once—so they are told—were nightmares that "set aswirl the mind of China" until "belittled" by craftsmen who dealt them the "drug of Form." Purchased as souvenirs—"We took to lunch our monsters wrapped in silk"—these talismans come both to reassure and to accuse. First, the speaker wonders whether a practiced style of personality makes for a perfect social presence: "Are we less monstrous when our motive slumbers/Drugged by a perfection of our form?" The question could as easily refer, of course, to the poetic struggle between conspicuous form and shadowy intention, or even dark inspiration. Those two readings, the personal and the literary, are together poised in the poem's final lines, in their open competition between fascination and abhorrence, between

> our hungers and our dread
> That, civilizing into cunning shape
> Briefly appeased what it could not oppose.

Naturally it is an uneasy situation that an appeasing dread, linked with knowledge and form, substitutes for any stronger, permanent shield against the devouring . . . the devouring *what?* The monsters are never identified. Are they the wilds of the unconcious? the toils of guilt? the trials of love? the past? the future? The figure of speech is the real appeasement here. And throughout the book, in some of its best as well as in many of its weakest poems, there is a similar reticence. It is hard to say whether it is the result of a poem's ignorance of its own final purposes, or of an inadequacy of form to ambition, or of some collusion of the two. Beginning with *Water Street*, his poems increasingly show a clear-eyed understanding and ironic appreciation of themselves. And the long poems in *Nights and Days* demonstrate, in ways that these earlier poems never realize, how their hybrid form and variegated tone are more than adequate to the scope and demands of the material. But *The Country of a Thousand Years of Peace*—perhaps for the wrong reasons, his most enigmatic book until *Braving the Elements* (1972)—remains at once inviting and uncertain. The book's good manners seem to force the poet to hesitate before the new and surprising depths he has discovered.

II

The *Country of a Thousand Years of Peace* opens with an elegy for Hans Lodeizen, and closes with a dedication to him. Lodeizen (1924–1950), a Dutch poet, author of *Het innerlijk behand* (*The Inner Wallpaper*—shades of *Mirabell*), had come to America to do graduate work at Amherst, where Merrill met him in 1946. The two young poets kept up a friendship, by occasional visits and correspondence, until Lodeizen's death four years later. Their last visit, the pretext of the title poem's elegy, was recalled once by Merrill in a paragraph introducing the poem:

> In 1950, at the beginning of nearly three years abroad, I went to Lausanne for an hour with my friend the Dutch poet Hans Lodeizen. He had been reading George Sand's autobiography; there was Roussel on the phonograph and a Picasso etching of acrobats on the floor. The June sunset filled up his hospital room. He spoke with carefree relish of the injection they would give him presently. Before I left we agreed to meet in Italy sometime that fall. He had leukemia and died two weeks later, at twenty-six. It was my first deeply-felt death. I connected it with the spell of aimless living in Europe to which I was then committed and to which all those picturesque and novel sights corresponded painfully enough.

That death and the unfulfilled promise of an idealized friend so near his own age must have haunted Merrill: the meaningless death accusing, he implies, his then purposeless life. But the close, ennobling identification with Lodeizen precludes much guilt. As tutelary spirit of the book, he is apostrophized in "Dedication." The poem is placed last in the volume presumably to stress its sense of dedication as proclamation and resolve rather than as merely a memorial gesture. What it proclaims are privileged moments. Twice in this brief poem the equation of mind and mouth, of idea and speech, is made. These are moments of poetic inspiration— moments of which each preceding poem in the book has given evidence— that are characterized as both ecstatic and humbling, and linked by Merrill less with grief at Lodeizen's death than with gratitude for his example. In one image, his death is described as the Orphic "deep spring," the continually self-renewing source of poetic power; in another, Hans returns as a Rilkean angel. This is the heroic side of him that the title poem—less an elegy really than a tribute—emphasizes as well. There is a tone of angry bewilderment, not at his friend's eventual fate but at his treatment. Twice Merrill repeats "It was a madness" that Lodeizen be deprived of his death, so that each day was "somewhat/Less than you could bear." The final two stanzas, completing the poem's single-sentence contradiction of the "peaceful" commonplace of death, begin as a curious rebuttal of Auden. In his "Musée des Beaux Arts," Auden complacently says the Old Masters were never wrong about suffering because they realized its "human position." Merrill's "old masters of disease" are doctors, not painters, and they make him "cry aloud" at the intolerable human position in which they confine Lodeizen. They would kill him by keeping him alive; they

> Would coax you still back from that starry land
> Under the world, which no one sees
> Without a death, its finish and sharp weight
> Flashing in his own hand.

The doctors' Damoclean sword becomes the hero's emblem. Its finish and weight (the pronominal ambiguity cleverly giving those qualities to death as well as to the sword) might also be the lyre's, since the unnamed but apposite hero here is Orpheus.

Lodeizen is not Auden's falling boy, but the questing adventurer. And he signals a shift from the typical protagonist of *First Poems*—the child, the innocent, the victim—to a more mature, though not necessarily less vulnerable persona—often a lover, an artist, a martyr, "a young man." This is a step toward autobiography, or at least toward the more naturalistic possibilities of direct address. But a poem's speaker and the poet's self are rarely merged in this book, only paralleled. "I" is used as a point of view. When more intimate or complex or troubling matters are raised, a surrogate is introduced. "Saint" is an example. It is a poem about the artist's practicing for eternity, with overtones that are both erotic and deadly. There are two figures: the "you" that is the speaker's own reflexive self, and the titular saint, Sebastian. These figures are set against the background of a crowd—almost a chorus and not unlike the "old masters" in the Lodeizen elegy—first of the soldier's executioners, then transformed into the saint's worshippers. And just as the two crowds, hooded archers and mumbling old women, are ironic versions of each other, so too are the figures, the "young martyr" and the yearning poet, a single split personality. Sebastian has only an iconic reality, as a series of images or fantasies the speaker has of himself. The poem opens tentatively, its first word meaning both to lack and to desire, its second line equivocating:

> Wanting foreknowledge of eternity
> It may be you must learn
> From an illumination, from an ivory triptych,
> How the young martyr, stripped
> And fastened to the trunk of a fruit-bearing
> Tree, could in a fanfare
> Of tenderness for their reluctance summon
> Those hooded archers: *Come!*
> *The arrows! Come! He loves me best who nearest*
> *To my heart hits!* In love and fear
> They let fly.

Left unanswered here is the question of *why* you want that foreknowledge. And are we to understand it to be erotic bliss or aesthetic perfection? The "illumination" is no fixed image or goal, and the excited fable is sexual but only when it is not sentimental, in the manner of T.S. Eliot's "Death of Saint Narcissus." The martyr's ecstasy or divine possession is clearly a projection of the speaker's longing for "eternity"—but for actual sublimity, or for the lifeless perfection beyond the "heart"? The reader is encouraged (or forced, according to his temper) to imply from the manifest details the poem's latent dilemma. The speaker's "you"—a reference to his distance or even alienation from himself—is no martyr, no Aeolian lyre fastened to a tree and struck by the arrows of inspiration, his efforts bear no fruit. At this point, and after such knowledge, the poem begins again:

> Wanting endurance of that moment's
> Music, you are afraid. Below
> Your hotel window, the piazza blackens
> And hisses. You do not draw back,
> You hold it all in your eye's mind.

Looking up from the imaginary portrait of Sebastian that has so kindled his mind's eye, the speaker's double returns to meditate on reality—through a "hotel window" that opposes the mirroring page, the hissing a black parody of possible music. There is an evident disgust in the language he uses to describe the life before, or literally beneath him—those limping, dribbling, mumbling women. Their "hocus-pocus" and their "dyed breaths" and "human acids" are a mean inversion of the articulate energy to which the young man aspires, and with which the saint rises above them all "exuberantly" with a warning that could speak for them both: *"He kisses me who kills, who kills me kisses!* The poem then attempts a strange reconcilia-

tion. The three deaths—the romantic martyrdom, the worm-drilled baroque statue, and the poet's despair—give way to a timeless pastoral, a
classic "endurance":

> And what is learned? Just this:
> He is the flaw through which you can glimpse meadows
> Herds, the lover piping with bent head.

The moralized scene of instruction is another piece of dreamwork, and
combines the two men in a stylized innocence at once solipsistic and
homoerotic: the piazza becomes a meadow, the worshippers are changed to
a herd; the soldier-saint is mistaken for an idyllic text, the poet fancies
himself the piping lover. But again, the figures are separated, and the
poem returns to an ironic contemplation of itself, this time with a bitter,
imprisoned finality:

> Full of the scene, you turn back in
> To serve your time. The damask bed
> Creaks under you. The board groans, the stone
> wrinkles—
> Eternity refusing to begin.

The poem seems unresolved because it cannot make up its mind, does not
care to. On the one hand, it evokes the sources of pain and power, and
diffidently suggests a literary solution. On the other hand, its ends or
ambition refuse to begin, and the poem turns into the familiar modern
fable about the impossibility of its own accomplishment.

"Saint" is followed in the book by "The Charioteer of Delphi,"
essentially the same poem but plainer and less febrile. Merrill has taken
the famous statue and reimagined its athlete as Phaeton—like Lodeizen
and Sebastian another youthful victim, the memory of whose downfall
still scorches. He has further conflated that sun-myth with Socrates's story
in the *Phaedrus* of the winged steeds of reason and passion. The poem,
then, begins with a question about its own subject—"Where are the horses
of the sun?"—and continues by tracing the initial "havoc" caused by "the
killing horses" from the myth of the dazzled son to actual memories shared
by the inquiring speaker and the child he protectively addresses. The
poem's self-conscious layering merely augments, by postponing, its
conclusion:

> Broken from his mild reprimand
> In fire and fury hard upon the taste
> Of a sweet license, even these have raced
> Uncurbed in us, where fires are fanned.

Invariably, the best poems in *The Country of a Thousand Years of Peace* have a similar taste for sweet license, for an abandon and risk belied by their superficial self-confidence. Despite alluring or even learned trappings, they pursue resolutely what another poem calls "the inner adventure," and what "The Charioteer of Delphi" identifies as "fires." Several poems in the book enlarge upon the metaphor. "Fire Poem" is one. Like "The Cruise" with its encrystaled monsters, or "Laboratory Poem" with its chilling climb through violence into "exquisite disciplines," "Fire Poem" takes up the conflict between passion and intelligence, between ardor and ashes, the song of once-burned innocence and twice-shy experience. After a theatrical introduction—the speaker and his companion seated before the hearth's stage, a scene replayed in *The Fire Screen* (1969)—the fire itself speaks:

> If as I am you know me bright and warm,
> It is while matter bears, which I live by,
> For very heart the furnace of its form:
> By likeness and from likeness in my storm
> Sheltered, can all things change and changing be
> The rare bird bedded at the heart of harm.

The language here is deliberately intense. Since we are first told that the fire "Built brightness in the eye already bright," it is fair to assume that the fire's italicized sermon might as well be a reverie by the speaker himself—or by the "laughing child" who, entranced by the prospect of transformation, "Reached for the fire and screamed." Like the charioteer, the child is burned. The phoenix-like possibilities of "change and changing," the escape from mere "likeness," that the fire announced are at once forgotten in the disillusioning pain and fear: "fire thereafter was the burnt child's name/For fear." Even—or, especially—the symbolic function of language, to reclaim and transform phenomena, is lost. In a sense, then, "Fire Poem" is a self-consuming artifact, and it is because the vision is literalized and wrongly acted upon that experience hurts and words fail. Much later, such playing with fire will earn Ephraim's rebuke: "LOOK YR FILL/BUT DO DO DO DO NOTHING."

A similar point is made, in a lighter vein and in reverse, by "The Doodler." It is a poem about "communing"—consciously with others over the telephone, and unconsciously with the self as the speaker idly doodles on a pad while talking. (The model of psychotherapy is clear but not stressed.) The first half of the poem draws the connection between the isolated human features obsessively figured out—kohl-daubed eyes, profiled noses, lips pursed and raised to anyone's but his—and the distant voices on the line, except that the drawings seem "more animate/Than any new friend's voice." The regressive inner adventure then beings with his admission that "nothing I do is at all fine/Save certain abstract forms. These come unbidden." What wells up is not an involuntary memory of Merrill's own, but the apparatus of a poem—"Stars, oblongs linked, or a baroque motif"—that finally assembles the "least askew of ikons" whom "The Doodler" first sets out to greet. It is an image with a life of its own—or so the poet imagines—who even begins to decipher the designing poet as *"He-Who-endures-the-disembodied-Voice."*

> Far, far behind already is that aeon
> Of pin-heads, bodies each a ragged weevil,
> Slit-mouthed and spider-leggèd, with eyes like
> > gravel,
> Wavering under trees of purple crayon.
>
> Shapes never realized, were you dogs or chairs?
> That page is brittle now, if not long burned.
> This morning's little boy stands (I have learned
> To do feet) gazing down a flight of stairs.

The situation here anticipates that of "Lost in Translation," where the young Merrill pieces together the puzzle revealing the page-boy. The little boy brought to light by "The Doodler" has no immediate autobiographical significance, but is a shape of things to come in Merrill's work, a realized shape of his own past. And the image's associations are crucial. The boy's emergence as both a recognizable figure and as a resonant symbol (what he *stands* for) is linked with the poet's own ability—his having "learned/To do feet." That achievement uncovers the past and its emotional dimensions, though this little boy's loneliness—like that of Proust's Marcel at the top of the stairs—is left for now in outline. "Lost in Translation" concentrates retrospectively on the child's private "void." This poem goes on, in a concluding quatrain whose miniature apotheosis spans alpha to omega ("A." to "O"), to celebrate the excited power:

> And when A. calls to tell me he enjoyed
> The evening, I begin again. Again
> Emerge, O sunbursts, garlands, creatures, men,
> Ever more lifelike out of the white void!

A whole career, an evolving world of figures, emerges in a kind of triumphal pageant from out of the page's white void—an echo of *"le vide papier"* in Mallarmé's *"Brise marine."* That emptiness is not only imaginative potential or experiential loss; it is the poet's subconscious as well, both image-repertoire and word-bank. They are tapped by not trying; stylized forms, not arbitrary self-expression, yield the responsive image—not an image skimmed from the moment, but one retrieved from lost time. By having learned here to *endure* the disembodied voices from the subconscious, and then patiently to portray their lifelike images, the poet—reinforced by A.'s approval—has every reason to begin again.

III

"You reflect and I rejoice," says the doodler of the image he has made—a line that draws attention to the fact that the white void may also be construed as a mirror. Several poems in *The Country of a Thousand Years of Peace*—"Mirror" and "In the Hall of Mirrors" especially—introduce an object that comes to have a central importance for Merrill, as an emblematic prop in many of his best poems and as his recent trilogy's proscenium. Actually, this book abounds in "glassen surfaces," several of them related to the mirror but without its thin silver mask. In "The Octopus," for example, the "vision asleep in the eye's tight translucence" is compared to an octopus behind an aquarium's plate glass—not unlike Hugo's remark that language itself is *"Tantôt comme un passant mystérieux de l'âme, tantôt comme un polype noir de l'océan pensé."* Merrill sets up a fine interplay in the poem between perception and creation, between reflecting surfaces and reflected depths, narcissistic attractions and visionary possession. The *monstre sacré* here is what rises to the surface: at one level an observor's dream of convulsive divinity, at another level the image of the octopus that the poet coaxes out by the "lusters" of his poem's associations. In another poem, "Some Negatives: X. at the Chateau," the translucent eyeball is replaced by a camera lens and its "images of images." The anti-world on film—again, a version of the subconscious—winds that speaker through a series of now paradoxical flashbacks:

> Where skies are thunderous, by a cypress walk
> Copied in snow, I have you: or
> Sitting beside the water-jet that here
> Is jet. You could be an Ethiop with hair
> Powdered white as chalk . . .
>
> Your charming face not lit
> But charred, as by dark beams instructing it
> In all to which you were the latest heir.

As the poem continues, its tone grows more unsettling. The leap from "charming" to "charred," for instance, is even more negative than its obvious inversion. And the "ghostliness" the speaker guesses in the pic-

tured woman comes to seem alternately more haunted and more menacing
than one first suspects. As a malign, potentially monstrous dream-image,
the woman may be linked with other death-dealing female figures in the
book—Naomi in "Laboratory Poem," Salome, and the vampire in "A
Narrow Escape." Further, she can be traced to the myth of Medusa that
pervades *First Poems*, a myth that turns on a compelling horror overcome
by having been reflected.

On the other side of the looking-glass, then, the life beneath the
life is deeply ambivalent and to that extent disturbing. As in "The
Locusts," it can be vacantly pastoral, the imagination's paradise:

> . . . a limpid source to peer
> Deep into, heaven-sent
>
> Mirrorscope, green, wet,
> All echo, orchid, and egret
> In pure transports recalling you.

Or, as in the poems I have just mentioned, it can be a threatening source
of psychological and emotional engulfment. These mirroring roles for the
poet, Narcissus or Perseus, are ones Merrill frequently tries on in his early
books. And the rivalry between them is one he must have been alert to
from the start; even as an undergraduate at Amherst, he had the lead in a
student production of Cocteau's *Orpheus*—a play in which a broken
window and a standing mirror figure prominently, the mirror as a doorway
for the hero to descend into the underworld and for Death, a glamorous
woman in an evening gown, to enter the stage for her victims. By the
time he came to write the trilogy's harmonic romance, he seems to have
resolved the dilemma. It is his early books that are especially set upon by a
Fury the poet only gradually interiorizes as a paramour.

This characterological ambivalence, the speaker's shifting attitudes
and roles, and the equivocal female figure, occur within individual poems
as well as between them. "The Day of the Eclipse" is an interesting
example of this. The poem divides in two, a cause-and-effect sequence
from the first nine stanzas to the concluding seven. At the outset, the
poet is alone, or at least detached, behind the summer's thin gold life
mask of sun on his face. The familiar composition of place he can
recall—dunes, gull, rower, "the mirror of the tide's/Retreat"—contrasts
with today's atmosphere of impending eclipse. His senses are uncertain;
his spirit troubled. At this point, there is an odd vision:

> There is a lone, burned child to watch
> Digging so furiously for fun
> As to stir up a chaos into which

> They both might slip, their muscle yield
> To something blinder and less skilled
> Than maggots, and their boniness
> Flex, fracture, effervesce,
> Before the lacy vortex can be healed.

This child is, as it were, the mirror's mercury, the psychopomp leading the poet through the black field on the other side of transparent reality, conducting him through the pattern of death and resurrection Merrill's poems have favored from the start. And he is a figure who recurs, in different guises, from the ripples in the basin's "coldly wishing surface" in "The Lovers" on to Ephraim and Mirabell, whenever the mirror's hermetical associations are introduced. In this poem, the imagined downfall—half feared, half desired—is then enacted above. Like the sun, "He rises, peers up through smoked glass./A black pupil rimmed with fire/Peers back." The burned child here becomes a black pupil—the poet's own inward gaze and futile solipsism. In the tenth stanza, the "girl of whom he has been aware all summer" abruptly appears. "He knows that she belongs to a far more/Exciting world," that she may be that "unique caryatid/Of the unthinkable" he has conjured from the sky's void and would court as his muse. But she is elusive, and remains "Companionless in a skylit shack," like the "ageless woman of the world" at the end of "The Book of Ephraim," or Mother Nature in *Scripts for the Pageant*. The poet remains curiously indifferent, paralyzed even, and instead of approaching her can only identify himself with the "mounds of matter cold and blind/She loves, how even they respond/To the least pressure of a shaping hand."

The blandness of his response here—her shaping hand so much less vital than the earlier furious digging into the chaos of the self—is paralleled by the delirium of the poem titled "Amsterdam" and by the stilted fervor of "The Greenhouse." The city and its canals are themselves seen as a vast mirror in "Amsterdam," by virtue of the poem's epigraph—"*Au pays qui te ressemble*," from "*L'Invitation au voyage*"—which adds to Baudelaire's invocation of "*Mon enfant, ma soeur*" Merrill's own implied and reflected presence. After describing the city as one where "desire is freed from the body's prison," an apparition of that desire in the imagination's labyrinth—distilled as moon, mirror, Medusa—turns the tourist into a voyeur:

> Into a black impasse deep in the maze
> A mirror thrusts her   brilliant severed head,
> Mouth red and moist, and pale curls diamonded.
> A youth advances towards the wraith, delays,
>
> Squints through the window at a rumpled bed.

The dream-encounter that follows, in four parenthetical stanzas, though it might be with absence itself or with an abstracted ideal ("the sheer gold of nobody's hair" is its only token), and is more probably the self's apprehension of the soul, is then tentatively, yet pointedly identified when the poet awakens:

> Next day, is, it myself whose image those
> Sunning their own on the canal's far side
> Are smiling to see reel . . . ?

This difficult poem—Merrill admits in the course of it that "a future sleuth of the oblique," more a type of the psychoanalyst than the literary critic, will be its best reader—then turns itself inside out. Macabre motifs accumulate, as if to signal the death-in-life of this particular inner adventure. In one extraordinary gesture, that links by its echo of the second stanza the poem and the mirror, the poet's own brilliant head is severed: "My head has fallen forward open-eyed." And in a kind of reverse eclipse,

> By dark the world is once again intact,
> Or so the mirrors, wiped clean, try to reason . . .
> O little moons, misshapen but arisen
> To blind with the emotions they reflect!

The balance between deflection and reflection here seems both destroyed by new knowledge and restored by the verse's closure. The Orphic overtones of the poem, used here to stress the relationship between the poet and his poem's own underworld of tangled memories and fantasies, are prominent too in "The Greenhouse," which opens with "So many girls vague in the yielding orchard" who cling to the poet and "Trailingly inquire, but similingly, of the greenhouse." What seems at first to be a frieze of *jeunes filles en fleurs* gradually emerges as an animated metaphor for the poet's own green thoughts. These wilt during his allegorical descent "under glass," until he finds himself in "the least impressive room":

> It was hotter here than elsewhere, being shadowed
> Only by bare panes overhead
> And here the seedlings had been set to breeding
> Their small green tedium of need:
> Each plant alike, each plaintively devouring
> One form, meek sprout atremble in the glare
> Of the ideal condition.

This hothouse forcing-room is both hellish and brooding. The unsteady tone—a blend of condescension ("tedium") and fear ("devouring")—in effect forces the poet to interrupt himself as he contemplates the paradoxical lost paradise: "the fiercer fading/Of as yet nobody's beauty." Once again, the terrible mother is transformed into a benevolent muse; the poet seeks to rescue what he would be devoured by. As in several poems in *The Country of a Thousand Years of Peace*, Merrill's latent private anxieties are manifest in familiar and recurring mythic formulas.

The whole matter of *reproduction* is raised in "The Greenhouse" and, naturally, in the book's other mirror-poems as well. As early as *First Poems* Merrill had been worrying the problem: the opposing demands of art and life. His belief in what Yeats called the perfection of the work was never in question. But the perfection of the life, insofar as that tends toward the creation of an actual and ethical family, seems to have troubled Merrill from the beginning—as it continues to in such poems as "Childlessness" in *Water Street*, and "The Emerald" in *Braving the Elements*, both of which seek to counter the hectoring expectations of others. Each sort of perfection claims to be an argument against time, but the generative task threatens Merrill's privileged status as only child in his own family romance, and as unique artist embodying himself in words. "In the Hall of Mirrors" is the most extreme and literally dazzling treatment of the problem in *The Country of a Thousand Years of Peace*. In a nearly condescending self-appraisal, Merrill once told an interviewer of the "buried meanings" that unconsciously shape and eventually sustain his poems, and he linked this with "some kind of awful religious streak just under the surface" in himself. Among the examples he then cited is "In the Hall of Mirrors": it is "a fairly obvious case. It was written during the 1950s when the 'myth' poems were popular. It's about the expulsion from Eden." Such a frank interpretation is, as usual, evasive; it buries the meaning in myth. The loss of paradise, or fall from natural grace, is not this poem's "buried meaning," merely its conceptual scaffolding. The myth of the Fall, from which Merrill's account of the Broken Home draws much of its power, would more appropriately describe the plot of a later poem, "18 West 11th Street." This poem is at once more complex and less resolved than its plot, and more private than its analogous myth. The setting described in the opening stanzas can be seen, in the light of Merrill's own explanation, as an Edenic *locus amoenus*:

> The parquet barely gleams, a lake.
> The windows weaken the dark trees.
> The mirrors to their bosoms take
> Far glints of water, which they freeze
> And wear like necklaces.

> Some pause in front of others with
> Glimmers of mutual admiration.
> Even to draw breath is uncouth.
> Steps make the silver marrow spin
> Up and down every spine.

The reader may be tempted here to ignore, for the sake of the fable, the deceiving force of the figuration, its stress on the reflected glories of artifice: the mirror a mother, the floor a lake, the lake a *rivière*, the experience embossed on a spine like any book's. There is no breath of life; all complexities of mire or blood are, like mirrors, silvered. This is no country for "Anything personal or commonplace," as the reptilian guide "hisses" to the couple who next enter the hall. Lured by such pride and by the "good offices" of their guide's bad eminence, they are drawn into the room's infinity effect:

> In one glass brow a tree is lit
> That multiplies itself in tiers,
> Tempting the pair to populate
> Those vistas from which visitors
> Ricochet in fours,
>
> Eights, sixteens, till the first two gaze
> At one another through the glazed crush
> Of their own kind, and the man says,
> 'Complex but unmysterious,
> This is no life for us.'

The glazed crush that nearly obscures the original pair here anticipates the "fleet blur of couples/Many of whom, by now, have reproduced" that is "inflicted" on the shatterproof glass shielding Giorgione's *Tempesta* toward the end of *The Book of Ephraim*. In this poem, once he knows the trick, the man is bored by the repetitions. Worse, he realizes that each of the multiplying likenesses before him represents a diminishment of the self. His companion is drawn even deeper into the dilemma. She looks beyond the obvious if primal image of this *stade de miroir*, beyond the repetition compulsion. Unsatisfied by the infinity effect's parodic anti-paradise, she searches for imaginary and therefore "grander" images of the self:

> The woman, making no reply,
> Scans the remotest mirrors within mirrors
> For grander figures,
>
> Not just those of herself and him
> Repeated soothingly, as though
> Somebody's wits were growing dim—
> Those! Those beyond!

The reactions, then, of those whom Merrill with a mischievous irony asks us to fancy our First Parents are not contradictory but complementary. Both conspire against the generative task: he derides it, she seeks to transcend it. When their guide—and one sees now why the Biblical spoiler is here a hermetic guide—says " 'Time to go,' " there is of course no reluctance or regret in their compliance. That order comes, I think, too abruptly in the poem, so that it seems to follow as an immediate consequence of an original sin of some sort of overweening narcissism. But there is no crime here, no punishment, no "expulsion." There is, instead, a rejection of mere reproduction in favor of the poet's grander expressive figures—one of which closes the poem:

> And in the solitary hall
> The lobes of crystal gather dust.
> From glass to glass an interval
> Widens like moonrise over frost
> No tracks have ever crossed.

The couple having taken their solitary way, the hall—a prototype of the trilogy's Empty Ballroom (the *Galerie des Glaces* was, after all, used as a *salon de fête*)—is empty of all but the by now familiar trope: the artistic compact, the white void, the frozen pool, the page to be written.

"In the Hall of Mirrors" begins with a refined idea of the finished book (the silvered spine), and ends by returning to the blank page of possibilities. In a sense, those are also the contrasted properties of the book's best known poem, "Mirror": the mirror's knowing polish and the opposite window's engaging openness. But there is no simple dialectic being proposed here. Though not inaccurate, it would be too reductive to read this poem as a debate between the reflective mind and the perceiving eye, or between the poem's surfaced depths and the novel's broad perspectives, or between a perfected, stale art and natural, generational life. The poem is too astute to deal exclusively in such standard contrasts. From its abrupt opening lines—which, with their overtone of threatened individuality, seem at first to be autobiographical—this dramatic monologue is a brooding study of frustration and transfiguration. The poem begins with a sort of moral prologue, a typifying episode of barely suppressed violence:

> I grow old under an intensity
> Of questioning looks. *Nonsense,*
> I try to say, *I cannot teach you children*
> *How to live.—If not you, who will?*
> Cries one of them aloud, grasping my gilded
> Frame till the world sways. *If not you, who will?*

The violence in that passage is symptomatic of the confused anger that seems to have provoked the exchange. There are strange reversals in this poem's mirror-world. Instead of taking Merrill's preferred role of vulnerable child or artist, the mirror's disembodied voice is that of a surrogate parent, his role not that of an Oedipal tyrant but of an aging father confessor. As if having given rise to it by allowing them a look at themselves, he shares the helplessness of his children. This poem is one of such redoubled and interchanged perspectives, in fact, that we do well to remind ourselves of its possibilities of address. Whenever a mirror is questioned, who is asking what of whom? Those "questioning looks" were presumably first directed at the children themselves, as introspection rather than injunction—though that is what the question becomes when repeated. The problem presented—*how to live*—is as much his as theirs, as much aesthetic as moral: how to come to life, as how rightly to live. And the reiterated question—"*If not you, who will?*"—may stress the urgency of the children's despair, or stand as an aural image of the mirror's visual reflecting, but the echo also reminds us of the stake the mirror has in the answer to it—much as a poem makes demands on the readers who presume to search it for what will suffice.

    With its irregularly metered lines and pleated apocopaic rhymes, "Mirror" has an unstanza'd, blocky look and a conversational fluency. Even so, the poem has three distinct sections. The prologue, which nervously issues the moral and aesthetic demand and establishes the complex relationships, is balanced by an answering and resolving epilogue. Between these two sections (11.) is a compressed, novelistic chronicle of the mirror's "children." Three generations of their secret lives is what the mirror knows, much as in this description by Hawthorne a mirror holds and represents the interior life of the House of the Seven Gables: "As regards its interior life, a large, dim looking-glass used to hang in one of the rooms, and was fabled to contain within its depths all the shapes that had ever been reflected there." Merrill's mirror begins with the room's still life: "Between their visits the table, its arrangement/Of Bible, fern and Paisley, all past change,/Does very nicely." Whether that dated arrangement is incidental or is a series of metonymies for religion, domesticated nature, and decorative art, the mirror is associated with what is fixed, conventionalized, "past change." The world of change, the works and days of human beings, are the window's province. In fact, the italicized *you* specifically links the window's temper with the children's importunate *you* at the start of the poem. As in Hardy's extraordinary poem "Moments of Vision," whose mirror "makes of men a transparency," here too the window and its human traffic are, in the mirror's view, all too easily seen through. The mirror's tone, from the bemused subjunctive to the waspish irony in "takes thought," is clearly condescending:

> If ever I feel curious
> As to what others endure,
> Across the parlor you provide examples,
> Wide open, sunny, of everything I am
> Not. You embrace a whole world without once caring
> To set it in order. That takes thought.

What then follows is a montage of details from real life. And if we read into them a courtship and marriage, adultery ("her first unhappiness") and divorce, then the costume drama here is another version of Merrill's own Broken Home:

> Out there
> Something is being picked. The red-and-white
> bandannas
> Go to my heart. A fine young man
> Rides by on horseback. Now the door shuts. Hester
> Confides in me her first unhappiness.
> This much, you see, would never have been fitted
> Together, but for me. Why then is it
> They more and more neglect me? Late one sleepless
> Midsummer night I strained to keep
> Five tapers from your breathing. *No,* the widowed
> Cousin said, *let them go.* I did.
> The room brimmed with gray sound, all the
> instreaming
> Muslin of your dream . . .

This uncanny nocturne—the senses's five tapers extinguished, the elegiac *correspondence* of the smoke's gray sound, the window's very reality turned to dream under the force of instreaming imagination—has a forlorn quality to its modulations. Both the ellipsis and the notable shift in tenses in the scene, from continuous present to past ("strained," "said," the decisive "I did"), marks the end of one movement, and should alert us to other changes. After all, there is a submission here and an unspoken recognition on the mirror's part—as, in Merrill's family romance, his artistic vocation is linked to his parents's divorce, so that "I did" (or *made*) is a parodic consequence of "I do." The commanding "widowed/ Cousin" (an antitype of Madamoiselle in *Divine Comedies*) might as well be a *windowed* cousin, whose authority the mirror obeys—as later it is amenable to a faceless will. The ellipsis signals, then, what the mirror had hitherto resisted, a *change*—of heart, of function, of values. That change is what gives the irony in the next lines its edge. The children turn to "muse" upon the window, and looking out at its mute poesy make the remark that concludes the poem's middle section:

> Years later now, two of the grown grandchildren
> Sit with novels face-down on the sill,
> Content to muse upon your tall transparence,
> Your clouds, brown fields, persimmon far
> And cypress near. One speaks. *How superficial*
> *Appearances are!*

That dismissal, which on different readings of the poem may sound contemptuous or resolute or stricken, is a response but not an answer to the prologue's question: *If not you, who will?* But by concluding the historical interlude—which comprises, in a manner of speaking, the "appearances" of the poem itself—the realization frees both the mirror and the reader to return to the greater issue: *how to live.* The final third of "Mirror" recapitulates a familiar sequence of experiences. Of course the answer involves a transformation. The children have, in effect, turned the window into a mirror by their attitude, which frames the scene into a landscape, and in this section the mirror literally sheds its identity and becomes a window. But I think, too, that the final lines of the poem bring us back to the notion of *dedication,* a commitment that opens and closes *The Country of a Thousand Years of Peace* and animates it throughout. It starts with a swoon. The old order is disturbed. The mirror sinks to the pitch of a negative sublime:

> Since then, as if a fish
> Had broken the perfect silver of my reflectiveness,
> I have lapses. I suspect
> Looks from behind, where nothing is, cool gazes
> Through the blind flaws of my mind. As days,
> As decades lengthen, this vision
> Spreads and blackens.

In seeking to account for this new and threatening vision, the mirror utters the lines that give this poem its eerie power:

> I do not know whose it is,
> But I think it watches for my last silver
> To blister, flake, float leaf by life, each milling-
> Downward dumb conceit, to a standstill
> From which not even you strike any brilliant
> Chord in me, and to a faceless will,
> Echo of mine, I am amenable.

These are tricky lines. The mirror begins tentatively. And the painful process of blistering so turns on the possibilities inherent in language ("leaf by life") that the change seems a transformation, even a reincarnation. The mirror's once brilliant chords lose, with a Stevensian flourish "each milling-/Downward dumb conceit." "In the Hall of Mirrors" trades its silver for untraced frost, or pristine contingency. Here, the dumb conceits or ineffectual tropes yield to a higher power, "a faceless will, /Echo of mine." Does this imply a rejection of narcissism—the mirror's reflecting pool of self-regard giving way to sweet Echo "that liv'st unseen/ Within thy airy shell"? Or is the faceless will the tall transparence of life itself to which the poet declares himself amenable—open, responsive, dedicated? Both perhaps. It is the self and—"Echo of mine"—more than the self these lines declare, accepting determinism *and* exaltation, experience *and* language.

It is characteristic of Merrill—in this poem, and in his later, more accomplished poems—to work not with a set of opposites but with a series of dissolves. In "Mirror," for instance, there is a continual exchange of perspectives, both literal and figurative. Even within the confines of a monologue, the reader is invited to watch the poem's subject through a constantly shifting framework: now mirror, now window, now picture-frame; figure to ground, contour to color, threshold to aftermath; the white oblong of the page outlining the black block of print that is the poem itself. Counterpointing these rapid, at times simultaneous variations of perspective is the slower, more decisive alternation of daybright and nightblind states of mind. The poem twice grows dark, twice moves from ferment to standstill, from perfect silver to blind flaw, from conscious order to the static chaos of the unconscious. The grasping, wide open world at the start of the poem sinks "Late one sleepless/Midsummer night" to a strained, dreamy impulse to cease, as it were, upon that midnight. At the end of the poem, the mirror again yields; the brilliant silver flakes to a blackness the mirror takes as blankness. A "faceless will" here replaces the commanding female figure in the first encounter. It is more menacing and abstract because internal—or rather, internalized. The mirror's powers of reflection are overthrown from within, and become in the end a black pane—a transfiguration of the primary pain that has suffused the poem, from the questioning looks at the start, to Hester's unhappiness and the smoking tapers. The mirror, then, amenable to this process, is another of the figures of the artist in *The Country of a Thousand Years of Peace*. This poem ends where the book's title-poem ends: in "that starry land/Under the world, which no one sees/Without a death."

DAVID LEHMAN

Elemental Bravery: The Unity of James Merrill's Poetry

. . . break, blow, burn, and make me new.
— DONNE, "Holy Sonnets"

For nothing can be sole or whole
That has not been rent.
— YEATS, "Crazy Jane Talks With the Bishop"

With the visionary gleam that informs his cosmic commedia, James Merrill appears to have taken a great many readers by surprise. The critic who might once have damned Merrill with faint praise—by extolling him as "merely" a master craftsman—no longer has that luxury, if luxury it is to deny oneself the pleasures of texts in which, as in the novels of Jane Austen and Henry James, an education of the feelings takes place under the tutorship of language. "The Book of Ephraim," *Mirabell*, and *Scripts for the Pageant* are as elegant of surface, as fastidiously well-wrought, as any of Merrill's previous writings, but there should now be less room for misunderstanding. The "poems of science" Merrill has fashioned achieve a remarkable synthesis of levity and gravity; their gay, buoyant atmosphere contrapuntally sets off the seriousness of their hieratic intent. If Merrill's tone remains that of the dandy, his attitude that of the aesthete abroad (who feels "American in Europe and

From *James Merrill: Essays in Criticism,* edited by David Lehman and Charles Berger. Copyright © 1983 by Cornell University Press.

exotic at home"), one can scarcely ignore the news he now brings us from heavenly circles of limitless circumference, whose centers are everywhere.

"Mind you, it works best as metaphor," Merrill's vision does, as he himself remarks of his model of "the psychic atom." Still, the wedding of science fiction and poetic truths for the sake of dealing with ultimate questions as well as with the pressures of an immediate reality—this is a larger ambition than we are accustomed to, and an ambition largely brought off. And surely one must admire the performance, the skill with which Merrill has approached a problem memorably defined by one of his voices from beyond:

> DANTE'S LUCK LAY IN HIS GULLIBLE
> & HEAVENLY WORLD   WE MY BOY DRAW FROM 2
> SORTS OF READER: ONE ON HIS KNEES TO ART
> THE OTHER FACEDOWN OVER A COMIC BOOK.
> OUR STYLISH HIJINKS WONT AMUSE THE LATTER
> & THE FORMER WILL DISCOUNT OUR URGENT MATTER
>   (Mirabell)

Uncomprehending or dismissive responses are indeed inevitable. With his Ouija board apparatus, lost continents, and black holes, this most urbane of poets had made himself vulnerable on several counts. But I would argue that it is precisely thanks to the taking of this risk, to the fusion of "stylish hijinks" and "urgent matter," of comic book and art, that Merrill's great breakthrough has occurred. It seems to me, moreover, that the breakthrough has come not as an about-face but as the culmination of a lifetime of trials and tremors; there is, I will undertake to show, an essential unity to Merrill's career. Toward the "lessons" of *Mirabell* and *Scripts*, Merrill began doing his homework long ago. He has schooled his sensibility to aim at high romantic ideals, or at a network of them: the apprehension of angels on earth, the recovery of paradises misplaced or extinct, the redemption of time, the outwitting of mortality.

In securing Merrill's place as an American original, the trilogy compels us to take a retrospective look at his career and, in doing so, to question our biases, to wonder how so many could fail for so long to recognize as virtues this poet's metaphysical wit and his prodigious formal resources; a melancholy conclusion points to the devaluation, in our time, of the verbal gestures that give Merrill's poetry its distinctive finish. Like Emerson's Rhodora, these gestures are their own excuse for being, but their existence is far from gratuitous. To the contrary, Merrill's formal choices and his visionary insights present a classic chicken-and-egg problem in causality. His "means" and his "meanings" coincide (*Divine Comedies*); the pun, so characteristic of its author, is as much an instrument of truth as an element of style or a quirk of mind. From the start Merrill's reflexive attentiveness to a word's multiplicity of meanings signaled a concomitant interest in the overtones of an action or event: what life proposed, language disclosed. Pleasurable in itself, Merrill's wordplay is thus inseparable from the tasks his sense of poetic vocation demands of him. The trilogy represents an apotheosis of the effort to extend the scrutiny of self to the point that the examined consciousness —no less than "the life lived" and "the love spent" (*Water Street*)—acquires the shape and clarity of a work of art. By the same token, the earlier books may now be seen to chart the progress of the poet toward a vision as difficult to endure as to earn, the living record of one who transformed himself from "maker" to "creator" with no consequent loss of craft, whose outbreaks from the jail of form result in new forms every bit as exacting as those they supplant, designed to enhance poetic freedoms rather than diminish them.

To call the trilogy a comedy is to fix its mode, not to circumscribe its flight. It might be argued that the comic impulse derives much of its energy from the perceived push-and-pull between gravity (or gravitation) and levity (or levitation), and Merrill's poetry is indeed poised between the thrill of escape from the earth's magnetic force and the relentless insistence of our corporeal natures, dragging us back to earth. The pattern is defined in the comic archetype of the stargazer who falls into a ditch, although in the versions of this motif found in Chaucer, Sidney, and Swift the accent falls on the assertion of our "clayey lodgings" that make a mockery of all spiritual aspiration. Not so in Merrill's poetry. There the "erected wit" stands a good chance of rescuing the "infected will": never has Merrill excluded the possibility of a true transcendence, beyond even the project of uniting sense and soul, Cupid and Psyche, the Sultan and Scheherazade. Even before "Ephraim," his work is rife with intimations of an immortal world in which, at a stroke, two clichés renew themselves— "whatever will be, will be right." (Not for nothing is JM said to be the "faithful representative" of an obscure nineteenth-century editor of the works of Alexander Pope.) "Form's what affirms," Merrill affirms in "The Thousand and Second Night" (*Nights and Days*), and so, finally, does the comic impulse, with its hope of order restored, its happy ending implicit from the start. It holds out the promise that buoyant chatter can redeem weighty matter, that wit is everlasting and dust but for a time, that the stuff of tragedy, endured and absorbed, can be transmuted—by a conceit Rilke would have enjoyed—into the musical "scale of love and dread" played on a "thinking reed" by "the great god Pain" (*Braving the Elements*).

In his poetry, Merrill characteristically cuts the figure of the suave host whose conversational brilliance and fondness for camp humor disarm the invited guest, so that the pouring of spirits at dinner's end finds him half-drugged already "in laughter, pain, and love" or "wit, affection, and despair," as the case may be. In "A Tenancy," the poem that closes *Water Street*, Merrill makes this tight-lipped pronouncement:

> If I am host at last
> It is of little more than my own past.
> May others be at home in it.

As "The Book of Ephraim" gathers momentum, the "others" who make their home in Merrill's salon include Zulu chieftains and "pallid Burne-Jones acroliths": like a friendly organism, the poem harbors and offers nourishment to all who call. But I do not mean to dwell overlong on this biological sense of "host"; it is pertinent that *hospes*, the Latin root of the word, signifies "host," "guest," and "stranger," for each fairly describes an aspect of the poet. He has ever been his own "perfect stranger"; he now plays host to a host of spirits, "familiar" and strange at once, while he himself is the guest in a heaven Ephraim defines as "THE SURROUND OF THE LIVING." To be host is not to deny other duties: from his privileged position at "the angelic secretariat," he takes dictation from Auden and other "ghostwriters": but then, Merrill's sense of hospitality is hardly conventional.

An additional sense of host can help correct a common misconception of readers who, upon opening *Mirabell*, will instinctively suspect the poet of pulling their legs. Such a reader will wonder whether Merrill gave strict credence to the messages spelled out by the willowware cup on his Ouija board; perhaps he or she will associate the work's otherworldly population with the mock-heroic machinery of *The Rape of the Lock*, will question the "scientific" basis of the poem, or will simply think the whole thing rather silly. Next, reassured by the way the poet has anticipated these reactions, impressed by the skepticism that marks the poet's persona, the reader will decide that Merrill consulted the board in much the same way that Yeats took note of his wife's sleeptalking, as a kind of Jungian trick, a way of coaxing the imagination. No doubt several of these responses have something to commend them, but committed readers will go further. They will begin to see that for Merrill the Ouija board is no more a trick than the Eucharist would be for devout Catholics. I draw my simile not only from the ecclesiastical sense of "host" but from the value Merrill everywhere places on the forms of ritual, the processes that prepare one to receive a vision of, and communion with, divinity. To be sure, Merrill's religiosity is quite explicitly that of the aesthete. Asked how "real" his "new mythology" seemed to him, Merrill has given this reply:

"Literally, not very—except in recurrent euphoric hours when it's altogether too beautiful not to be true." If the relation between beauty and truth proposed here should strike familiar Keatsian chords, that is no accident; the romantic element in Merrill's work—its Platonic confidence, its sensuality of language—will prompt many to see Keats's capable hand pushing Merrill's pen in pursuit of his theme, "an old, exalted one: / The incarnation and withdrawal of / A god."

Reviewing Merrill's career, one is struck by the consistency with which the poet has turned to this theme, by the frequency with which his poems function as rituals designed to welcome and witness the divine visitation and to mourn over its aftermath. Not since Rilke has a poet trained his vision with such determination to explore the realms of the angels, confident that superior eyesight can discern their presence here on earth. "Life was fiction in disguise," and as a corollary proposition, "the stranger is a god in masquerade": subscribing to the defense of masks and fictions mounted by Oscar Wilde in *The Critic As Artist*, Merrill never forgets that the purpose of the disguise is to foster ultimate recognition, that the unmasking scene crowns the masquerade ball. Consider these lines from "A Dedication," the poem that serves as the valedictory close to *The Country of a Thousand Years of Peace*; the poet is communing with the newly-dead Hans Lodeizen, a figure of importance in the trilogy as well:

> These are the moments, if ever, an angel steps
> Into the mind, as kings into the dress
> Of a poor goatherd, for their acts of charity.
> There are moments when speech is but a mouth pressed
> Lightly and humbly against the angel's hand.

Significantly, the angel is rendered as a Shakespearean monarch, bearing a likeness to Henry V in disguise among his troops. "His state is kingly," we are meant to see, and his charity a form of *caritas*; standing and waiting, the poet is struck speechless in his praise.

The "evidently angelic visitor" returns twice in *Water Street*, both times in the context of a work of art half-perceived and half-created by the poet. In "Angel," the figure appears "in finely woven robes, school of Van Eyck," in the painting hanging "above my desk"; in the angel's gestures and "round, hairless face," the poet reads a text "demanding praise, demanding surrender," forbidding profane speech. In "A Vision of the Garden," the poet recollects the childhood incident when, using his breath for ghostly writing on a chill windowpane, he drew the features of an angel doomed to "fade in mist"—features that will someday, he adds, be embodied in a flesh-and-blood "you." Nor is the figure absent from succeeding volumes; if anything there is a proliferation of guises by which he may be apprehended. An unlikely reincarnation occurs in *Braving the Elements*, in "Days of 1935": the poet's remembered fantasy of being kidnapped at age nine by "Floyd and Jean," gangster and moll. To them he becomes, in one of the poem's poignant reversals, deeply attached; and in an eery echo of the "mouth pressed / Lightly and humbly against the angel's hand," the boy struggling with his captor leaves "my toothprints on his hand, / Indenture of a kiss."

David Kalstone reports on a hidden agenda to Merrill's career, to which the titles of his volumes attest:

> It would be interesting to know at what point Merrill saw a larger pattern emerging in his work—the point at which conscious shaping caught up with what unplanned or unconscious experience had thrown his way. In retrospect a reader can see that *Braving the Elements* (1972) gathers behind it the titles—with full metaphorical force—of Merrill's previous books. In *The Country of a Thousand Years of Peace*, *Water Street*, *Nights and Days*, and *The Fire Screen*, he had referred to the four elements braved in the book which followed them. (*Divine Comedies* extends it one realm further.)

The elements thus braved resurface in *Scripts for the Pageant*, only now they have been elevated into a quartet of angelic essences. "Samos," the magnificent canzone at the heart of that volume, weaves a pattern of the "Promised Land" out of the elements and our ability to engage them; the poem's five recurrent end words are "water," "light," "fire," "land," and "sense" (*Scripts for the Pageant*). If there is a teleology at work here—if "sense" somehow leads to "ascents"—one way to measure it is by reference to the poet's progressively more successful attempts at prolonging his brief encounters with those divinely appointed messengers who came at first unbidden and eventually by way of response to his conscious summons. Perhaps the most extraordinary change in Merrill's poetry since *Divine Comedies* is its scale, its epic extension of a lyric impulse; by dint of an arduous soul-making, vessel-breaking progress, Merrill has managed to sustain the epiphanies that had previously proved as delicate and evanescent as Walter Pater's privileged moments or those of Stephen Dedalus.

It had always seemed an implicit truth in Merrill's poetry that the god's incarnation must be followed by his withdrawal. Hence, in works preparatory to "The Book of Ephraim"—in the past that serves as prologue—the ecstatic occasion is tinged with regret at its imminent loss. Beauty, as Stevens put it, is momentary in the mind; the word "moments" occurs no fewer than three times in the nine lines of "A Dedication." Alas, the poet seems to lament, the vision cannot endure—to paraphrase Auden, it does not seriously intend to stay; more exactly, we can endure it only briefly.

Yet even in defeat the poet takes away such knowledge as heralds future victory.

"Charles on Fire" comes close to making a parable from the (necessarily) interrupted vision, the blaze of brightness that blinds the viewer back into the cave but, once seen, ignites the determination to gain a return match, to stage a second showing. The poem records precisely the sort of epiphany Pater had in mind when he wrote, in *The Renaissance*: "A sudden light transfigures a trivial thing, a weathervane, a windmill, a winnowing flail, the dust in the barn door; a moment—and the thing has vanished, because it was pure effect; but it leaves a relish behind it, a longing that the accident may happen again." Like "A Narrow Escape" (*The Country of a Thousand Years of Peace and Other Poems*), "Charles on Fire" has a *Symposium* setting—somewhat ironically, given the wise man's reticence at dinner's end. By the time of *Scripts*, the party will have grown into a full-fledged banquet, an ongoing and movable feast that numbers Plato himself among the gregarious "guest-hosts"; but here we are granted only an isolated moment of illumination bracketed by darkness. In a second respect as well, "Charles on Fire" resembles "A Narrow Escape" and the seven other poems Merrill published in 1954 under the title *Short Stories*: it tells a tale in little, claiming the stuff of short fiction for the province of verse, just as "The Book of Ephraim" would later perform the functions of a novel. I quote the poem in full:

> Another evening we sprawled about discussing
> Appearances. And it was the consensus
> That while uncommon physical good looks
> Continued to launch one, as before, in life
> (Among its vaporous eddies and false calms),
> Still, as one of us said into his beard,
> "Without your intellectual and spiritual
> Values, man, you are sunk." No one but squared
> The shoulders of his own unloveliness.
> Long-suffering Charles, having cooked and served the meal,
> Now brought out little tumblers finely etched
> He filled with amber liquor and then passed.
> "Say," said the same young man, "in Paris, France,
> They do it this way"—bounding to his feet
> And touching a lit match to our host's full glass.
> A blue flame, gentle, beautiful, came, went
> Above the surface. In a hush that fell
> We heard the vessel crack. The contents drained
> As who should step down from a crystal coach.
> Steward of spirits, Charles's glistening hand
> All at once gloved itself in eeriness.

> The moment passed. He made two quick sweeps and
> Was flesh again. "It couldn't matter less,"
> He said, but with a shocked, unconscious glance
> Into the mirror. Finding nothing changed,
> He filled a fresh glass and sank down among us.

In "little tumblers finely etched" and "filled with amber liquor," the poet's alter ego serves up a trope for poetry, for that kind of poetic making whose desired end is the burnished artifact, frozen in its elegance, into which go a few rare and expensive drops of "spirits." It is a poetry that keeps up appearances; and, in the sense of "physical good looks," "appearances" are what the after-dinner conversation turns to. At one time, we learn, these may have sufficed, as the delicate objet d'art might once have satisfied its maker. Indeed, the group agrees, uncommonly handsome physiognomy might still be said "to launch one." At this point in the poem, Merrill instinctively renews the somnolent metaphor in "launch": having been christened, having had the queen break a bottle on his hull, the initiate is now sailing somewhat against the current, through the "vaporous eddies and false calms"—the misleading appearances of calm—that are all that stand between him and turbulent waters. The figure is extended in the beat diction of the bearded young man, who issues a crucial proviso: "Without your intellectual and spiritual / Values, man, you are sunk." Both *sunk* and *man*, the two slang words in the statement, work overtime. Looks might launch the man, but staying afloat is a "spiritual" matter.

No sooner has our host poured the liquor than the same young man—ironically, since he has been the one to insist upon the "spiritual" side of things—takes a sudden interest in appearances and fashion, flaming the brandy as is done "in Paris, France." (A lovely touch, naming the country conveys a sense of the speaker's innocence and enthusiasm; he has the arrogance of youth—of one who has only recently been "launched.") His action results in an appearance of a wholly unexpected kind, an emblem of the angelic realm; in lieu of a toast, there is a divine hush:

> A blue flame, gentle, beautiful, came, went
> Above the surface. In a hush that fell
> We heard the vessel crack. The contents drained
> As who should step down from a crystal coach.

These lines do more than conduct us to the story's denouement. If, in the poem's terms, the sea represents that element of flux upon which our material lives toss and turn, fire is the agency of the spirit, of all that "couldn't matter less." Dancing "Above the surface," the "blue flame" comes as a revelation; it has all the attributes of an epiphany, that is, a flashing forth of divinity, of darkness made visible. Extending the poem's sailing metaphor, the "blue flame" also suggests the bluish aura or glow visible around the masts of a ship during an electrical disturbance: the phenomenon known as St. Elmo's Fire, after the patron saint of sailors. The ship in question is no longer seaworthy, however; it has metamorphosed into an altogether different sort of vessel, one that cannot weather the storm. The glass, though it collaborated with the flames and the brandy to make the epiphany possible, can neither survive the moment nor contain it. The glass cracks; the fire that purifies destroys. But in its flickering instant a social occasion has turned into a religious mystery, as physical appearances have given way to a spiritual apparition. From circumstances that must, at least at first, seem unlikely, Merrill has extracted "the makings of a miracle," in Elizabeth Bishop's phrase; from the milieu of manners, he has derived the forms of ritual and ceremony so dear to him because they connect the realms of art and of spirit. And if, as a result, the host's serving of "spirits" may be taken as a trope for the poetic process, it is the vessel-shattering flame that has turned an inconsequential anecdote into a parable.

Harold Bloom has demonstrated that, as found in the doctrine of the Lurianic Kabbalah, the theme of the cracking of vessels furnishes an antecedent myth for the literary artist's "breaking of forms," an account of creation that the secondary or "belated" artist must reenact. According to the Kabbalah, God first created "*kelim*, 'vessels', of which the culminating vessel was *Adam Kadmon* or primal Man." But the creative light was too strong, or the vessels too fragile, for the majority of them shattered instantly to pieces. It is axiomatic—the very products of holy energy cannot contain it, cannot stay whole. Fortunately, by stages one can grow to absorb such heavenly light as, in its original force, cannot but burst the beholder, splintering his vision as if it were no sturdier than a child's eyeglasses lying smashed and forlorn on a worn gymnasium cinderpath. Creation can be restored, the dispersed light gathered, only by a process of restitution that, in Bloom's words, calls for "acts of meditation, acts that lift up and so liberate the fallen sparks of God from their imprisonment in the shards of the *kelippot* [broken vessels of evil]." That these acts of meditation are "at once psychic and linguistic," that "defense mechanisms and rhetorical tropes" accomplish the work of restitution, hammers home (for Bloom) the pertinence of the analogy for an understanding of poetic creation. It would be impossible, in so brief a summary, to do justice to Bloom's reasoning. But even as I have sketchily described it, the myth of blinding light, broken receptacles, and redemptive meditation cannot fail to illuminate a vital aspect of "Charles on Fire" and the tendency it exemplifies in Merrill's poetry.

Indeed, whether or not the allusion lay beyond the poet's conscious intention, "Charles on Fire" seems invested with a knowledge of kabbalistic doctrine. Just as "God's name was too strong for his words" and therefore smashed the *kelim*, so here the "blue flame" shatters one of the "little tumblers finely etched"; just as the divine sparks of light disperse, so here the "contents" drain from the glass. The destruction is holy nevertheless, for it yields the glimpse of an angelic presence, "As who should step down from a crystal coach." The very syntax of this royal simile recalls the moment of Merrill's first angelic encounter:

> . . . an angel steps
> Into the mind, as kings into the dress
> Of a poor goatherd, for their acts of charity.

The visitation has taken place, however unseemly the circumstances, and it has swiftly made itself felt. Precisely where the vessel has cracked, a lane to the spiritual realm has opened—we remember that these lines from Auden's "As I Walked Out One Evening" occur in the "Quotations" section of "The Book of Ephraim":

> The glacier knocks in the cupboard,
> The desert sighs in the bed,
> And the crack in the tea-cup opens
> A lane to the land of the dead.

Now Charles, "Steward of spirits" in both senses, experiences a momentary transfiguration, even as he resumes his duties as host; preparatory to sweeping up the spilled "contents," his "glistening hand" has "gloved itself in eeriness," has added an invisible layer to his skin. Only for a moment, to be sure: and it passes, as the flame itself "came, went," pausing only for the length of a comma. The change in Charles does not survive "a shocked, unconscious glance / Into the mirror," which confirms our host's return to flesh and to the world of looks and appearances; the other "host," the sacred guest, has departed, if he was ever there—he existed by intimation alone, by the proxy work of a simile. And now, with the conclusion of the poem, the metaphor of shipwreck is brought to port: "He filled a fresh glass and sank down among us."

I have analyzed "Charles on Fire" in such detail not only because Merrill's intricate conceits demand and reward the closest possible attention but because this paradigmatic epiphany mirrors so many of the concerns and habits we encounter in the trilogy. There, as here, the consuming wish to entertain the angels (in the additional sense of entertaining an idea) is as fundamental as Merrill's penchant for elevating social gestures, parlor games, apparent accidents, even a guest's gaucheries, into acts and activities of mystical significance, performed, pondered, repeated as rituals, as invitations extended to the divine unknown. Thus from figures on wallpaper, demoniac beings spring to imaginative life; thus a photocopying machine can supply the requisite mirror and flash of light that, in an ironic update of Proust's memory triggers, bring spirits rushing to the scene. Nor does the question of appearances go away after "Charles on Fire." Merrill is still asking it in the celestial context of *Mirabell*: "Will it ever, ever solve itself, / This riddle of appearances in Heaven?" "This riddle," which can be solved by paradox alone, refigures the diners' dilemma in "Charles on Fire"; it revises that poem's gloomy conclusion on the uneasy relations between spirit and corporeal form. How, JM wonders during one of the early lessons, can his bodiless tutors be said to resemble the bats on his wallpaper? His skepticism merits an "A PLUS" from the spirit of Maria Mitsotáki, who exposes "THE FICTION THAT THEY HAVE APPEARANCES THEY DO NOT." Nevertheless, though he exists "in the realm of no appearances," JM's favorite bat promptly turns into a peacock and manifests himself as such. From "Charles on Fire," whose mirror signaled a failed metamorphosis, we have arrived at a place where mirrors—and where the mind's mirrorlike systems of reflection and speculation—enable spirits to "appear," allow contact to be made with them, and can even revamp bat into peacock, "741" into foppish "Mirabell," a number into a name.

In the journey of his making, the Merrill of *Nights and Days* seems in retrospect to have been governed by Hölderlin's wistful observation (in "Brod und Wein"):

> Denn nicht immer vermag ein schwaches Gefäs sie zu fassen,
> Nur zu Zeiten erträgt göttliche Fülle der Mensch.

> [For not always can a frail vessel contain them,
> Only from time to time can man bear the plenty of the gods.]

But he has also learned that he must endure—and more, he must work to bring about—the shattering of vessels, the *shevirah hakelim*, before he can embark upon those redemptive acts of meditation that will restore his blissful seat at "the angelic secretariat." He will have to subject to a visionary blaze the vessels of his craft; he will have to stretch to the breaking point the sculptured verse forms that resemble "little tumblers finely etched." In the books that lead up to *Mirabell* and *Scripts for the Pageant*, Merrill has taken just this course. His poetry seems to have burst out of contours lovingly etched; the forms he has mastered he shatters, and out of a gathering of splinters a new heavenly order has emerged. It is surely appropriate that the epigraph of *Scripts* contains a reference to the delicate glass the groom must shatter with his foot during the Jewish wedding ceremony: for the climax of that book occurs when JM and DJ, scribe and hand, break a mirror in order to release the imprisoned spirits of Auden and Maria. It is also to the point that the word "break," in conjugated or participial form, recurs throughout *Mirabell* and more than once signals an actual break in the flow of words, a rupture between verb and object. Two examples:

> Broken—for good?—of its imperious
> Slashing at capitals, our cup points out
> A gentler dictum . . .

And, two pages earlier, in an italicized letter addressed to DJ:

> *How about breaking (remember*
> *that old dream?) the trip with a glimpse of Stonehenge*
> *& Avebury?*

It is a rupture, we learn, that necessitates the surgery DJ must undergo. He had suffered it when—no accident!—he carried up some flights of stairs the immense Victorian mirror that proved indispensable to the Ouija ceremony; the pain of the breakage constitutes the cost, for him, of admission to the celestial seminars. JM, for his part, has been told he will have an "ARTISTIC BREAKTHRU." But inevitably the message containing this prophecy or promise itself "Breaks off. Is broken off," mid-sentence, before the speaker could complete the thought. Some sort of fragmentation must, it seems, precede or accompany a vision of unity. After all, the author of "The Broken Home" was also, and first, the product of one. No accident: there is a special providence in the fall of a sparrow—or in the breaking of a trance, a limb, a code, a home. "Nothing can be sole or whole," said Crazy Jane to the Bishop, "that has not been rent."

Of this pattern Merrill's story "Peru: The Landscape Game" takes charming notice. An account of a trip to Peru, the story was conceived and composed *before* the trip took place, in the writer's effort to provide proof against disappointment, anticipatory imaginings to compensate for the inadequacies of actuality. The story's generative conceit is "that psychological game in which each person describes a house he then leaves in order to take an imaginary walk. One by one he discovers a key, a bowl, a body of water, a wild creature, and finally a wall. Free association is invited at any stage, and nothing explained until the last player has spoken." What kind of bowl springs to Merrill's mind as, the night before flying to Lima, he plays the game? Not golden but a "mixing bowl,

cracked—fearing botulism, I kick it out of my path." A humorous translation of the line occurs a page later, in this exchange:

> "What was it your bowl meant?" K yawned, up in the room.

> "I'm a good mixer. But liable to go to pieces."

In the Jungian code the story proposes as an interpretive key, the bowl
stands for Art.

JUDITH MOFFETT

"The Changing Light at Sandover"

Then Sky alone is left, a hundred blue
Fragments in revolution, with no clue
To where a Niche will open. Quite a task,
Putting together Heaven, yet we do.

—From "Lost in Translation"

I have received from whom I do not know
These letters. Show me, light, if they make sense.

—From "From the Cupola"

The *Changing Light at Sandover* is Merrill's grandest achievement. Into its more than five hundred pages has gone everything he knows about writing poetry, everything he believes about living among other people in the world, all his deepest-held values, fears, convictions, and prejudices, spread among passages of "revelation" spelled out on a Ouija board. Not everyone will wish, or know how, to approach that sort of book, and not everyone who approaches will feel welcome; the material takes getting used to. But many readers may well feel they have been waiting for this trilogy all their lives.

Beginning about 1955, when Merrill and his friend and lover David Jackson first moved to Stonington, they often diverted themselves with a Ouija board—a commercially manufactured one at first, later a larger one homemade from cardboard. A Ouija board, as described in

From *James Merrill; An Introduction to the Poetry*, edited by Judith Moffett. Copyright © 1984 by Columbia University Press.

The Seraglio (where Francis Tanning grew addicted to the use of one) is "a smooth wooden board on which had been printed the alphabet, the Arabic numerals, and the words YES and NO. At the top was the likeness of a female face, Oriental in spirit, lit from beneath: she peered down into a crystal ball wherein misty letters had materialized." The board is used to get in touch with the "spirit world"; the mortals below ask questions, the spirits reply by spelling out messages with a pointer on which each player allows the fingers of one hand to rest lightly. (Instead of the planchette that comes with a bought board, Merrill and Jackson preferred the handle of an inverted teacup.)

　　Some pairs of players, without consciously controlling the pointer, get very much livelier results than others do; and for a time JM and DJ (in the board's shorthand) made a regular parlor game of *their* extraordinary ability to summon the souls of the dead. Both the temporarily and permanently dead—for they were instructed in the rudiments of a cosmology whereby souls are reborn until advanced enough to embark upon the nine Stages of heavenly progression. The two grew ever more fascinated with the phenomenon; as to what it meant they remained in the dark. But the game had its disquieting, not to say sinister, aspects. Where in fact *were* these messages coming from? *Should* the whole affair have become so seductive that for a time DJ and JM found themselves living more within the spirit world than in their own? A poem in *The Country of a Thousand Years of Peace*, "Voices from the Other World" (written in 1955), describes how, finally, they began to call upon the spirits less often "Because, once looked at lit/ By the cold reflections of the dead . . ./ Our lives had never seemed more full, more real. . . ." But the board continued to play a background role in their lives, and eventually the substance of twenty years' irregular conversation with one favorite voice became the basis of "The Book of a Thousand and One Evenings Spent/ With David Jackson at the Ouija Board/ In Touch with Ephraim Our Familiar Spirit."

　　The Book of Ephraim appeared as the greater part of *Divine Comedies*, in 1976. *Mirabell* followed in 1978 and *Scripts for the Pageant* in 1980; these three Books, plus a Coda, make up the trilogy published in one volume in 1982 under the collective title *The Changing Light at Sandover*. *Ephraim* covers the decades between 1955 and 1974. The second and third Books and the Coda document another obsessive involvement with the board lasting roughly from June 1976 into late 1978, and need to be considered separately from *Ephraim* for several reasons. Not reasons of style: the entire trilogy displays the same wit, formal skills, economy, and lyric power as the very best of Merrill's previous work. Nor of overt theme:

all were originally undertaken as a warning against nuclear disaster. But *Ephraim* was composed and published, in *Divine Comedies*, with no thought of anything to follow. In manner of composition it resembles the shorter narrative poems of that volume multiplied by ten or twelve. The varied experiences with the Ouija world have been thoroughly interpenetrated in *Ephraim* with the rich whole of the poet's life, and with the sea-changes of twenty years' unconscious ripening, to emerge in "timeskip and gadabout" form as a lengthier counterpart of "Lost in Translation" or "Chimes for Yahya." Time, and the material, had even allowed for a certain amount of manipulation and invention, improvements for the poem's sake on the literal truth.

Mirabell and *Scripts*, and the Coda, were composed very differently. A routine chat with the spirits, after Ephraim's book had been completed, was abruptly intruded upon one day by dread powers bringing JM a daunting new assignment: "UNHEEDFUL ONE   3 OF YOUR YEARES MORE WE WANT   WE MUST HAVE POEMS OF SCIENCE   THE WEORK FINISHT IS BUT A PROLOGUE." Having impulsively accepted this charge, Merrill then found himself obliged to give up enormous amounts of time—his own and David Jackson's—to daily sessions of transcribing dictation at the board, struggling to make sense of it, and later tossing the messages lightly with details from his and DJ's ongoing lives as he drafted the POEMS OF SCIENCE he had been commissioned to create. The result is that while *Ephraim* reads like the rest of Merrill's work only more so, the other two Books progress by fairly (*Mirabell*) or rigidly (*Scripts*) chronological schemes to set forth material Merrill has not himself consciously chosen: a bizarre creation myth involving, among other things, Atlantan centaurs and huge radioactive bats which are at once both "life-size" earthly creatures and subatomic particles; four angels who conduct a seminar; and much gossip, often licentious, about the famous dead.

Though the assignment absorbs and enthralls the two mediums in time, Jackson initially reacts to it with fear and Merrill with dismay ("Poems of *science?* Ugh."). The poet makes an effort, a successful one, to talk himself round:

> Not for nothing had the Impressionists
> Put subject-matter in its place, a mere
> Pretext for iridescent atmosphere.
> Why couldn't Science, in the long run, serve
> As well as one's uncleared lunch-table or
> *Mme X en Culotte de Matador?*

This is no new line of thought for Merrill, who had always liked opera's emphasis on sound over sense, and that of French art songs, and who

quotes Andrew Marvell in *Scripts* (from Heaven) as saying "THE LINE! LET
IT RUN TAUT & FLEXIBLE/ BETWEEN THE TWO POLES OF RHYTHM AND RHYME/ &
WHAT YOU HANG ON IT MAY BE AS DULL/ OR AS PROVOCATIVE AS LAUNDRY."
But the argument had always served *his* ends before—that is, he could cite
it when he wanted to safeguard a subject with lyrical obscurity. Nowhere
does *Mirabell* sound merely dutiful in the writing, but parts—the bat's
numerology, above all—are plainly thrust upon a reluctant poet whose
choice of material when writing *Ephraim* had been free. And both *Mirabell*
and *Scripts* tax the mediums with doctrine that—at least at first—offends
them: the No Accident clause, the elitism clause, the prophecy of a
"thinning" to come. Two shades—W. H. Auden and Maria Mitsotáki—
are permitted to assist in their instruction, which makes the project more
appealing, and much of their resistance eventually evaporates. Still, when
Auden blandly urges Merrill "ON WITH THE WORK! THRILLING FOR YOU JM,"
the younger poet retorts:

> And maddening—it's all by someone else!
> In your voice, Wystan, or in Mirabell's.
> I want it mine, but cannot spare those twenty
> Years in a cool dark place that *Ephraim* took
> In order to be palatable wine.
> This book by contrast, immature, supine,
> Still kicks against its archetypal cradle . . .
>
> I'd set
> My whole heart, after *Ephraim,* on returning
> To private life, to my own words, Instead,
> Here I go again, a vehicle
> In this cosmic carpool. Mirabell once said
> He taps my word banks. I'd be happier
> If *I* were tapping them. Or thought I were.

But the case is easily overstated. While *Ephraim* has been shaped at
the center of Merrill's singular art and self in some sense that the other
two Books were not, these can hardly be said to be *all* by someone else.
The given subject matter determines the direction of the narrative; the
daily transcriptions force a structure upon it. But in and about these
Lessons is ample room for Merrill to say how he feels about it all, to talk
with David, pay calls, travel between Stonington and New York, Athens,
California, and one way and another—shocked, alarmed, distressed, over-
joyed, stimulated by what comes across the board—to reveal a great deal
about his sense of the meanings of his life. Merrill has described "the way
the material came" in an interview: "Not through flashes of insight,
wordplay, trains of thought" in the ordinary manner of poetic composition

(and, overall, of *Ephraim*), "More like what a friend, or stranger, might say over a telephone. DJ and I never knew until it had been spelled out letter by letter. What I felt about the material became a natural part of the poem, corresponding to those earlier poems written 'all by myself.' "

It was expected that he edit the transcripts, recast the passages to be used into meters assigned to the various speakers, and polish the whole into something that would read smoothly. Sometimes this meant quite a lot of work, sometimes almost none; as DJ describes it:

> I was freer to enjoy the whole experience with the dictation than JM was. . . . great passages of it that I thought were just ravishingly beautiful, Jimmy was seeing as useless to the text, or a little too much of a good thing. And it must have been maddening for him to think that he couldn't, you know, improve upon something that was very nice; sometimes it already fitted into his syllabic scheme.

But the sense of being driven to the task was unrelenting:

> They dictated it. All of the *Scripts*—it was very much a regimen. . . . We had to do it—it started in on this cycle talking about time and the series of moon cycles. We had to get this given amount done in them, and we had to come back at this given moment. They were precise about their schedules, as they were about when the poem would be finished, when it would be published, everything.

Merrill's own sense of how he "Quarried murky blocks/ Of revelation" from the transcripts to build the second Book is described early in the third:

> *Mirabell*—by now more Tower of Babel
>
> Than Pyramid—groans upward, step by step.
> I think to make each Book's first word its number
> In a different language
> (Five is *go* in Japanese), then stop
>
> Sickened by these blunt stabs at "design."
> Another morning, Michael's very sun
> Glows from within the section
> I polish, whose deep grain is one with mine.

Of the three Books, *Mirabell* seems in one way to have been the most difficult to write. As the poet has described it:

> With "Ephraim," many of the transcripts I had made from Ouija board sessions had vanished, or hadn't been saved. So I mainly used whatever came to hand, except for the high points which I'd copied out over the years into a special notebook. Those years—time itself— did my winnowing

for me. With *Mirabell* it was, to put it mildly, harder. The transcript was enormous. What you see in the poem might be half, or two-fifths, of the original. Most of the cuts were repetitions: things said a second or third time, in new ways often, to make sure we'd understood. Or further, unnecessary illustrations of a point. . . .

    With *Scripts*, there was no shaping to be done. Except for the minutest changes, and deciding about line-breaks and so forth, the Lessons you see on the page appear just as we took them down. The doggerel at the fêtes, everything. In between the Lessons—our chats with Wystan or Robert [Morse] or Uni [the trilogy's resident unicorn]—I still felt free to pick and choose; but even there, the design of the book just swept me along.

Increasingly the great labor grew compatible, even joyous, till Merrill could acknowledge that while writing *Scripts* "I woke up day after day beaming with anticipation."

    Though he recoiled from the word, so mammoth a poem could not be managed without "design." The Ouija board itself provided the basic frame of each Book: one section for every letter of the alphabet in *Ephraim*, which covers a calendar year; one (with decimal subdivisions) for each number from 0 to 9 in the book of number-happy *Mirabell*; and a set of Lessons for the three major divisions—YES (ten), & (five), and NO (ten)—of *Scripts*, a fit scheme for that monument to ambiguity, corresponding to the plot's electric plusses and minuses, Whites and Blacks. A proliferation of voices from the Other World made further device imperative if the work were not to become hopelessly confusing. Merrill solved the principal problem (with help from WHA) in *Mirabell* 7.9: rough pentameter, "our virtual birthright," for the human characters living and dead; and for the bats, who think in fourteens, "WHY NOT MY BOY SYLLABICS? LET THE CASE/ REPRESENT A FALL FROM METRICAL GRACE." Five stresses by fourteen syllables, of course, borrows from the internal yardstick of the dyed-in-the-wool sonneteer. In *Scripts* a unicorn/ centaur speaks a fair imitation of four-stress Anglo-Saxon alliterative meter. Greater powers—God, Nature, the angels—are bound to no metrical pattern and never use rhyme (apart from certain ceremonial occasions, and from Archangel Michael's clumsy couplet-making). Nor do the bats rhyme; but the humans often fall into couplets or stanzas as if for comfort. Tag phrases distinguish the many upper-case human voices from one another: "MY BOYS" or "MY DEARS" for Auden, "MES ENFANTS" for Maria, "MES CHERS" for Ephraim, "LADS" (and baby talk) for Robert Morse, only George Cotzias calls DJ "DAVE," and so on. The variations of the effortlessly coalescing and dissolving lyric passages are too numerous to list; and if the middle distance of *Mirabell* does sometimes display what Helen Vendler tolerantly calls "a sheer willingness to bore," the verse of the trilogy's hundreds of pages consistently outdazzles everything critics can think to say about it.

II

As the foregoing should make clear, *Mirabell* and *Scripts* are the unforged record of a lived experience; for the nature of their "revelation" Merrill cannot, in the ordinary sense, be held accountable. By the terms of his commission he may—indeed must—paraphrase, condense, question, even criticize, as well as change prose to poetry. But he is not to decide which ideas to keep and which to exclude: is not to censor, embellish, nor in any way distort the *sense* of the revealed text. Thus restricted, he can take no more responsibility for its nature than John Constable could for the concepts of *cow* or *hundred-year-old oak* when he set out to paint the landscapes of East Anglia. Actually, the material revealed was such as to plague JM with skepticism (and DJ with fear) through much of the work. The first transcriptions strike them respectively as preposterous and terrifying; their harmless parlor game has changed character so drastically, in fact, that the question of *belief*—easily shrugged off in *Ephraim*—now reasserts itself again and again. To Auden's rhapsodizing in *Mirabell* 2, Merrill replies in exasperated couplets:

> Dear Wystan, VERY BEAUTIFUL all this
> Warmed-up Milton, Dante, Genesis?
> This great tradition that has come to grief
> In volumes by Blavatsky and Gurdjieff?
> Von and Torro in their Star Trek capes,
> Atlantis, UFO's, God's chosen apes—?
> Nobody could transfigure stuff like that
> Without first turning down the rheostat
> To Allegory, in whose gloom the whole
> Horror of Popthink fastens on the soul,
> Harder to scrape off than bubblegum. . . .
>
> I say we very much don't merit these
> Unverifiable epiphanies.

As the experience continues, appalling and ravishing him by turns, Merrill's doubts trouble him less and less, and near the end of *Scripts* his assent has become all but total:

> Beneath my incredulity
>> All at once is flowing
> Joy, the flash of the unbaited hook—
> *Yes, yes, it fits, it's right, it had to be!*
> Intuition weightless and ongoing
>> Like stanzas in a book
> Or golden scales in the melodic brook—

Readers, of course, may more easily believe in Merrill's riveting experience than in the divine authenticity of its source, or the truth of its prophecy. "For me," Merrill has said himself (of *Mirabell*), "the talk and the tone—along with the elements of plot—are the candy coating. The pill itself"—the poem's apocalyptic message, its insistence on determination and elitism—"is another matter. The reader who can't swallow it has my full sympathy. I've choked on it again and again." His own sense, illustrated by the quotation, of his role of Poet as distinct from his role of Scribe is a distinction readers should bear in mind. Thinking of the two roles as Mind Conscious and Unconscious is one very workable way of reading the poem—as if all of *The Changing Light at Sandover* were an inexhaustibly elaborate dialogue between Merrill's waking intelligence and its own unconscious sources of feeling, myth, and dream, with David Jackson as essential catalyst (and supplemental unconscious story-trove).

DJ himself reports that, to the engrossed mediums, "Whether all that dictation came out of our collective subconscious or not finally became less and less of real interest. Rather as if a flying saucer were to land on one's front lawn, would one ask, 'Where's it *from?*' as one's first question?" Readers unable or unwilling to fight clear of this question of source, or the related one "What does it mean?" risk spoiling their initial plunge into the trilogy's elemental weirdness—needlessly, because its Message and its meaning are not the same. Large tracts of Message— Mirabell's mathematical formulas, kernels of concept that refuse to crack, Lessons that often seem pure pretext for extravagant spectacle, parts of the System no sooner grasped at last than made pointless by revision—will certainly frustrate an approach to the poem which is too doggedly literal. *The Changing Light at Sandover* is, and expects to be read as, an immensely complex Overmetaphor packed more tightly with lesser metaphors within metaphors than a plutonium atom is with atomic particles. It's best to assume that what doesn't seem to make literal sense right away makes dramatic or metaphorical sense, or none that matters intellectually. "MAKE SENSE OF IT" Merrill is told and told in *Scripts*; but why should the sense wanted be merely verbal? As Vendler has noted, "Merrill's primary intuition is that of the absolute ravishment of the senses"—those senses restored to the dead souls only at the highest heavenly Stage, and (in "YES" Lesson 7) identified one by one with the very angels. Musical and visual sense is the sort to look for in a baffling passage, like seeing a very fine operatic adaptation of *Dracula* sung in a foreign language.

Many years ago, Merrill wrote in "To a Butterfly," "Goodness, how tired one grows/ Just looking through a prism:/ Allegory, symbolism./ I've tried, Lord knows,// To keep from seeing double. . . ." Now in *Mirabell* he addresses the radioactive bats intemperately:

> How should you speak? Speak without metaphor.
> Help me to drown the double-entry book
> I've kept these fifty years. You want from me
> Science at last, instead of tapestry—
> Then tell round what brass tacks the old silk frays.
> Stop trying to have everything both ways.
> It's too much to be batwing angels *and*
> Inside the atom, don't you understand?

But truly the bats can speak no other way: "we get an effect of engines being/ Gunned in frustration, blasts of sheer exhaust." (This passage is one of those exceptionally easy to read as an argument between conscious Poet, who thinks he ought not to depend so heavily on metaphor, and unconscious Scribe, who knows himself unalterably addicted to it.) Only toward the end of *Scripts* does Merrill gratefully allow Auden to persuade him that metaphor-making can itself be a form of freedom, that (as WHA has already asserted, late in *Mirabell*) "FACT IS IS IS FABLE":

> But if it's all a fable
> Involving, oh, the stable and unstable
> Particles, mustn't we at last wipe clean
> The blackboard of these creatures and their talk,
> To render in a hieroglyph of chalk
> The formulas they stood for?   U   MY BOY
> ARE THE SCRIBE   YET WHY: WHY MAKE A JOYLESS THING
> OF IT THROUGH SUCH REDUCTIVE REASONING?
> ONCE HAVING TURNED A FLITTING SHAPE OF BLACK
> TO MIRABELL, WD YOU MAKE TIME FLOW BACK?
> SUBTRACT FROM HIS OBSESSION WITH 14
> THE SHINING/DIMMING, PHASES OF OUR QUEEN?
> CONDEMN POOR UNI TO THE CYCLOTRON
> AFTER THE GREENS U'VE LET HIM GALLOP ON?
> Dear Wystan, thank you for reminding me
> The rock I'm chained to is a cloud; I'm free.

Like the elements of the sonnet form, metaphor is in Merrill's marrow-bone. And to speak of it thus returns us full circle to the perceptions that took shape in his Amherst honors thesis and in *First Poems*: that earliest perception of metaphor as ice, sheeting the black abyss, making pain bearable, and of the thin blue eggshell of appearance with the tiny dead claw broken through. From that cracked robin's egg to "THE WHOLE FRAIL EGGSHELL" of the Earth "SIMPLY IMPLODING AS THE MONITOR'S/BLACK FILLS THE VACUUM MOTHER N ABHORS" is but a step thirty years in length.

When it appeared as part of *Divine Comedies*, *The Book of Ephraim* had seemed about ready to put masks by, as if Merrill at last had found a way to make his peace symbolically with *this* world's reality by forswearing the spirit world for good. But Poet has a way of insisting on resolutions to which Scribe has not assented. The oedipal fire supposedly extinguished by Francis Tanning in *The Seraglio* blazed on, and metaphor has cheerfully persisted in doubling Merrill's vision despite the wish voiced twenty years before *Mirabell* in "To a Butterfly." And now, with the publication of *From the First Nine* and *The Changing Light at Sandover*, in two volumes, the import of *Ephraim* has been shifted; we are directed to consider it not as the last and most complex work along one line of development but as the first and simplest on another. It is, of course, both—and ought rightly to be printed last in the first volume as well as first in the second.

Renounce the Other World, spiritual metaphor and twin of this "one we feel is ours, and call the real . . ."? Strip the real world, never so loved as now, of her thin gold mask at last? Not if the Powers that decide such matters have anything to say about it—and in fact They have found all this to say.

III

And so the old themes whose conflicts *Divine Comedies* had seemed to resolve burst forth again, their vigor all restored, in *Mirabell* and *Scripts for the Pageant*. Literally, those resolutions were true enough. But some of the themes had shaped Merrill's outlook in profound psychological ways all his life, just as they had been shaped *by* his life. They are evidently not to be cast off merely because their actualizing source in life is neutralized. Now, though, the scale is grander and the mode transcendent, for none of them—masking and illusion, passion and sexuality, parents, aging, childlessness—need be life-size or earthbound any longer.

The spirits continually reaffirm that there are no appearances in Heaven; they can see JM and DJ in mirrors, and whatever their mortal "representatives" see, but never one another. The meaning of *mask* in such a realm cannot be literal, yet masking of many kinds, and the pretense of sparkling appearances, are perpetual; should this trilogy ever be adapted for the stage with skill it should play splendidly, but the costume budget would need to be generous beyond dreams. The whole poem is constructed of deceptions-for-a-purpose, successively unveiled as the mediums become able to tolerate what they will hear. Often the purpose is dramatic: quarrels between angels, rehearsed and staged to drive the Lesson home, or two characters finally revealed to be one and the same. Heavenly doctrine gets revised like drafts of a poem; Ephraim makes mistakes corrected by Mirabell, who must be corrected in his turn. The numerous pageants, fêtes, and masques overlay the revelation of "the Black" with imaginary spectacle as the schematic order of instruction overlays the revelation of Chaos—gilt or ice above the void. And much about Heaven remains permanently hidden, unfathomable.

But no secrecy now obtains between these mediums and us; and the sense of their shared life realized here forms a powerful chemical bond between reader and poem, tiding us over the "stretches of flats in the exposition of the mythology." JM and DJ began together as lovers, and the "FORTUNATE CONJUNCTION" (as Ephraim calls their partnership) has withstood the stresses of Athens and Santa Fe. Passion was the keynote of Merrill's life and of his art when he and DJ first got through to Ephraim, or he to them, and continued to be its keynote for another twenty years. But, by the mid-seventies, radical social changes had affected that part of his life at the same time it was being reclaimed by trustier, less violent loves. *The Book of Ephraim* makes abundantly clear that their familiar shares, and rejoices in, his mediums' homosexuality. No more now of that sickness of self felt in "After the Fire"; nothing of the obsessive "dirt-caked" and "dirty-minded" talk New Mexico had produced. Strato himself is vividly evoked in *Ephraim*, in terms that recall that "animal nature" passage of "Chimes for Yahya":

> Strato squats within the brilliant zero,
> Craning at his bare shoulder where a spot
> Burns "like fire" invisible to me.
> Thinking what? he studies his fair skin
> So smooth, so hairless . . .
>
>   Strato's qualities
> All are virtues back in '64.
> Humor that breaks into an easy lope
> Of evasion my two poor legs cannot hope
> To keep up with. Devotion absolute
> Moments on end, till some besetting itch
> Galvanizes him, or a stray bitch.

(This being seldom in my line to feel,
I most love those for whom the world is real.)
Shine of light green eyes, enthusiasm
Panting and warm across the kindly chasm.
Also, when I claim a right not written
Into our bond, that bristling snap of fear. . . .

Some of the funniest lines in *Mirabell* are "spoken" by Auden's widow
Chester Kallman, who complains about how Auden treats him in Heaven,
about a fickle heavenly lover, about the life in Johannesburg into which
he is about to be reborn—all in a style suggesting that the subject of
homosexuality and the gay world, off the leash at last, went slightly mad
with unconfinement:

> But you're coming back,
> It's too exciting! PLEASE TO SEE MY BLACK
> FACE IN A GLASS DARKLY? I WON'T BE
> WHITE WONT BE A POET WONT BE QUEER
> CAN U CONCEIVE OF LIFE WITHOUT THOSE 3???
> Well, frankly, yes. THE MORE FOOL U MY DEAR
> You shock us, Chester. After months of idle,
> Useless isolation— ALL I HEAR
> ARE THESE B MINOR HYMNS TO USEFULNESS:
> LITTLE MISS BONAMI OOH SO GLAD
> TO FIND ARCADIA IN A BRILLO PAD!
> LAUGH CLONE LAUGH AH LIFE I FEEL THE LASH
> OF THE NEW MASTER NOTHING NOW BUT CRASH
> COURSES What does Wystan say? TO PLATO?
> HAVING DROPPED ME LIKE A HOT O SHIT
> WHAT GOOD IS RHYME NOW

Extended passages like this one enliven *Mirabell* and *Scripts*, and the
trilogy is liberally salted throughout with witty camp chit-chat. Willing at
last to exploit this source, Merrill has drawn upon it with a free hand.

But the subject of proclivity is not only a rich new well-spring of
comedy; the long-stoppered avowal will swell and swell, and grant a still
more deeply seated wish. "Why," wonders DJ early in the *Mirabell* Lessons,
"did They choose *us*?/ Are we more usable than Yeats or Hugo,/ Doters on
women . . . ?" An explanation ensues:

> LOVE OF ONE MAN FOR ANOTHER OR LOVE BETWEEN WOMEN
> IS A NEW DEVELOPMENT OF THE PAST 4000 YEARS
> ENCOURAGING SUCH MIND VALUES AS PRODUCE THE BLOSSOMS
> OF POETRY & MUSIC, THOSE 2 PRINCIPAL LIGHTS OF
> GOD BIOLOGY. LESSER ARTS NEEDED NO EXEGETES:
> ARCHITECTURE SCULPTURE THE MOSAICS & PAINTINGS THAT

FLOWERED IN GREECE & PERSIA CELEBRATED THE BODY.
POETRY   MUSIC   SONG INDWELL & CELEBRATE THE MIND . . .
HEART IF U WILL. . . .

NOW MIND IN ITS PURE FORM IS A NONSEXUAL PASSION
OR A UNISEXUAL ONE PRODUCING ONLY LIGHT.
FEW PAINTERS OR SCULPTORS CAN ENTER THIS LIFE OF THE MIND.
THEY (LIKE ALL SO-CALLED NORMAL LOVERS) MUST PRODUCE AT LAST
BODIES   THEY DO NOT EXIST FOR ANY OTHER PURPOSE

"Come now," the mediums demur, "admit that certain very great/ Poets and musicians have been straight." Self-despising homosexual behavior was displaced onto Panayioti in "After the Fire" and onto the Enfant Chic in *The (Diblos) Notebook*; in like manner this unblushing speech issues from Mirabell's mouth—or beak; Mirabell has turned, the instant before he makes it, from a bat named 741 into a peacock, in a kind of coming-out party of his own. The doctrine of homosexuals as evolution's crème-de-la-crème transforms the childlessness that once grieved JM into a trade-off beneficial, even essential, to his poetry. It also accounts for the gay-subculture ambience created in this poem by so much camp talk, and makes sense of a circumstance which would otherwise seem decidedly peculiar: that once they reach the formal-lesson stage, nearly all the poem's significant characters are male and gay. (The one who appears to be neither will ultimately reveal herself as both.) Two straight men added to the cast of *Scripts* are friends who died with *Mirabell* half-written and the "YES" dictations of *Scripts* completed; the poem fits them to a scheme whose shape is already fixed. Which cannot prevent JM from feeling, as he knows his readers must, that

> A sense comes late in life of too much death,
> Of standing wordless, with head bowed beneath
>
> The buffeting of losses which we see
> At once, no matter how reluctantly,
>
> As gains. Gains to the work. Ill-gotten gains . . .
>
> Well, Robert, we'll make room. Your elegy
> Can go in *Mirabell*, Book 8, to be
> Written during the hot weeks ahead;
> Its only fiction, that you're not yet dead.

The dead souls most important to the entire poem are two: W. H. Auden, and Maria Mitsotáki, an Athens friend who was the subject of a *Fire Screen* poem, "Words for Maria." JM's peace with his own mother has been ratified. His father died in 1956. The death of DJ's aged parents is the first major event of *Mirabell*; indeed, these impending deaths are what send them back to the Ouija board after an absence of more than a year ("As things were,/ Where else to look for sense, comfort, and wit?"). Helen Vendler, wise in this as in much else, writes:

> In the usual biological cycle, parents die after their children have become parents; the internalizing of the parental role, it is believed, enables the parents to be absorbed into the filial psyche. In the childless world of *Mirabell*, the disappearance of parents, or parental friends, is the disappearance of the parental and therefore of the filial; JM and DJ can no longer be "boys" but must put on the mortality of the survivor.

Both childless like the mediums in (this) life, WHA and MM make idealized parent-figures, their two-sided humanity masked beyond the kindly chasm of death. As Merrill has said in an interview, "In life, there are no perfect affections. . . . Yet, once dead, overnight the shrewish wife becomes 'a saint,' frustrations vanish at cockcrow, and from the once fallible human mouth come words of blessed reassurance. . . . Given the power . . . would I bring any of these figures back to earth?" Vendler amplifies: Auden and Maria "are the people who call JM and DJ 'MES ENFANTS' (Maria, known as 'Maman') or 'MY BOYS' (Auden). When these voices fall silent, there will be no one to whom the poet is a child." A (twinned) only child: Maria, we learn in *Mirabell*, "Was hailed on arrival by 'HORDES OF POLYGLOT/ SELFSTYLED ENFANTS . . . BUT NOW A DECENT/ VEIL IS DRAWN & I HAVE NONE BUT U.' "

These voices, even these, fall silent at poem's end—but only after the parents' and children's love has been perfected, like that of Dante and Beatrice, by its three-year ceremony of guidance, enlightenment, and farewell. Beyond this silence gleams the tantalizing hope of a rendezvous with Maria in 1991, Bombay, The World. And as the surrogate parents move inexorably toward their departures, behind them grow and fill out the personified figures of Mother Nature and God/Sultan Biology: all-powerful and capriciously destructive, even murderous, on the one hand, heartbreakingly loveable on the other, like parents as perceived by small children. By the terms of the myth, their "divorce" would destroy their third, last, human child and his green world; and the poet, struck by parallels between the broken home he grew up in and the present situation of all humanity, angry and afraid as no child of divorced parents is ever too old to be, evokes himself when young once more. "Between an often absent or abstracted/ (In mid-depression) father and still young/ Mother's wronged air of commonsense the child sat," he writes, and goes on to build the metaphor, cosmic by domestic detail, which will culminate in Earth-shattering divorce. "*That* was the summer my par—YR PARALLELS/ DIVERGE PRECISELY HERE," insists Maria. "HUSH ENFANT FOR NO MAN'S MIND CAN REACH/ BEYOND THAT HIM & HER THEIR SEPARATION/ REMAINS UNTHINKABLE." JM, if not entirely convinced, is convinced at least that Maria is right to stop this probing, terrifying line of thought. "Barbarity," he agrees, pulling himself together, "To serve uncooked one's bloody tranche de vie . . ./ Later, if the hero couldn't smile,/ Reader and author could; one called it style." Or called it metaphor, ever and always at work to make any new form of the oldest, most chronic pain bearable.

IV

The *Prophetic Books* of William Blake and the *Vision* of Yeats come tentatively to mind when one considers all this, for *The Changing Light at Sandover* is a masterwork of great eccentricity. Unlike Dante's *Comedy* or *Paradise Lost*, those other major poems which purport to address man's role in the universal scheme, the value "system" given poetic expression here is not shared by an entire culture. Unlike them, it is not a morality tale. It substitutes yes-and-no ambiguities for moral absolutes. Sin is equated with the giving *and receiving* of pain, evil and good recognized on the cosmic level alone, outside the power of individual human beings (in a wholly deterministic universe) to choose, or to enact unless "cloned" to do so. Personal salvation then cannot be at issue; the issue is global survival. The poem accounts for the chief obstacles to survival—overpopulation and nuclear holocaust—in original ways, but does not propose, in the manner of science fiction, original ways of implementing the obvious solutions. Certain virtues—kindness, courtesy, devotion, affection, modesty, tolerance, tact, patience, plus intelligence, talent, and wit—are celebrated, many of these broadly shared with western religions; yet the values they embody are, lacking spiritual principles to back them up, social rather than spiritual values. ("LANGUAGE," says WHA, "IS THE POET'S CHURCH.") Neither deep religious sensibility, nor political savvy, nor philosophical inquiringness are at work in Merrill's poem, setting it off sharply in tone from Dante's and from Milton's.

The chief difficulty in viewing the trilogy as *western* religious myth is its insistence that innate class, on Earth as in Heaven, determines who can take steps to prevent the world from blowing up. Only elect "Lab souls" of sufficient "densities," preprogrammed or *cloned* in Heaven between lives, can do God's work on Earth to build an earthly Paradise; only they will read this poem's Message with comprehension:

A MERE 2 MILLION CLONED SOULS LISTEN TO EACH OTHER WHILE
OUTSIDE THEY HOWL & PRANCE SO RECENTLY OUT OF THE TREES.
& SO FOR U THE HARDEST RULE: THE RULE OF THE RULERS.
POLITICIANS HAVE LED MAN DOWN A ROAD WHERE HE BELIEVES
ALL IS FOR ALL   THIS IS THE FOOL'S PARADISE   ALL WILL BE
FOR ALL ONLY WHEN ALL IS UNDERSTOOD.

The absolute amount of "human soul densities" is finite, and has had to
be pieced out in recent history with "animal densities" of dog and rat to
cope with the glut of children. Holocaust is a present danger precisely
because power has fallen into the hands of leaders with a high proportion
of animal soul densities—"Rat souls"—who too easily lose control of their
high-spirited but destructive impulses. And lately, therefore, accidents—
slippages in the works—have infiltrated the realm of NO ACCIDENT. To
restore balance, save the earth from utter destruction, and bring Paradise
upon it, a thinning of the population is essential.

If the positive and negative charge within the atom is a metaphor
for this global drama, the drama is in turn a metaphor for something
vaster. The cosmic conflict of Good, or White, forces represented by God
Biology—Earth is, so to speak, his representative, he Earth's patron, in a
Galactic Pantheon—are at war with horrific forces called simply "the
Black" (as in black holes), whose nature is utter nothingness: "The Black
beyond black, past that eerie Wall—/ PAST MATTER BLACK OF THOUGHT
UNTHINKABLE," elsewhere defined as "ATOMIC BLACK/ COMPRESSED FROM
TIME'S REVERSIBILITY," a phrase which resists conceptualization. Michael
identifies it "IN MAN'S LIFE" with "THE DULLWITTED, THE MOB, THE IDIOT IN
POWER, THE PURELY BLANK OF MIND"; perhaps these make time flow back-
ward by reversing the evolutionary ascent of life through time toward the
development of an ever larger, more convoluted brain. On his second visit
Michael had stated resoundingly, "INTELLIGENCE, THAT IS THE SOURCE OF
LIGHT. FEAR NOTHING WHEN YOU STAND IN IT." It follows that when the
idiot rules you stand in darkness, and are afraid.

"Time's reversibility" remains a conundrum; but forward-flowing
time is easy to see as Black in the context of Merrill's earlier work. "Why
should Time be black?" he asks, having answered his own question
through thirty years of poems wherein Time is the agent of aging, and of
steadily diminishing beauty and passional capacity, and the destroyer of
kindly masks and illusions. When Paradise comes upon Earth "THEN TIME
WILL STOP": man will be immortal.

The poem's cryptic Message, however, is not identical with its
meaning, as readers with any density of soul at all can see. Part of its
meaning is its wit and style. The rest lies where the most meaning has

always lain in Merrill's work: in the loves between human characters in life and beyond death, and in their losses; and especially in the evocation of twenty-five domestic years with David Jackson, which Thom Gunn has called "the most convincing description I know of a gay marriage":

> The men's life together is presented to us in detail which is almost casual: we see them choosing wallpaper, keeping house, traveling, entertaining, and above all sitting at the Ouija board. It is not a minor triumph and it is not an incidental one because, after all, it is the two of them in their closeness who have evoked the whole spirit world of *Ephraim* and *Mirabell* [and *Scripts*], or perhaps even created it.

Those "genre" glimpses of JM and DJ watering on the terrace, discussing the sense of a knotty transcript, going about their days together while *not* collaborating across the Board, are the most affecting, most authentic part of the entire story unstifled here, and the most human. *Have* they created the Other World, in its infinite richness and strangeness, between them? *The Book of Ephraim* includes an explanation suggested by JM's former psychiatrist: "what you and David do/ We call folie à deux"—a way of talking to one another from behind the mask of the Ouija board. The ex-shrink leads his ex-patient to speculate that Ephraim is an imaginary offspring produced in lieu of a real one to satisfy the biological urge to procreate, seeing that "Somewhere a Father Figure shakes his rod/ At sons who have not sired a child." The explanation tidily foreshadows Mirabell's: homosexuals, being poorly suited to make children, are well-suited therefore to make poetry. *Ephraim*—and all that follows where he led—*makes sense* as the child of JM's and DJ's love and pro/creativity, conceived through their union at the Ouija board.

"Jung says—or if he doesn't, all but does—/That God and the Unconscious are one," we read in *Ephraim*, Section U. To theorize that in *The Changing Light at Sandover* two unconsciouses, linked skillfully by long practice, have played God by creating a cosmic vision still leaves a great deal unexplained. How, for instance, did DJ and JM know that Nabokov was dead—news that reached them first via the Board? More centrally, what is it these two do that others fail to do, which yields such astonishing results? When we leave JM at the close of the Coda, nervously preparing to read the completed trilogy to the heavenly host assembled (one auditor per letter of the alphabet), his situation is both so familiar in its Proustian stance and thematic preoccupations, and so outré in its total concept, as to baffle and defy any simple explanation. Even if the two did make all of it up unconsciously, an experience has befallen them scarcely less amazing and wonderful than if, like the prophets of old, they had heard God's voice address them aloud. And if God and the Unconscious are one—? As Merrill has observed, "if it's still *yourself* that you're drawing upon, then that self is much stranger and freer and more far-seeing than the one you thought you knew." Put another way, in another place: "If the spirits aren't external, how astonishing the mediums become! Victor Hugo said of *his* voices that they were like his own mental powers multiplied by five." He adds that his time among the spirits has "made me think twice about the imagination,"—a reminder that Section S of *Ephraim* begins where this essay may properly conclude:

> Stevens imagined the imagination
> And God as one; the imagination, also,
> As that which presses back, in parlous times,
> Against "the pressure of reality."

CHARLES BERGER

"*Mirabell:*" *Conservative Epic*

To speak of *Mirabell* as an apocalyptic poem forces us to ask: what kind of apocalypse is this? Here the Latin synonym "revelation" might be more to the point, since *Mirabell* is nothing if not a continuous series of revelations, glimpses behind the screen, confessions of unorthodox conversations, which, strangely enough, often tally with more orthodox renderings. Apocalypse, in our current usage, tends to convey a stronger flavor of violence than does revelation; apocalypse and catastrophe verge upon becoming synonymous. And yet *Mirabell*, though it does relate a version of catastrophic creation in its account of how the dark angels ruined an earlier version of our world, nevertheless also embodies a vision of the universe as being continuous rather than discontinuous. In *Mirabell*, as in Merrill generally, the message (or faith) that man will survive is the triumphant anti-climax to fears of his annihilation. Though he traffics with the dead, Merrill has little gift or inclination for instilling a sense of dread. He is indeed more at home with Congreve than Marlowe. Merrill belongs to that branch of modernism— Stevens and Joyce are his confrères in this—which has no instinctive relish for violence, apocalyptic or otherwise, as a means of redeeming humanity. Although *Mirabell*, as the purgatorial poem of the triad, includes some accounts of purgative catastrophes, Merrill displays little taste for such "necessary" measures as the thinning-out of unwanted gene-bearers. Indeed, Merrill seems embarrassed by ideology in general, whether normative or not.

The lack of a sense of dread in Merrill's universe extends to the way he reacts to the evidence that he is chosen by the spirits, an honor

First published in this volume. Copyright © 1985 by Charles Berger.

that might trigger limitless bouts of paranoia in a writer such as Pynchon. JM and DJ utter their perfunctory disclaimers at being the bright center of the dark world, the audience for the sublime events of natural theater (such as the hurricane whipped up to impress them), but they adjust rather easily to such displays of favoritism. Even the assertion that there are NO ACCIDENTS, which would set a paranoid howling with fear and delight, presents only an intellectual stumbling-block, soon enough incorporated into the lesson plan. Merrill can react this way because such news squares with his sense of how things really are. For him, poets do indeed constitute the center of our culture. Merrill suffers little of the self-contempt common to many post-modern poets. He knows, of course, that the poet in our culture is deemed a marginal figure—after all, *Mirabell* opens in a small-town parlor, home of poet and reader alike—but he is not therefore inclined to rage against this judgement, or to accept it as a partly valid assessment of poetry's true place. Thus, the bizarre flights of perspective in *Mirabell* from high to low, sublime to trivial, prophetic to ordinary, are negotiated with surprising ease. Another possible reason for Merrill's equanimity in the face of his culture's judgement has to do with his cosmopolitanism. Merrill seems the least explicitly "American" of our major contemporary poets, the least afflicted with the ambition to speak to and for America. One gets the sense in Merrill, especially in a cosmic or universal drama such as *Mirabell*, that America itself is peripheral. It is only too easy to forget that the events of *Mirabell* transpire during the Bicentennial summer of 1976.

Now, one of the striking features of *Mirabell* is the way its spirit-messages tend often to confirm, rather than discredit, traditional myths. The chief shock value of the trilogy comes from its insistence upon a literal grounding for what has hitherto been received as figurative truth—at least by most poets and readers. We are not told that the old myths are false, but that they are truer than we dare to think. Despite the bizarre occasion of the poem, Merrill is not really advocating a counter-tradition so much as rearranging known elements within the sacred storehouse of myths. The strenuousness of Merrill's vision comes from its burden of affirmation, not denial. For most readers, the chief discomfort induced by *Mirabell* will likely turn out to be its thematic naivety, rather than its immense formal sophistication. But the deepest question for the critic of Merrill's trilogy—perhaps especially for *Mirabell*—is to what extent Merrill may be called a genuine revisionist of the mythopoeic tradition. Does he refigure what he repeats? In this regard, the distance imposed by the upper-case fourteeners employed by Mirabell and Co. creates a nearly unbridgeable gap that indicates the difficulty for Merrill of translating what he transcribes. And yet, these upper-case pronouncements also serve to stabilize the text, given Merrill's penchant for vertiginous punning in his "own" voice. This poet of infinite nuance seems almost to compel the writ of upper-case law, if only to contain the proliferation of meaning below. Merrill, master of the lapidary style, yields to the true tablets, the stony engravings from on high.

Another way to approach the extraordinary range of discourse in *Mirabell* is to place the poem within the context of other modern and post-modern attempts at polyphonic epic. Merrill is an interesting case because he combines the fidelity to personal history of a Lowell or Berryman with writing on a much more sublime scale. His religious rhetoric, whatever its sponsorship, may be seen as belonging to the continuing modernist effort to accommodate a lost hieratic discourse in the absence of an overt ideological justification for such thought. The upper-case portions of *Mirabell* function in a manner similar to the blocks of quotations (or allusions) in the *Cantos* or *The Waste Land*. Mirabell's upper-case messages survive as relics of a lost cosmological order and the process of presenting them in the poem can be viewed as a conserving act of retrieval.

Merrill's poetic pantheon might at first incline one to place him with Yeats, and the trilogy is indeed often compared to *A Vision*. But Yeats is a greater celebrant than Merrill, more attuned to the sacred. Despite everything, Merrill remains a secular epiphanist, committed to the Poem of Science. Such a poem liberates mythology from its grounding in a particular culture, resulting in a pure ideology of myth assigned to a prehistorical era. By mythologizing history, Yeats and Pound opened the way to dangerous, even Fascist, notions of past wholeness, lost origins, true cultural centers. "V Work" is Merrill's equivalent of the privileged cultural enterprise, which Yeats assigns to "Byzantium" and Pound to "Provence," among other places. The sacred spot becomes an invisible laboratory. And while the ahistorical and impalpable nature of Merrill's central myth reduces its sacramental value, it does bestow upon it the prestige of pure anteriority. Mirabell and the fallen spirits have gone before, and thus they can legitimately warn us.

These warning voices place *Mirabell* squarely within a modernist tradition that continues the ancient function of the epic as a vehicle for instruction. For an age that prided itself on renouncing Victorian didacticism, a not inconsiderable amount of modernist verse epic is devoted to lecturing the reader, either by foregrounding aesthetic touchstones or by outright preaching. The pronouncements of Merrill's instructors combine aesthetics and pedagogy, for the voices of *Mirabell* recapitulate past myths (e.g. the Fall, Arcadia) in order to instruct mankind in the mythic or aesthetic patterning of cosmological history, and also to warn against the pride that might destroy the Greenhouse. Eliot and Pound had enough of a bad conscience about the didactic to develop techniques that would seem to allow the redemptive parts of the tradition to resurface, almost unconsciously, in their own poems. Capacious minds could encompass all of the aesthetic past that mattered, so the argument ran; the right quotation would arise at the right time, unwilled. Merrill develops a fascinating myth or method to account for the return of such archaic material. And even as he instructs us, he reveals himself to be instructed. (Rarely, indeed, has a poet given such a full account of his text's method of production.) In a strange way, Merrill thus rationalizes the presence of the archaic in the modernist long poem without resorting to the notion of the poet's great containing mind, though it would be easy for critics to locate all that happens at the Board within Merrill's own capacious poetic intellect. And, although *Mirabell* includes much autobiographical experience of Merrill's, it also more than hints at the price to be paid for allowing the mind of the poem to be thus invaded by outside voices. What Merrill calls THE STRIPPING PROCESS takes place; this is another word for the kind of epic impersonality Eliot raised to the status of a poetic ideal. In one of the poem's central passages, we see JM reacting, "horrified," to news that Scribe and Hand, though crucial for the present, will be dissolved as discrete personalities and incorporated into the next evolutionary stage of the cosmic scheme. They will not be lost, for nothing is lost in Merrill's universe; but all accidental qualities of the self will be sacrificed (giving another, grimmer meaning to the credo NO ACCIDENTS). The JM who speaks in the following passage is akin to Dante the Pilgrim, actor within his own narrative, addressing us from a more human, pathos-ridden perspective, which the Poet who later composed the work has presumably transcended:

> WHA IN OUR MASQUE EXPERIENCED WHAT? THE WIND LET
> OUT OF HIS BEING   HIS (M) PERSONALITY GONE   ITS
> LOSS A COMPLETENESS IN THAT DANCE UNDER THE POWERFUL
> LIGHT FLOODING THE LENS
>   JM (still horrified begins to see):
>   This loss you call completeness is *lived through?*
>   Soul, the mortal self, expendably
>   Rusting in tall grass, iron eaten by dew—
>   All that in our heart of hearts we must
>   Know will happen, and desire, and dread?
>   Once feeling goes, and consciousness, the head
>   Filling with . . . vivid nothings—no, don't say!

A A A PLUS & NOW WE ADMIT
OUR SEMINAR IS THIS STRIPPING PROCESS.

So, even if we cannot know the dancer from the DANCE, we at least have the compensating comfort of knowing that life conforms to an orderly pattern. But nowhere is Merrill's totalizing aestheticism better seen than in his vision of language as the underlying score of the dance. Poetry, music, science—the central constituents of cultural V work—are all united by language, as Mirabell's breathtaking hymn at the opening of Book 8 makes clear:

WHEN WE SEE THE SQUATTING APES WITH NO
CODIFIED LANGUAGE NOTHING BUT GIBBERISH GRUNT & SQUEAK,
THEN MERELY BY TURNING YR WAY OUR TIMELESS ATTENTION
LISTEN, HOW NOT TO REVERE GOD B WHO IN HIS WISDOM
SAID: MAN WILL RULE! FASHION ME A MAN & LET HIM SURVIVE!
SO WHAT IS MOST REWARDING OF MAN'S V WORK? HIS CULTURE
& THIS? HIS ENTIRE LIFE-FABRIC WOVEN OF LANGUAGE.

No vision of language as the prison-house is put forward in *Mirabell*. Instead, language is the GARDEN, and the mission of man's V work is to extend this paradise until it encompasses the whole of the greenhouse Earth. The sacred role of language applies also to talk—at least of the inspired kind—as Mirabell tells JM and DJ, perhaps to assuage the fears of poet and scribe that their epic is growing too talky:

WHEN BY CANDLELIGHT YOU MEET & TALK DO U
EVER THINK OF THE 2 BASIC APECHILDREN WHO IN PRE
CARNIVOROUS PRE IN FACT FIRE DAYS MET FOR ONLY
ONE REASON WHICH THEN, SAD TO SAY, OFTEN RAN DOWN A LEG?
WHAT A CLIMB WHAT A LEAP U MAKE BACK INTO ALTITUDE
MAN'S RAMIFYING TREE MINUTELY SHAPED THRU THE AGES! . . .
THEY NEVER TIRED OF TALK FROM THAT INSTANT.

A convenient justification, the reader might murmur, but the epic poet of whatever age is surely allowed to claim divine prerogative for his own procedures. Further on in the eighth book of *Mirabell*, we get a more subtle characterization of poetry's role in the scheme of things. Relating God B's command—MAKE REASON—and the Luciferian application of that injunction in the hubristic work of Nefertiti and Akhnaton, when ALL CULTURE FOCUSSED ON ONE/ GLOWING UNIFYING VISION (with the result that the world was nearly destroyed), Mirabell describes a saving revision of that imperative in the next stage of creation:

GOD B SENT MAN
THE IDEA: TO CREATE, A REASOND INDIRECTION.

NOW THRU THE ARTS OF SCIENCE   POETRY   MUSIC   IN SLOW
ACCUMULATIVE FASHION MAN'S GARDEN TOOK SHAPE.

So poetry and its sister arts arise as a means of retaining, yet also deflecting, man's energetic impulse to attain the goals of his reason. Science-as-technology threatens to destroy even as it achieves, but in the reasoned indirection of science-as-art there is a respect for the Earth, a preservative or conservative element which builds without destroying.

In the final pages of *Mirabell*, the full power of poetry is revealed through the chant of the archangel Michael. As the hour of revelation approaches, JM and DJ prepare to receive the angel's message. Theirs is an ascetic rite, involving abstinence and submission to the silent forces of nature: "Things look out at us as from a spell / They themselves have woven." The "baby pyramid" they acquired after hearing the story of Akhnaton and Nefertiti cracks ominously in the heat of the August sun, leading the poet to wonder: "And will light learn / To modify its power before our turn?" But he needn't have worried, for when the angel does speak, it is in the accents of the poets. As Wordsworth says: "By our own spirits are we deified," a line that can be much brooded upon as a way of glossing the ending of *Mirabell*:

I AM MICHAEL
I HAVE ESTABLISHED YOUR ACQUAINTANCE & ACCEPT YOU. COME NEXT TIME
     IN YOUR OWN MANNER. SERVANTS WE ARE NOT.
I LEAVE NOW AS THE LIGHT LEAVES AND WIND MY PATH OVER ITS TRACK
     ON EARTH   I AM A GUARDIAN OF THE LIGHT
LEAVE THIS FIRST OF THE FIRST TWO MEETINGS IN A CYCLE OF TWINNED
     MEETINGS IN A CYCLE OF TWELVE MOONS
LOOK!   LOOK INTO THE RED EYE OF YOUR GOD!

Michael bequeaths himself to the same soil that Whitman bequeathed himself to at the end of *Song of Myself*. (The angel may know something that Merrill himself hasn't fully realized yet, since the human poet has little overt interest in Whitman. But the most important thing to observe about Michael's chant is that it is a paean to poetry, leading us to wonder: do poets speak like gods, or gods like poets? Who has priority? Michael begins his chant by addressing us from THE WINEDARK SEA OF SPACE. The Homeric epithet, transferred to celestial seas, reminds us of Mirabell's claim that Homer's epics were a literal gift from the gods. By invoking the source of Western poetry at the beginning of his own speech, Michael also reminds us how dependent Merrill's gods are upon the imaginings of human poets. Merrill's divine aestheticism culminates in the direct echo of Keats in the archangel's summary declaration: AND THAT IS ALL

YOU NEED TO KNOW OF YOUR PHYSICAL INCARNATE HIS-
TORY. The cup on the board has been transformed into the Grecian
Urn. The fact that Merrill's gods so blatantly echo the poets (and let me
suggest that these echoings, rather than the poem's rehearsal of anonymous myth, constitute its true power), does not automatically consign
those gods to the status of fictions. If anything, it works the other way,
exalting the role of the poet to dangerous heights.

For this last reason especially, Merrill is likely to have few imita-
tors, at least in the mode of the trilogy. His greatest influence may lie in
how he compels us to rethink the claims made for poetry—not for the
sake of demystifying the poet's work, but for aggrandizing it. Merrill
openly revives the category of the outrageous, making us see how it was
present all along in the works of other poets. Playing Merrill's Board game
with any degree of seriousness makes it that much harder to negotiate the
boundary between the literal and the figurative elsewhere. The late poem
of Stevens, "Large Red Man Reading," illustrates the uncanny shadow
Merrill now casts on earlier poems:

> There were ghosts that returned to earth to hear his phrases,
> As he sat there reading, aloud, the great blue tabulae.
> They were those from the wilderness of stars that had expected
> more.
>
> There were those that returned to hear him read from the poem
> of life,
> Of the pans above the stove, the pots on the table, the tulips
> among them.
> They were those that would have wept to step barefoot into
> reality,
>
> That would have wept and been happy, have shivered in the frost
> And cried out to feel it again, have run fingers over leaves
> And against the most coiled thorn, have seized on what was ugly
>
> And laughed, as he sat there reading, from out of the purple
> tabulae,
> The outlines of being and its expressings, the syllables of its
> law:
> Poesis, poesis, the literal characters, the vatic lines,
>
> Which in those ears and in those thin, those spended hearts,
> Took on color, took on shape and the size of things as they are
> And spoke the feeling for them, which was what they had lacked.

Knowing Merrill makes it harder to slip easily into the fabular frame of
this poem without recognizing the sublime strangeness of its claims. There

are signs enough in the poem of how Stevens keeps his distance from the supernatural (the opening "There were," a variation on the formulaic story indicator "There was," is only the first of these), but the reader's experience of Merrill makes Stevens' boundaries both easier to spot and more difficult to reconnoitre, aware as we are of the pitfalls avoided. Stevens brings the dead to him merely in living as and where he lives. No journey to Hades is necessary to summon the spirits, and the only blood offering that the Red Man brings is his own full-bloodedness. The dead in Stevens' poem are compelled to return in order to hear the poet read from the earthly Book of Life, as if the heavenly volume were found wanting. The dead long for the domestic as well as the vatic, both perhaps being present in the notion of "*Poesis, poesis*, the literal characters." The dead are spent and need the tones of the living, while the somewhat inhuman author needs them as his truly appreciative audience. Stevens' poem reads so intriguingly alongside Merrill's for, obviously, Merrill read *it*. Only now, a reader can almost convince himself that the voice of the Large Red Man Reading is but another example of Merrill's astonishing ventriloquism.

LESLIE BRISMAN

Merrill's Yeats

In an exciting introduction to James
Merrill, Helen Vendler associates the poetic technique of voices from
another world with the poet's essentially elegiac subject matter:

> Nothing so compels poets to complication [as the thought of death].
> And if what they conjure up to talk to them from the dark is a voice
> recognizably their own but bearing a different name, they (and their
> readers) are peculiarly consoled by the reflected Word. So Milton found
> his own best voice speaking back at him under the name of Phoebus
> Apollo and St. Peter; so Dante fell into colloquy with his elder self,
> Virgil; so Yeats invented his "mysterious instructors" who dictated to
> him and his wife his elaborate system of history and the afterlife. . . .

In general, it is not true that a poet thus finds "his own best voice" in the
sense that the lines put into the mouth of the conjured precursor or master
are the poet's best lines or those most representative of the poet's true
spirit. But it may be true that Milton, for example, found a voice most
distinctly his own in the returns he makes in *Lycidas* after the inadequate
thunderings of Apollo and Peter—and that, more generally, the device of
projecting (or rejecting) a certain aspect of self as the voice of a precursor
moves a poet to a stance most uniquely his own.

In certain ways, Yeats represents for Merrill not only a number of
specific literary debts but a vision of an old self that much of Merrill's
verse is concerned to refashion and transcend. Yeats introduced the Ouija
board and its mysterious instructors, and Merrill's supreme trilogy, *The
Changing Light at Sandover*, owes and pays a debt to Yeats for paving the
way to our familiarity with these "metaphors for poetry." There is also the

Yeatsian esthetic of "perfection of the work" chosen as a sad but noble alternative to "perfection of the life," and one senses the precedent, perhaps the sanction of the author of "Pardon, old fathers . . ." when encountering those poignant recognitions in Merrill's work that there will be no wife, no child, no patter of any but metrical feet. Like Yeats, master of dialogues of selves and souls, Merrill can "do the police in different voices," to borrow T.S. Eliot's phrase, itself borrowed from Dickens; and like Yeats, Merrill gives us voices of authority that seem to belong to an "internal police," a bevy of super-ego voices rising from the poet's own id. Beyond all this, perhaps, is a sublimity of style most extraordinary when tied to a pun or a memory, two modes of compacting meaning into a limited space or time. Merrill's wit is a Yeatsian, aristocratic wit, coupled with a high seriousness and a graceful manner seldom equaled in the work of Auden, Merrill's other great precursor.

Yeats speaks, in *Scripts for the Pageant*, a deliciously Yeatsian tribute to Merrill's power of evoking the voices of the past and overgoing them at their own intonations:

> O SHINING AUDIENCE, IF AN OLD MAN'S SPEECH
> STIFF FROM LONG SILENCE CAN NO LONGER STRETCH
> TO THAT TOP SHELF OF RIGHTFUL BARD'S APPAREL
> FOR WYSTAN AUDEN & JAMES MEREL
> WHO HAVE REFASHIONED US BY FASHIONING THIS,
> MAY THE YOUNG SINGER HEARD ABOVE
> THE SPINNING GYRES OF HER TRUE LOVE
> CLOAK THEM IN HEAVEN'S AIRLOOM HARMONIES.
>
> (The Last Lessons)

Without actual quotation, this short passage captures a number of tricks of the old voice. It is, above all, an old voice—the "old rocky voice" of Yeats, still yearning ("O") and aware of its limitations ("if"). Nature's comparatively ordinary image for the aspiring mind a few lines earlier, "there scrambles up / stiffly at first a figure on all fours," becomes, in Yeats's voice, an unusual and very Yeatsian figure for voice, "SPEECH / STIFF FROM LONG SILENCE." This is the poet who spoke of giving up the apparel of a dressy style for the greater enterprise of going naked, but who found, in invigorated images like "coat upon a stick," a mode of awareness of decay and death that seems to transform the flesh it dispar-ages in the very accuracy and poignance of its attention to it. The poet who "mocked mockers after that" combines his perspective on mockery in the sense of ironic detachment with mockery in the sense of fashioning, refashioning an image, not a shade. And the final pun on *airloom* as both heirloom (preservative of the past) and air-loomed (ethereal) captures the high tension that was Yeats's own between the desire for transcendence and the all-too-human veneration of traditions and traditional things of this earth. Beyond the sheer fun of this pastiche, then, is a figure of pathos undiminished by his brief appearance in comic context. Elsewhere in *Scripts* Yeats speaks through DJ, who answers the question "Does Yeats suffer now?" by responding about his own hand while talking about the master's: "It doesn't hurt . . .":

> . . . often before I know the message
> I feel its beauty, its importance. Tears
> Come to my eyes. Is that Yeats being moved?
> (The Last Word on Number)

Though there is a playful victory over Yeats in making him a figure who misses the mark and incarnates his spirit in DJ's hand rather than Merrill's own (Yeats "still making the wrong sense," as DJ says) there is also a great tribute here to Yeats's sense of the beautiful and the important—Yeats's pathos beyond his mystical vision of cycles of history or his sprezzatura in coping with age and death. The greatest "trick of the voice," to borrow again Gloucester's sense of what makes Lear Lear, may be the intonation of profound sorrow behind the raging "I'll not weep!" that Yeats shared with the much-moved Lear.

Yeats represents, then, not only enormous imaginative vision but a capacity for pathos that he often goes out of his way to control or to represent as best controlled. I believe that Merrill's turn to the device of the Ouija board is therefore a turn not just to the Yeatsian metaphor for poetry but to a Yeatsian mode of muscular control over emotion so voiced. Though Auden is the poet most there, most often overlooking the cards and actually kibbitzing or instructing the players, Yeats's spirit hovers over the entire enterprise of *The Changing Light at Sandover*. Two grand lyrics, published in *The Country of a Thousand Years of Peace* (1959) and *Braving the Elements* (1972) (the first part of the trilogy, *The Book of Ephraim*, was published in 1976), find Merrill preparing for the long poem by toying with its machinery and something of his relation to Yeats. In the first of these, "Voices from the Other World," he pits Yeatsian urbanity against the desire for something as "cold and passionate as the dawn," and actually ends with two lines Yeats could have written: In the wake of the voices from the other world, "Our lives have never seemed more full, more real, / Nor the full moon more quick to chill." The second of these poems is "Willowware Cup," and I believe it establishes the "medium" of the voices in the long poem not only by describing the teacup used on the Ouija board but by covertly describing a relationship to Yeats that involves both great attraction, and great need to represent Yeats as a figure for a past or a rejected self, over and against which Merrill will define what is most his own. Here is the poem:

> Mass hysteria, wave after breaking wave
> Blueblooded Cantonese upon these shores
>
> Left the gene pool Lux-opaque and smoking
> With dimestore mutants. One turned up today.
>
> Plum in bloom, pagoda, blue birds, plume of willow—
> Almost the replica of a prewar pattern—
>
> The same boat bearing the gnat-sized lovers away,
> The old bridge now bent double where her father signals
>
> Feebly, as from flypaper, minding less and less.
> Two smaller retainers with lanterns light him home.
>
> Is that a scroll he carries? He must by now be immensely
> Wise, and have given up earthly attachments, and all that.
>
> Soon, of these May mornings, rising in mist, he will ask
> Only to blend—like ink in flesh, blue anchor
>
> Needled upon drunkenness while its destroyer
> Full steam departs, the stigma throbbing, intricate—
>
> Only to blend into a crazing texure.
> You are far away. The leaves tell what they tell.
>
> But this lone, chipped vessel, if it fills,
> Fills for you with something warm and clear.
>
> Around its inner horizon the old odd designs
> Crowd as before, and seem to concentrate on you.
>
> They represent, I fancy, a version of heaven
> In its day more trouble to mend than to replace:
>
> Steep roofs aslant, minutely tiled;
> Tilted honeycombs, thunderhead blue.

The opening two words of the poem are already a little poem in themselves, one in which a fine turn of language not only reflects but constitutes the poem's attitude to a social problem—or rather, to a poetry of social concern. The words "mass hysteria" represent a snobbish social attitude (contempt of immigrants) mocked by the poem's own literalism, the fact that it is talking about chinaware, not Chinese. One obvious distinction between Merrill the lyric poet on the one hand and Yeats and Auden on the other is Merrill's almost total obliviousness to politics.

Merrill's stance will be questioned and (in parts two and three of the trilogy) almost ignored by the higher voices that "take over," putting not just the persona JM but the poet himself under Auden's influence. But Merrill begins, and at various moments in *The Changing Light at Sandover* is reinvigorated by the thought that the truest mental warfare is fought neither in the newspaper headlines nor on the frontiers of science but at the teacup's edge—in refining the boundaries between memory and desire, between aestheticism and concern. "Hysteria" is a disturbance in the human reproduction "plant," and "mass hysteria" is a poetic way of talking about mass production of cheap teacups. Yet if the true subject of this, as of all poems, is the particular victory of a poetic birth over the death of clay (the undifferentiation of the dust from which we come and the undifferentiation of mass production), then the vehicle is ironically closer to rather than further from the poem's core than is the ostensible "tenor." We can call this reversal, this achievement, the opening irony of the poem, and one accessible to a reader who lingers over the first two words in context even without what I believe to be the buried allusion:

> I have hear that hysterical women say
> They are sick of the palette and fiddle-bow,
> Of poets that are always gay. . . .

Yeats's "Lapis Lazuli" turns against the hysteria of social concern and towards the composure of art. For Yeats, the figures sculptured in a piece of stone will represent the tranquility beyond attachment to things and persons, the tranquility of fine performers who "do not break up their lines to weep." Merrill's figures painted on cheap china remind us, as it were, that Lear himself and even the player reciting Aeneas' speech in *Hamlet* do indeed weep and make weep, that it is as much the function of poetry to move us to tears as to regain a final composure over womb-felt agony. I think Merrill's poem is written specifically against Yeats's, but in this we must see a larger opposition, a new emergence from the "gene pool," an emergence distinguished from the mere replica of a prewar pattern. The quarrel with Yeats means an agon with the death that is repetition of aesthetic production without new emotive life, a repetition that is figured as mass production without the individual womb. Though a concern for individualization often takes the form, in Merrill's poetry, of the special heightening of personal reminiscence to symbolic status, actual authenticity to a particular person or time is not really an issue. It matters no more for Merrill's "Willowware Cup" that "Lapis Lazuli" is a pre-World War II pattern than it does for Yeats's poem that a zeppelin suggests World War I bombing; Yeats's poem represents a certain aristocratic aestheticism we always want to call "pre-war," though the war changes. "Lapis Lazuli" illustrates a stance toward art which one can glean from Merrill's poem without Yeats, but which one understands all the more poignantly for the new poet's need not to succumb to a "dated" indifference.

Though one can read Merrill's poem without "Lapis Lazuli," it helps to have Yeats. It helps to have Yeats's description of two Chinamen climbing upwards towards wisdom, if only to have a basis to ask why Merrill chooses a scene his poem interprets as being that of a father saying farewell to his daughter and her lover. In teaching the poem, to ourselves or to others, we need to come upon the awareness that Merrill has chosen his scene neither "out of the blue" nor out of Yeats's lapis lazuli blue but out of the need to contrast the most heart-felt sorrows with their two-dimensional artistic representation: The womb is stirred for the loss of children or lovers who go on to lead their own lives—whether one has a womb or not. Hence the melancholy of Merrill's comment on the father: "He must by now be immensely / Wise, and have given up earthly attachments, and all that." Merrill may be said to be reacting ironically against Yeats-as-poetic-father and against the detachment of Yeats's Chinamen, but the psychological defense of reversal or turning against his own, all-too-human self in the dismissive phrase "and all that" exposes Merrill's deep heart's core—what he wishes to claim as a pathos all his own, characteristically brushed aside by Yeats.

At this point Merrill's poem takes a turn so uniquely his that calling it an X-ing out of a precursor's move or a creation *ex nihilo* leaves the lines equally awesome in their power and originality. This father, "rising in mist," is imagined to ascend not into a "half-way house" of Yeatsian wisdom but into the incarnate form of homoerotic desire, the sailor detained from his ship. For Yeats, the Greek wind that blows into the verse paragraph preceding the turn to the lapis lazuli stone itself brings only the detached beauty of classic sculpture—handsome bodies covered with "draperies that seemed to rise / When sea wind swept the corner." For Merrill, however, the turn to a Greek thought becomes an occasion for an image of such poignance as to hold its own against all clichés about Greek love, sailors' flight, and the impermanence of passion tattooed only skin-deep. The departing "destroyer" is both ship and lover, the "stigma throbbing intricate" are both those of the needle and those of the phallus—or rather the heart, for it is truly the holiness of the heart's affections, not the nature of sexual orientation, that is the poem's topic. If these stigma throb "Only to blend into a crazing texture," they throb not for fancy's sake, in order to connect tattooing to the cracked surface of chinaware the way Yeats associates "every accidental crack or dent" in the lapis lazuli with a line of the landscape. They throb beyond the patternings of poetry to give birth to human meaning, human feeling, that "crazes" the mind by upsetting and complicating it.

Writing of the turn to the stone itself in "Lapis Lazuli," Jon Stallworthy comments,

> The transition from the handiwork of the Greek sculptor to that of the Chinese is made without a word of explanation; simply with the space between paragraphs. A jump so daring could only be brought off by a master poet at the height of his confident powers. He outstrides his readers, but knows he has them on a leash.

One could almost argue that Merrill had in mind not only Yeats's transition but Stallworthy's comment on it, for it seems vain to praise Yeats's transition beside the shocking starkness of Merrill's:

> Only to blend into a crazing texture.
> You are far away.

The first line of the couplet completes the old, carried-over thought and connects the disquiet of the (fleshly) landscape with the disquiet of the (china) sky. Then, suddenly, one is lifted as though by the scruff of the neck from scrutiny of images across the immensity of space separating the representation of desire from an ultimate "thou." Perhaps it would be wrong to identify "you" as Yeats, just as it would be wrong to specify "you" as D.J. or another object of desire. But granted that Merrill's poem emerges as a love poem while Yeats's aspires to an excited reverie somehow beyond desire, this "you" is not *a* lover but the You behind poems—or rather, towards whom one can say all poetic discourse is directed. Neither father nor lover, "real precursor" nor "real friend," this "You" comes into being in the crazed texture of poems as we turn. This means that *the* turn of the poem is a turn against Yeats, against an ideal of detachment that Merrill is associating, through "Lapis Lazuli," with Yeats. The turn away is also a turn to—to the affirmation of desire for a "you," to desire itself. Like Jesus invoking the Father in the Lord's prayer through the act of forgiving those who trespass against him, the poet discovers power and kingdom and glory in forgiving the "you" who has trespassed in the sense of having walked across and out of the poet's life. Yeats's wise men themselves walk away from the world of desire as they climb a mountain of transcendence. And the poet anticipates them, racing ahead to the half-way house they are headed towards, never to reach: "and I / Delight to imagine them seated there." For Merrill, however, transcendence means overgoing absence through apostrophe. The spirit of this transcendence becomes the bread and wine of the life of the affections:

> But this lone, chipped vessel, if it fills,
> Fills for you with something warm and clear.

"If it fills" may be a strange and wonderful concession to the vagaries of desire, but behind that expression of chance is the certainty of the rejection of Yeatsian detachment, the coldness of his beautiful stone. The warmth and clarity Merrill substitutes are the warmth of the heart's affections and the clarity of its imagination. While there is no doubt something platitudinous in our calling "this lone, chipped vessel" a figure for the poem itself, or every poem, Merrill's phrase does go beyond what Harold Bloom calls the "breaking of the vessels" to discover, in the new trope, a form of what the kabbalists called *tikkun* (restoration) and modern Hebrew calls *tikkun olam* (social action, literally "restoration of the world"). What is restored, to undo a Stevensian trope, is a world of human meaning, of human feeling—a not-so-foreign song.

In the final four lines of Merrill's poem, we move beyond the "daemonization" or empowering of the spirit that brought us face to face with the poem's "you." The penultimate couplet has about it a special poignance we can associate with a more distanced outlook on desire: It used to be that dimestore china was easily replaced, and it used to be (in a fantasy of sexual plenitude in a time of innocence) that homoerotic relationships were disposable because replaceable—"more trouble to mend than replace." This is not a comment on changing mores nor even, I think, about growing old, but an awareness of the deepening of the version of heaven that the poem itself has to offer. Merrill's poignant turn to mending itself mends a crack in the Yeatsian design. Yeats's carefree optimism seems like a carelessness with history: "All things fall and are built again / And those that build them again are gay." Merrill's poem lingers more over the awareness of how necessary but how hard it is to mend, to build again.

It is, of course, a misunderstanding of "gaiety" in the sense of willed good-humor rather than homoerotic desire that Merrill is correcting in correcting Yeats; Merrill is not swerving from Yeats by posing a new sexual meaning of "gay" against the old, Nietzschian mode of acceptance. But I think there is an attempt to sum up, as the quintessentially Yeatsian attitude to death, a gaiety that transfigures by rising above the involvement in the passions. In *Scripts for the Pageant* the angel Raphael, also known as Elijah, discloses a revelation that gives us a Yeatsian "still small voice" beyond all that thunder:

> WE STARED FORTH FROM IT AT YR MOUNTAIN:
> IT IT IT SPOKE   THEN TOOK A HUMAN SHAPE
> ALL MASSIVE ROCK & GREEN WITH BOUGHS FOR LASHES
> OF SUCH I MUST SAY WICKED MERRY EYES!
> I DO BELIEVE OUR SPRINGTIME WILL BE GAY
> IN THE OLD SENSE.

The mountain, I think, is not just Mt. Lykabettos but the old granite face and rocky voice of Yeats. With "wicked, merry eyes" he represents gaiety in the old sense, the hardened sensibility of one who learned to cast a cold eye on life, on death. It is against this wisdom of old age that Merrill's "younger" sense of gaiety restores the pathos and the importance of the life of the affections.

One has to misread or misrepresent Yeats, to forget about his "Crazy Jane phase," in order to have Yeats represent an asceticism of any sort; but it is fair to say that Yeats never turned to the fund of what might be called "sensual memory"—an association of the world of the senses and the poet's personal past—with anything like the regularity and liveliness of Merrill. The penultimate couplet of Merrill's poem takes us not to Yeats nor to a still more mythic world of free sex but to a realm of human feeling we most apprehend in seeing it lost:

> They represent, I fancy, a version of heaven
> In its day more trouble to mend than to replace.

What Merrill restores in this exquisite couplet is a sense of just how much trouble it is to mend a relationship, but how necessary that mending is in a world of age, of decay, of time. For with poems as with persons we are nowhere at all if we are still contemplating the possibility of choosing another object of attention. It is for this reason that the willowware cup makes such a striking contrast to the lapis lazuli that represents the conservatism, the moneyed sophistication, the high art of the Yeats that Merrill mends rather than replaces.

The dominant chinaware color is "thunderhead blue," emblematic of a crisis that is clutched in place of a lover: The departure is held sacred and "present" by being repainted as a storm evermore about to be. This is no lapis lazuli blue, emblematic of emotional isolation from our tragic scene, the scene "held off" only in the sense that the poet stands aloof from it. In one of Auden's "Twelve Songs," a rejected lover speaks of her "dear John" in third person, and for four stanzas he enters the refrain like a spirit of distance and distaste: "But he frowned like thunder and he went away." Though Merrill may have had no thought of Auden's rejection lyric when he wrote his own and chose "thunderhead" as his shade of blue, Auden's touching transposition of the refrain to second person for his poem's last line, "But you frowned like thunder and you went away," suggests the preservative quality of the elegiac "you" encoded in Merrill's poem in the turn to the *you* in the phrase, "You are far away." With or without the transcendence of one particular loss through allusion to another, or another mode of representing loss, "thunderhead blue" suggests the transcendence of the sensory world when one sees—and continues to see—the thunder in a frown, the cloud in a cup. That is, with or without allusion, there is all the difference between the Yeatsian dismissal, "let all things pass away," and the Audenesque holding on in the illusion of presence by addressing an absent one, "You are far away."

Yet one more expression of the will to "hold on" may be encoded in the lovely image of "tilted honeycombs" of Merrill's last line. Miniaturized here may be one more of this poet's characteristic efforts to make some small house out of the life lived—as opposed to the honeycomb sweetness that Yeats derives from leonine transcendence of passion in "Vacillation." Merrill's protest against Yeats is a protest against a Yeatsian high attitude to middle age, an attitude not always taken by Yeats but epitomized in the transcendence of earthly passion at the end of "Lapis Lazuli." Much of Merrill's great trilogy, especially *Scripts*, is under the influence of Auden, and I think it is Auden more than anyone else who deflected Merrill from the grand and more Yeatsian enterprise of *The Book of Ephraim*. But, to adapt what Helen Vendler says of Milton in reviewing *The Book of Ephraim*, Merrill found his own best voice speaking back at him under the name of Yeats. Or rather, Merrill found his own best voice in speaking back to Yeats. The grand Yeatsian cry of "Vacillation," "Let all things pass away!" becomes, in Merrill, an antithetical cry to hold on to even the most common of experiences and things. The world is too old, or life too short, to take the old high way. When Merrill points his common willowware cup on the Board, it spells the knowledge that death is common, and life less impossible to mend than replace.

Chronology

1926   Born in New York City, March 3, 1926, to Charles E. Merrill and Hellen Ingram Merrill.

1946   *The Black Swan.*

1947   Graduates from Amherst College, after service in U. S. Army (1944–45). Writes B. A. thesis on metaphor in Proust.

1951   *First Poems.*

1954   Moves to Stonington, Connecticut, where he shares house with David Jackson. Residence in Stonington is permanent. Second house in Athens for many years, now in Key West.

1956   *The Immortal Husband.*

1957   *The Seraglio.*

1959   *The Country of a Thousand Years of Peace.*

1962   *Water Street.*

1965   *The (Diblos) Notebook.*

1966   *Nights and Days*; National Book Award.

1969   *The Fire Screen.*

1972   *Braving the Elements.*

1973   Bollingen Prize.

1974   *The Yellow Pages.*

1976   *Divine Comedies*; Pulitzer Prize.

1978   *Mirabell: Books of Number.* National Book Award.

1980   *Scripts for the Pageant.*

1982   *From the First Nine.*

1982   *The Changing Light at Sandover.*

Contributors

HAROLD BLOOM, Sterling Professor of the Humanities at Yale University, is the author of *The Anxiety of Influence, Poetry and Repression* and many other volumes of literary criticism. His forthcoming study, *Freud: Transference and Authority*, attempts a full-scale reading of all of Freud's major writings. He is the general editor of *The Chelsea House Library of Literary Criticism*.

RICHARD HOWARD—poet, translator, critic—is best known for his books of poems, *Untitled Subjects* and *Findings*, for his translation of Baudelaire, and for his capacious commentary upon contemporary American poetry, *Alone With America*.

RICHARD SÁEZ teaches comparative literature at the City University of New York, and has published essays on seventeenth-century Continental literature and on contemporary poetry.

DAVID KALSTONE teaches English literature at Rutgers University. He is currently editing the letters of the late Elizabeth Bishop.

HELEN VENDLER is Professor of English at Boston University and at Harvard. Her books include studies of George Herbert and of Keats.

STEPHEN YENSER teaches at the University of California, Los Angeles. His writings include *Circle to Circle*, a study of Robert Lowell.

JOHN HOLLANDER is Professor of English at Yale. His books include *Spectral Emanations: New and Selected Poems, Rhyme's Reason* and *Powers of Thirteen*.

J. D. McCLATCHY teaches at Princeton. His books include *Scenes from Another Life*, a volume of poems and *Anne Sexton: The Artist and her Critics*.

DAVID LEHMAN, poet and critic, has edited *Beyond Amazement*, a book of critical essays on John Ashbery.

JUDITH MOFFETT teaches at the University of Pennsylvania. Her volumes of poetry are *Keeping Time* and *Whinny Moor Crossing*.

CHARLES BERGER teaches at Yale. He is the author of a critical study of Stevens, *Forms of Farewell*, and many essays upon contemporary poetry.

LESLIE BRISMAN is Professor of English at Yale University. He is the author of *Romantic Origins* and of *Milton's Poetry of Choice and its Romantic Heirs*.

Bibliography

Berger, Charles, and Lehman, David. *James Merrill: Essay in Criticism.* Ithaca: Cornell University Press, 1982.

Bishop, Jonathan. *Who is Who.* Ithaca: Glad Day Press, 1975.

Brown, Ashley. "An Interview With James Merrill." *Shenandoah* 19 (Summer 1968): 3–15.

Dickey, James. "James Merrill." In *Babel to Byzantium.* New York: Farrar, Straus and Giroux, 1968.

Donoghue, Denis. "Waiting for the End." *New York Review of Books* (May 6, 1971): 27–31.

Ehrenpreis, Irvin. "Otherworldly Goods." *New York Review of Books* (January 22, 1981): 47–51.

Ettin, Andrew V. "On James Merrill's 'Nights and Days'." *Perspective* (Spring, 1967): 33–51.

Harmon, William. "The Metaphors and Metamorphoses of M." *Parnassus: Poetry in Review* (Spring 1980): 29–41.

Kennedy, X. J. "Translations from the American." *Atlantic Monthly* (March 1973): 101–03.

Labrie, Ross. "James Merrill at Home: An Interview." *Arizona Quarterly* 38 (Spring 1982): 19–36.

McClatchy, J. D. "Lost Paradises: The Poetry of James Merrill." *The Paris Review* (Fall / Winter 1976): 305–20.

———. "The Art of Poetry, 31: James Merrill" *The Paris Review* (Summer 1982): 184–219.

Merrill, James. *First Poems.* New York: Alfred A. Knopf, 1951.

———. *The Immortal Husband.* In *Playbook: Five Plays for a New Theatre.* New York: New Directions, 1956.

———. *The Seraglio.* New York: Knopf, 1957.

———. *The Country of a Thousand Years of Peace.* New York: Atheneum, 1959.

———. *The Bait.* In *Artist's Theatre: Four Plays.* Edited by Herbert Machiz. New York: Grove Press, 1960.

———. *Water Street.* New York: Atheneum, 1962.

———. *The (Diblos) Notebook.* New York: Atheneum, 1965.

———. *Nights and Days.* New York: Atheneum, 1966.

———. *The Fire Screen.* New York: Atheneum, 1969.

———. *"The Landscape Game."* Prose 2 (Spring 1971).

———. *Braving the Elements.* New York: Atheneum, 1972.

———. "Driver." In *The Poet's Story*. Edited by Howard Moss. New York: Simon and Schuster, 1973.

———. *The Yellow Pages*. Cambridge, Ma.: Temple Bar, 1974.

———. "Object Lessons." *New York Review of Books* 22 (July 17, 1975): 12–17.

———. *Divine Comedies*. New York: Atheneum, 1976.

———. *Mirabell: Books of Number*. New York: Atheneum, 1978.

———. *Scripts for Pageant*. New York: Atheneum, 1980.

———. "Divine Poem." *The New Republic* 183 (November 29, 1980): 29–34.

———. *From the First Nine: Poems*. New York: Atheneum, 1982.

———. *The Changing Light at Sandover*. New York: Atheneum, 1982.

———. "Condemned to Write About Real Things." *The New York Times Book Review* 87 (February 21, 1982): 11–13.

Moffett, Judith. "What is Truth?" *American Poetry Review* (Sept./Oct. 1979): 12–16.

———. "Sound Without Sense: Willful Obscurity in Poetry." *New England Review* 3 (Winter 1980): 294–312.

Nemerov, Howard. "The Careful Poets and the Reckless Ones." *Sewanee Review* 60 (Spring 1952).

Parisi, Joseph. "Ghostwriting." *Poetry* (Dec. 1979): 161–173.

Sheehan, Donald. "An Interview with James Merrill." *Contemporary Literature* 9 (Winter 1968): 1–14.

Sloss, Henry. "James Merrill's 'Book of Ephraim'." *Shenandoah* (Summer 1976): 63–91, and (Fall 1976): 83–110.

Spender, Stephen. "Can Poetry Be Reviewed?" *New York Review of Books* (Sept. 20, 1973): 8–14.

Vendler, Helen. "James Merrill's Myth: An Interview." *New York Review of Books* 3 (May 1979): 12–13.

White, Edmund. "On James Merrill. *American Poetry Review* (Sept./Oct. 1979): 9–11.

———. "The Inverted Type: Homosexuality as a Theme in James Merrill's Poetry." In *Literary Visions of Homosexuality*. Edited by Stuart Kellog. New York: Haworth, 1983.

Acknowledgments

"James Merrill" by Richard Howard from *Alone With America* by Richard Howard, copyright © 1980 by Richard Howard. Reprinted by permission.

"James Merrill's Oedipal Fire" by Richard Sáez from *Parnassus* 3 (Fall / Winter 1974), copyright © 1974 by *Parnassus*. Reprinted by permission.

"Transparent Things" by David Kalstone from *Five Temperaments* by David Kalstone, copyright © 1977 by David Kalstone. Reprinted by permission.

"James Merrill" by Helen Vendler from *Part of Nature, Part of Us* by Helen Vendler, copyright © 1972 by the New York Times Company. Reprinted by permission.

"The Fullness of Time: James Merrill's *Book of Ephraim*" by Stephen Yenser from *Canto* 3 (Spring 1980), copyright © 1980 by *Canto*. Reprinted by permission.

" 'Mirror' " by John Hollander from *The Yale Review* (Winter 1981), copyright © 1980 by *The Yale Review*. Reprinted by permission.

"Monsters Wrapped in Silk: *The Country of a Thousand Years of Peace*" by J. D. McClatchy from *Contemporary Poetry* 4 (Fall 1982), copyright © 1982 by J. D. McClatchy. Reprinted by permission.

"Elemental Bravery: The Unity of James Merrill's Poetry" by David Lehman from *James Merrill: Essays in Criticism* by David Lehman and Charles Berger, copyright © 1983 by Cornell University Press. Reprinted by permission.

"The Changing Light at Sandover" by Judith Moffett from *James Merrill; An Introduction to the Poetry*, edited by Judith Moffett, copyright © by Columbia University Press. Reprinted by permission.

"*Mirabell*: Conservative Epic" by Charles Berger, copyright © 1985 by Charles Berger. Published for the first time in this volume.

"Merrill's Yeats" by Leslie Brisman, copyright © 1985 by Leslie Brisman. Published for the first time in this volume.

Index